D1121470

GREEN TECH

GREEN TECH
HOW TO PLAN AND IMPLEMENT
SUSTAINABLE IT SOLUTIONS

LAWRENCE WEBBER AND MICHAEL WALLACE

AMACOM AMERICAN MANAGEMENT ASSOCIATION

NEW YORK ▲ ATLANTA ▲ BRUSSELS ▲ CHICAGO ▲ MEXICO CITY
SAN FRANCISCO ▲ SHANGHAI ▲ TOKYO ▲ TORONTO ▲ WASHINGTON, D.C.

This publication is designed to provide accurate and authoritative information in regard to the subject matter covered. It is sold with the understanding that the publisher is not engaged in rendering legal, accounting, or other professional service. If legal advice or other expert assistance is required, the services of a competent professional person should be sought.

Although this book does not always specifically identify trademarked names, AMACOM uses them for editorial purposes only, with no intention of trademark violation.

Library of Congress Cataloging-in-Publication Data

Webber, Larry.
    Green tech : how to plan and implement sustainable IT solutions / Lawrence Webber and Michael Wallace.
        p.   cm.
    Includes index.
    ISBN-13: 978-0-8144-1446-0 (hardcover)
    ISBN-10: 0-8144-1446-X (hardcover)
    1. Data processing service centers—Energy conservation. 2. Green technology. 3. Information technology—Environmental aspects. 4. Microcomputers—Materials—Recycling. 5. Social responsibility of business. I. Wallace, Michael, 1960– II. Title.
    TJ163.5.O35W43   2009
    658'.05—dc22   2009009840

Printing number

10 9 8 7 6 5 4 3 2 1

CONTENTS

"Green" is a feel-good term. It has positive, earth-friendly connotations, often without much specificity—perfect for marketing purposes. *Sustainability*, on the other hand, is something we can measure and manage. We are sustainable when our use of resources does not permanently deplete or damage our supply, including natural resources, energy, and capital. Corporations that adopt sustainability as their goal will improve not only their environmental impact—achieving truly green results—but their financial outcomes as well.

Of course, electronics can never be absolutely sustainable. Steel, aluminum, copper, petroleum, and a laundry list of other materials that go into manufacturing IT hardware are not renewable resources. Organizations can become significantly more sustainable, though, according to the choices they make around planning, buying, managing, and retiring their IT assets. Greater sustainability almost always correlates with lower total cost of ownership (TCO). It is the high-tech version of the old-fashioned notion of frugality, which is how many organizations rationalize their sustainability efforts.

Senior management support over the long run is critical for sustainability initiatives, as the ROI horizon is usually at least as long, or longer, than the typical asset lifecycle. Though usually an IT responsibility, sustainable computing also requires ongoing participation from a variety of stakeholders, usually including Security, Procurement, Asset Management, Legal/Compliance, and Environmental/Health & Safety. With everyone around the table, the first step is to define explicit policies and set quantitative goals.

The EPA's cliché, "Reduce, Reuse, Recycle," is a useful signpost. Every sustainability plan should include provisions for lengthening asset life-cycles, proactive reuse as an alternative to buying new, and responsible recycling. Improved sustainability may be the virtuous consequence of frugal behavior, but in the United States, the opposite is true where recycling is concerned. Though every other industrialized country has ratified international law forbidding the export of hazardous materials to the developing world, in the United States, it is still perfectly legal to ship toxic-laden e-waste for processing in low-wage countries where environmental and worker safety laws are lax. Exporting will be cheaper—in monetary terms—than proper recycling, but the consequent environmental and human health damages are enormous. Since virtually every electronics recycler claims to be responsible, companies must choose service providers with the highest reputation for integrity and transparency to avoid becoming complicit in this toxic trade.

Even well-designed sustainability initiatives will falter without good governance. After initial policies and objectives are set, it is important to measure results and hold individuals accountable for achievement of goals. Fine tuning of policies and procedures is always necessary. As progress is made, recalibrate and set new goals. Regardless of the starting baseline, continuous, incremental improvement is the best strategy for moving an IT organization toward lasting sustainability.

As progress is made, communication of the good news—up, down, sideways, inside and out—is important to maintaining the budgetary and moral support necessary for an ongoing sustainability program. The metrics should be designed to quantify and support both the financial business case, and to tell the human interest side of the sustainability story too. Make sure all direct stakeholders are completely informed. Tell the end users; tell the Board; tell the shareholders and alert the media. Ultimately the mind-set required for sustainable practices must become part of the organization's culture, reinforced at an individual level, and viewed as part of the company's strategic strength. It's just good business.

Robert Houghton

Robert Houghton is President of Redemtech, a leading provider of Technology Change Management services to global companies (http://www.redemtech.com).

ACKNOWLEDGMENTS

Michael dedicates this book to his teacher and mentor, George Jenkins, whose encouragement and support have been invaluable over the years, and to his wife and best friend, Tami, for all her support during his many projects.

This book was made possible by the support of many different people, who all do their part to make the world a better place and who gave generously of their time to help make this a better book. The authors would like to thank Robert Houghton, President of Redemtech for sharing his insights into the business of IT asset disposal; Carey Sullivan from American Electrical Power (AEP), who explained a power company's role in Green IT. She also tapped the knowledge of the AEP Green Team (Kevin E. Walker, Eric Chorey, Kathy Stolte-Sawa, Patrick J. Collins, Christina Faust, Derek Myers, and Keith Meyers); Jim Puckett of the Basel Action Network for educating us on the issue of e-waste recycling overseas and for allowing us to reprint pictures showing the damage that it can cause; Rick Gideon, VP of Systems Operations at Ecommerce for sharing some innovative techniques for managing a data center; Mike Hogan of Fahlgren Mortine for making connections for us; Cheryl Plak and Jason Gloeckner of Emerson Corporation for sharing with us the latest in data center energy management, and Kevin Palmer for his insights on virtualization.

We would also like to thank Ronald Gooch of the Ohio National Guard, who explained to us the importance of leadership in the process of gaining individual compliance; Warren Chen from Seasonic, Inc. for his detailed explanation of the power supply industry; Marina Zeigler for her assistance in providing information about Antec power supplies; Larry's son Fred who applied his electrical engineering expertise toward explaining the detailed inner workings of computer components; and Michael's son Phillip for his help on the latest industry initiatives.

And last but not least we thank the world's best literary agent, Marilyn Allen, for all of her hard work in getting this project started, and the editorial team at AMACOM, Jacqueline Flynn and Jennifer Holder, who brought this project to a successful conclusion.

GREEN TECH

THE BASICS OF GREEN
COMPUTING

GREEN TECHNOLOGIES is a term that some business leaders believe espouses a back-to-nature philosophy and denounces all industry. However, the reality is much more positive than that. Green Technologies is the reduced environmental impact from running an Information Technology (IT) department. Green is just another term for the efficient use of technologies. (In this case, we are referring primarily to electronic equipment.) Efficient happens to also coincide with lowest cost and most environmentally friendly technologies.

"Green" technologies are nothing special. The key is to know what to look for. Equipment is considered green if it is efficient to operate and easy to dispose of at the end of its useful life. Green technologies save companies money, if viewed over their useful life. For example, an "80 Plus" grade power supply in a desktop computer will save about $30 per year in reduced energy consumption over a "standard" desktop unit. However, there may be a one-time additional cost of about $20 at its purchase. In addition, a computer designed for easy material separation at disposal is cheaper to discard at the end of its useful life than one built using a higher level of toxic materials.

There are three primary characteristics of Green Technologies. One or more of these can apply to an IT device (computer, printer, monitor, keyboard, scanner, etc.):

▲ It must use energy efficiently. A piece of equipment with a given level of capabilities can be designed and assembled with an eye toward low purchase price, easy disposal, or energy efficient operation. Unfortunately, many companies emphasize the initial purchase price and not the cost of running the equipment over its three or five year useful life. Therefore, most manufacturers focus on providing the lowest unit price.

▲ It uses the right size equipment for the job. Most people would not use a semitruck instead of an economy class car to drive back and forth to a distant grocery store. It would consume significantly more fuel to accomplish the same amount of work. (Ok, some people would drive the truck no matter what.) The same applies to IT systems. Often an oversized server is purchased to support an application either because it is the company standard or it was available when a server was needed. The larger device consumes more energy than a properly sized unit, yet provides the same amount of benefit to the company.

▲ It includes the cost for the proper disposal of unwanted equipment. Disposal is something rarely considered during a purchase. After all, it is years away. Yet the cost to properly dispose of a device is part of the total cost of unit ownership. Companies may be liable for the cost of landfill cleanup for improper disposal of equipment.

If you want to wrap up the essential messages of this book, it is to use less energy and to properly dispose of old equipment. That's it. Now you can close the book's cover. You now know the "what.." However, if you want to know the "how to do this," then you must read on.

The Energy Problem

If someone asked you the cost of providing electricity to your data center for a month, do you even know where to find the information? The primary cause of the electrical usage problem in a company is the disconnect between the people who are using electricity and the ones who are paying the bills. Employee behaviors are the result of a company's reward system.

The people consuming this resource have little incentive to economize; they simply assume it's available. The people who are paying the bills lack the time or technical understanding to debate its appropriate level of use.

Electrical consumption is a combination of what we are operating and how we operate it. For efficient electrical usage, which devices should we buy? Imagine shopping for new computers that were plastered with stickers such as those found on a new refrigerator—stickers that proclaim the average amount of energy used by that device in a given year. With this information, IT managers could make intelligent comparisons of the operational costs between devices with similar capabilities. That day has not yet arrived. Purchases are typically based on current company technical standards or lowest price. Energy consumption is not a determining factor.

Much of the electrical energy purchased by an IT organization is consumed by equipment sitting idle. Think not? When workers go home at night, the lights are turned off. Are all desktop PCs turned off as well? How about their monitors and printers? How much electricity is used while they sit around with no one to use them? Is this a wise use of a company's scarce financial resources?

Think about the data center. Rows of servers, disk drives, tape backup systems all humming along all day, every day. For most companies, the daytime hours are used in on-line inquiries, while evening hours are used for batch processing. Yet only certain servers are engaged in all of the processing. There could be long stretches of time when many others sit, slurping down electricity, generating heat that must be cooled. This continues hour after hour, kilowatt after kilowatt. We cannot flip computer switches on and off throughout the day. It takes time to start a computer and to warm up a laser printer. There is business value in having these tools always immediately available.

So what are the solutions? What are some practical actions to address these issues without hurting customer support?

Sometimes being green and saving energy go hand in hand. Have you ever replaced someone's bulky desktop CRT monitor with an LCD monitor? The LCD monitor's smaller size frees desk space for other things, so people are very happy to make the switch. (The image displayed on LCD monitors "appears" larger than it is, permitting the use of smaller screens.) As a side note, you just reduced the company's electrical expenses for that single device by two-thirds. The same goes with replacing desktop computers under a three-year refresh cycle. If the new machines are Energy Star compliant, then they will provide greater performance (being three years more technically advanced than the unit they replaced), while using even less electricity. A component of Energy Star compliance is that the equipment is set to automatically "go to sleep" (a reduced power state where everything in memory is saved). Of course, if this function is disabled, then much of the Energy Star benefit is lost.

Think about Power in a Different Way

Think of energy like any other material used to make something, with a computer as the factory. Just as a factory uses metal, parts, or glue to create something, computers use energy to create, process, or store data. This data has value to the company, so electricity should be an identifiable component of the cost of goods sold. However, since the cost of electricity is spread like pennies across a wide range of uses, it appears to be too small to count. Further, the cost of collecting individual device usage statistics would be unwieldy and too expensive to be practical.

True, each individual cost is small, but the aggregate cost is high. The problem is the disconnection between the person using the material (electricity) and the person paying the bill. When you shop for a new car, do you look at the vehicle's miles per gallon rating, or just buy the one whose shape appeals to you the most? If costs are important to you—as they are in business—then the miles per gallon rating is a key factor. However, if the fuel is free, then the equipment's efficiency becomes irrelevant to you.

So, idea number one is to begin thinking about electricity as a material that is consumed by the data center and the office desktop computers. Electricity is essential to complete our daily work. Therefore, it is just the cost of doing business. This is true. However, the issue is not that electricity is used, but rather how much is wasted.

Think back to the factory example. What if your factory purchased raw materials to make a product for retail sale, and 75% of the purchased material was scrapped—thrown away unused? How long could your company afford this? That means three out of every four components purchased were waste? That is how much electricity a desktop computer that is left on all of the time wastes per year. Electricity cannot be stored. It is consumed by equipment and the wattmeter is running, but no useful work was done for the money. Are you concerned yet?

How about another example? Have you ever walked into an office that was packed tight with boxes of files? These containers full of paper took up floor space (figure what you pay per square foot), restricted work, and were a fire hazard. What if the paper is moved out, but the files still exist on data center disk drives. Because managers and clerks insist that these files must be instantly available online, these disk drives often sit untouched and spin and spin and spin around the clock, even on holidays. In addition, they need to be cooled and, then, there is the expense of hardware maintenance. In addition, there are the back-up tapes created of the data on these storage drives. How much would you pay per year to store these files off-line for occasional use? Remember the disconnect between the people creating the equipment and the ones who pay the bills. The same holds true with the expense of backup media.

So, you see, there is more to Green Technologies than just flipping off the power switch. There may be significant opportunities for savings in an organization—without any impact on customer service. How can you resist such a promise! Again the topic is easy to understand—use less electricity. But how!

EASIEST SAVINGS

The author once worked at a factory where the executives closely timed every manufacturing step and scrutinized the pennies spent for every material used in the product. This was what they were familiar with. However, they lost many dollars in the shipping department because it was an expertise they did not have or wish to learn. Pennies saved on the shop floor were thrown away as dollars with every container shipped to a customer. Company executives may be uninterested in their electric bill because they do not see how to contain it. The easiest savings in an organization are found in the places that normally escape review.

Types of IT Energy Wastes

The cost of energy is the primary issue driving companies to "green." Although it has always been of concern, it has gained more attention during recent years. Several years ago, California began running out of generating capacity in the heat of summer. This resulted in rolling "brownouts," during which power remained available at a reduced level. For many electronic devices, such as light bulbs in your house, this lowered power level allowed operations to continue However, IT equipment depends on a clean, constant electrical supply. UPS units and generators struggled to fill this gap.

More recently, energy prices have been rising primarily as a result of increases in the cost of oil. Driven by an ever-expanding world demand, oil and natural gas prices are expected to keep increasing over time. A significant amount of the electrical power generated in the United States is derived from fossil fuels. As energy prices increase, so does the commercial cost of power. This rising cost should be combined with concerns over the impact on global warming from the greenhouse gases created when power is generated, have lead to a greater awareness of a company's energy usage. Expect your cost per unit energy to continue to rise.

Keep in mind that the central issue is not that electricity is being consumed, it is the large amount of it that is wasted every day. All companies now face three significant types of energy wastes:

▲ The cost to power equipment when it is not needed.

▲ Powering equipment far more powerful than is needed.

▲ Energy wasted as heat.

POWERING IDLE EQUIPMENT

The easiest waste to stop is the powering of equipment that is not doing anything. Most office desktop computers (and most of the computers in people's homes) are left running around the clock. This provides immediate access to this important appliance. It also enables the IT department to push software updates to company computers during the late night hours.

However, this wastes a lot of electricity. Few people are in the office at 2:00 AM, yet the equipment is chewing through as much electricity as it does throughout most of the day. Data Centers are another example. Few IT programs must keep running all of the time. Most computer servers and, even some disk drives, can save power by being idle from time to time, with minimal or no impact on customer service.

A variation of this is the excess amount of data that is kept in on-line disk storage, just in case it is needed. Over the past decade, the price per megabyte of disk storage has dropped dramatically. Where companies once closely watched the amount and source of data kept on its disk drives, it seems at times that all control has been lost. Multiple copies of the same data, many generations of historical data (that are no longer relevant), and the ever-expanding electronic mail storage all add to the ever- increasing electric bill.

Each of these examples of excess storage translates into disk drives. These devices are ever spinning around the clock every day of the year, year in and year out. Has the cost for this ever been compared to the value it provides to the company? Remember the disconnect between the people creating the bills and the ones paying them (and therefore responsible for reducing them).

POWERING EQUIPMENT IN EXCESS OF NEED

Many IT departments run applications that are more than 20 years old. These programs provide a useful function, are stable, and just seem to keep running. Think for a moment about one of these programs. In the beginning, it was installed on a new medium-sized server. Three years later, the servers were refreshed. The new servers were more powerful than the old ones, and the application was installed on the weakest model used in that upgrade. It still ran fine because its CPU and RAM requirements had not changed. Every few years, the same application is moved to an ever-more powerful refreshed server. Gradually, an application that once used 60% of a server's capacity is now using 5% of its capacity. It requires the same amount of electricity to operate as any other server of its class (actually, a bit less since it does not run very hard). How many of these underutilized servers do you have?

The solution to this in recent years has been to virtualize servers. This software allows one physical server to house many logical servers—each application running in a "logical" server thinks it is still on its own physical device. Of course, there is a cost for this software and its support. However, consider the electrical savings alone. If 20 servers are collapsed into one, then the electrical footprint is dramatically reduced.

ENERGY LOST AS HEAT

During the cultural fights between mainframe and server computers (which servers won), one of the taunts tossed at the mainframe supporters was that the machine was so huge it could heat the building. This is not an idle statement and, in many cases, the heat generated by the mainframe was used to provide some or all of the building's heat.

In rough terms, for every watt of electricity used to power equipment in a data center, another watt is required to cool it. Companies whose data centers reside in old buildings were feeling the floor space pinch. Proliferating servers were replaced with "blade servers." Blade servers did allow data centers to pack more servers into the same floor space, but often required running additional power feeds into the data center to keep everything running (and cooled) at once. It is not unusual to see a blade center rack whose power supplies exceed ten kilowatts.

Offices suffer the same issues in a more dispersed fashion. Have you ever walked into a room full of desktop computers (usually a training center) where the air conditioning had stopped working? It is very hot. The same holds true in offices. Computers left running when no one is around add significantly to a building's air conditioning load. The difference is that the equipment is spread over a larger area, and the heat created by individual units is not as obvious.

Finally, electronic devices depend on solid-state components. The primary enemy of solid state components is wide temperature variations—

very hot or freezing cold. (Now you know why the data center's temperature is maintained at something colder than a meat locker!) Equipment that runs hot all of the time is more likely to suffer a hardware failure than similar devices that run cooler. Reducing the number of hours per year that idle equipment is running will extend its useful life.

Reducing Energy Waste

In short, there are many ways that an IT department can reduce its power footprint without impacting customer service. The immediate benefit is a reduction in company power expenses. Now we are back to the disconnect between those who use the electricity and those who pay the bill. A connection must be created so there can be incentives for reducing costs. Without this connection, the IT staff will err on the side of caution. The current attitude is, "I have never been rewarded for reducing power but have been chewed out for a down server." Unless rewards are aligned with strategy, the IT staff may not participate in this important company cost-saving effort.

ONE COMPANY'S SUCCESS STORY

American Electrical Power (AEP) of Columbus, Ohio, is a major power producer providing 38,000 megawatts to 11 states and owns the nation's largest electricity transmission system, a nearly 39,000-mile network. In a company of this size, a lot of IT equipment is dispersed to many sites. Tracking everything and bringing it all under the company's power management program is a significant and ongoing challenge. Successful strategies include making AEP's Green IT program a performance goal across the IT organization, including departments and individuals, and promoting green initiatives. These goals were tracked and reported internally. In addition, AEP had a focus on enterprise-wide communication, including articles on AEP Now, the corporate Intranet, newsletters, and e-mails.

In 2008, AEP completed a Green PC pilot for all employees in Shared Services, which includes IT, Human Resources, and Business Logistics. To date, 2,700 PCs (86 percent) in Shared Services use the power saving mode for a savings of 544,299 kilowatt hours, or 974,295 pounds of CO_2, between May 1, 2008, and October 1, 2008. From a cost perspective, at an average commercial rate, this amounts to an annual savings of $117,000. In itself, this is plenty of business justification for this effort. However, it also reduced emissions by 2,338,000 pounds of CO_2 improving the air that we all breathe.

In the data center, AEP implemented VMware in the Windows server environment, thereby allowing IT to decrease the number of servers from 442 to 23. A similar conversion for Unix servers decreased the number of machines used from 170 to 75. At this point, AEP is analyzing the data. Final figures will be released with the 2009 Corporate Sustainability Report.

In addition to focusing on reducing wasted energy, AEP is conscious of downstream vendors and the ability to recycle IT purchases. Staff takes this into consideration as part of the total cost of the IT life cycle. Specifications are under consideration at this point. If the item has resale value, AEP's asset recovery group takes possession of the material. Cell phones and accessories are sent to a recycling vendor that pays AEP for materials it can resell. Other electronic items are properly recycled through Intechra LLC, which kept more than 155,000 pounds of AEP's electronic waste from landfills through a combination of remarketing and proper recycling.

Looking ahead, AEP CEO Michael Morris projects a diminishing electrical capacity in parts of the country over the next ten years, as a result of the difficulties in securing sites for new generating plants and the power lines to deliver the product to the market. These structures take a long time to construct. The challenge for the future is to work closely with communities to ensure that energy continues to be available to customers when they need it.

AEP accomplished this using a cross-functional IT department team led by the CIO and Senior Vice President, Kevin E. Walker. The team consisted of IT Directors and Managers in customer support services and IT Infrastructure.

How Much Electricity Is Enough

Electricity is a ubiquitous part of our lives. We use it all of the time every day, from the electric alarm clock that gets us up to the television that provides the weather reports to the light we turn out at night as we slip off to sleep. The smoke alarm, water heater, and refrigerator all use electricity (in varying amounts) around the clock. As anyone who has lived through an extended electrical outage over many days will testify, we never realize how critical electricity is to our daily lives until it is gone.

Electricity has an interesting characteristic. It must be used when it is created. It cannot be stored. Electrical utilities must predict how much electricity will be consumed at a given time and ensure that 99.9% of the total possible number is provided—even though no one will purchase a significant amount of it. Imagine the cost to create and then toss away a significant amount of your product every day!

Electrical blackouts happen. Complete outages are something most people have experienced at one time or another. The electrical generation industry is hard pressed to keep pace with the increase of electrical demand. One factor driving this increase is the rapid expansion of electronic devices into all aspects of life.

The same is true for industrial users. Facilities that depend heavily on large amounts of readily available power will locate near its source. Some aluminum smelters build electrical generation plants adjacent to their facilities primarily for their own use. Some companies with megasized data centers even locate to areas adjacent to hydroelectric generating dams.

So if companies would reduce their consumption of electrical energy, the demand for electrical generation would likewise be reduced. This would lead to a decrease (or slower growth) in the amount of greenhouse gases created—just so someone can leave his or her office PC on overnight.

CLIMATE CHANGE

At various times throughout earth's history, it has warmed and cooled. The question of our time is whether human activity on the planet is accelerating the rate of warming or possibly increasing its severity. Many educated and intelligent people argue on both sides of this issue. Of course, if you get two experts on any subject together in a room, they will argue just to be "right."

This discussion about climate change has focused on the creation of "greenhouse gases" as a significant cause. The gases originate from many sources, among which are the emissions from fossil-fueled electrical generation plants. As warming is capturing more of the public's attention, those who believe that people are causing the problem are pressing for reduction in these emissions. Cleaner air has been a long-term goal of everyone, including the electrical generation companies.

The impact of climate change reaches far beyond how warm it is outside. Climate change is a socially disruptive factor. International efforts to reduce greenhouse gases are resulting in the passage of new laws that will impact the ways in which companies conduct their operations. The best way to minimize these legal mandates is to act now. Green isn't hard to do—it is just a different way to look at things.

THE DISPOSAL PROBLEM

Our surplus electronic parts are poisoning the planet. Lead, cadmium, mercury, and other toxic substances used in the manufacture or computing equipment is escaping into the environment from improperly disposed equipment. The correct handling of these substances is essential to avoid long term health problems for people and damage to the environmental.

We live with a "throw-away" mentality. If a cell phone is broken, just get a new one. If a radio breaks, throw it away and buy a replacement. In most cases, it is cheaper to purchase a new item than to try and get the old one repaired. There are good reasons for this. The cost of the repair may be as much or more than the price of a replacement. Also, there may be a several week delay before the replacement arrives. At best, we give the broken device to someone who may repair it for their own use. However, in most cases, it is simply added to the local landfill.

Electronic equipment is created from many different materials. When the device ends up in the waste stream, these substances can escape into the environment, causing damage and potential health risks to humans and animals.

The issue is how to safely discard old electronic equipment. Recently, the disposal effort has shifted to how to recycle the materials in electronics to minimize the amount that is stuffed into landfills. Recycling potentially saves energy because it is cheaper to reuse a material than to dig it out of the ground, transport it, smelt it, and then ship it to the manufacturer. Recycling changes this to isolating the material, extracting it, and then shipping it for reuse.

Another factor driving disposal is the three-year desktop and server-refresh cycles used by most companies. New desktop computers, monitors, and servers are typically sold with a three-year warranty. During this time, parts and labor are provided (under certain circumstances) for free. Once this service has expired, it is believed that the technology has advanced to such as degree (usually two generations) that new equipment provides more reliable and faster service than the older device. This results in the movement of equipment with significant remaining useful life into the waste stream.

This brings up several significant issues:

▲ The "old" equipment may have many more years of reliable service left in it. Yet interest in this equipment is low. Since these desktop units and servers are no longer under warranty, the cost of an outside service company to support them must be included in a budget. Other companies are reluctant to purchase these older servers, since they are unknown quantities and may have been poorly maintained. The cost to purchase this used equipment, added to the cost to ship it, plus the technical labor to examine it comes close to the cost of a new unit with a full warranty support.

▲ Disk drives and anything that may hold company information cannot be passed on to another entity. The common practice is to crush them to render the platters unreadable. This significantly reduces the value of used equipment since a new replacement drive must be purchased before the device is usable.

▲ Disposal of the old equipment must be handled by a professional recycler. They will charge to pick up and haul away the equipment. If it can be resold, some of this money may be refunded. The recycler makes its profit from properly disassembling and shredding the components so that the basic materials can be extracted.

So why not just chuck the equipment into the dumpster and crush it before it is picked up? Who would know? Likely the very people you are trying to deceive. Improper disposal of electronic components may lead to extensive fines for your company. A single device showing up in a landfill with your company's asset tag still attached can be damning evidence. Serial numbers on the chassis and on internal components may also be traced back to an organization. The result may be the cost of remediating an entire landfill for potential toxic waste that was snuck in by other companies —just because the evidence of your action is apparent.

The Bottom Line

The chemical industry lived through a green transition years ago as it sought to reformulate many of its compounds to be more environmentally friendly to use and to discard. Today, few people use oil-based house paint thinned with flammable turpentine. Instead, they use water-based latex. So in a sense, it is now the IT industry's turn to clean up its act.

Green Technologies is about changing the way we do business, so that the company will save money while reducing its impact on the planet's environment. It is not hard to do. Some of the savings are immediate, such as reducing power usage. Some of the savings come later from properly recycling equipment and keeping toxic material out of the air, water, and soil that we all share. The best thing about Green Technologies is that costs are reduced without a corresponding reduction in customer service.

The biggest challenge to overcome is to shift the thinking of IT executives. First, they must look at the three- (or five-) year cost of operation when purchasing new equipment rather than focusing on a cash flow approach, in which available cash is used to purchase the least expensive equipment. This will allow the purchase of energy-efficient equipment and devices that are easier to recycle when no longer needed.

Second, IT executives must understand the legal impact of the disposal of equipment. Equipment that is disposed of improperly may be traced back to a company, thereby diminishing its public image. It may also result in fines from the local environmental enforcement authorities.

Third, organizations need to discover Green Technologies as a competitive weapon. If these actions are taken for your company's benefit, why not tell the world that as a side benefit of your actions, your company is also a "good citizen." An enhanced public image brings its own rewards in improved employee morale and a public belief that the company is a trustworthy business partner.

Green Technologies need not wait until someone powerful in a company takes notice. It can begin at any level of the organization, however small. Individuals can set the power controls on their computer to turn off when idle. They can delete (or move to offline storage) idle files and look for servers and applications to turn off. Sometimes a great idea, a great movement of people, begins with one humble believer. This is your chance to initiate something big! The first step is up to you.

An interesting thing about Green Technologies is that it allows a company to align itself with being environmentally friendly while simply running more efficiently. In effect, implementing Green Technologies saves company money while making it a better neighbor.

2 LEGAL MANDATES FOR GREEN

WHILE AS individuals most of us try to do the right thing when it comes to the environment, governments around the world have found it necessary to enact legislation to address the growing volume of e-waste. We all want the latest and most up-to-date electronics and computers, which means that there is a steady stream of old equipment that reaches its end of life each year. The U.S. Environmental Protection Agency (EPA) has published on its Web site the following statistics on the volume of e-waste generated in the United States:

▲ Of the 2.25 million tons of TVs, cell phones, and computer products ready for end-of-life (EOL) management, 18% (414,000 tons) was collected for recycling and 82% (1.84 million tons) was disposed of, primarily in landfills.

▲ From 1999 through 2005, the recycling rate was relatively constant at about 15%. During these years, the amount of electronics recycled increased, but the percentage did not because the amount of electronics sent for end-of-life management increased each year as well.

▲ For 2006 to 2007 the recycling rate increased to 18%, possibly because several states have started mandatory collection and recycling programs for electronics.

Clearly, government will have an increasingly active role in how we manage the end of life of our IT assets. While your local government may not yet have such regulations, the odds are pretty good they will by the time you dispose of the equipment you buy today. By knowing the potential legal issues that may affect your disposal choices when your computers and other IT assets reach their end of life, you can make better acquisition decisions today to improve your total cost of ownership.

Regulations in the United States

At present, no Federal mandate requires the recycling of computers and other e-waste. While there have been several attempts to develop a Federal policy covering e-waste, it has been left up to the individual states to enact their own electronics recycling, reuse, and recovery programs. The Federal government has encouraged the recycling of CRT displays by exempting intact CRTs from hazardous waste regulations (see RCRA below). Although the individual states decide how to handle their e-waste, several Federal laws do indirectly effect how e-waste can be disposed of, as computers and other IT assets can contain a significant amount of toxic materials.

RESOURCE CONSERVATION AND RECOVERY ACT (RCRA)

The Resource Conservation and Recovery Act (RCRA, pronounced "rick-rah") enacted by the federal government in 1976, bans the open dumping of solid and hazardous wastes. While not directed specifically at the computer industry, the RCRA ban on dumping hazardous waste into landfills can apply to computers and electronics. Many computer and other electronic components, such as CRT monitors, cell phones, PDAs, and so on, are considered hazardous under Federal law. Exemptions are made for the following circumstances:

▲ Resale or donation: CRT monitors that are resold or donated for continued use are not considered hazardous waste.

▲ Unbroken CRTs: To encourage recycling, the EPA does not consider unbroken CRTs to be hazardous waste unless they are stored for more than one year. The one-year storage limit applies only to collectors or recyclers, as the EPA feels the risk to the environment is low as long as the CRT is unbroken.

▲ Broken CRTs: Again to encourage recycling, broken CRTs are not regulated as hazardous waste as long as the following conditions are met:

  ▲ The container holding the broken CRTs is clearly labeled that it contains broken CRTs.

  ▲ The container or building that the container is in is designed to minimize the release of any hazardous material.

  ▲ Any container used to transport the broken CRTs must be designed to minimize the release of any hazardous material.

  ▲ The broken CRTs are stored for less than one year before they are recycled.

▲ Small quantities. Businesses and other organizations are permitted to dispose of up to 100 kilograms (220 pounds) of e-waste per month without having to treat the e-waste as hazardous material. As far as the Federal government is concerned, throwing out small quantities of e-waste into the normal trash is fine, but many states are making this illegal.

▲ Households. CRTs and other e-waste generated by households are not considered hazardous waste by the Federal government. Again, many states are passing stricter laws of their own to regulate e-waste at all levels.

Computer motherboards and other types of circuit boards are specifically exempted from federal hazardous waste rules. Intact new circuit boards are considered unused commercial chemical products, which as a category are not regulated. Intact used circuit boards are considered scrap metal, which again as a category is not considered hazardous waste. Circuit boards that have been shredded are not considered hazardous waste if they are containerized to be shipped to a recycler. The circuit boards must have had all components containing mercury and any batteries removed before being shredded or they will be considered hazardous waste.

The only time CRTs and other electronics are considered hazardous under federal law is when more than 100 kilograms (220 pounds) per month is disposed of at any single facility. In this case the CRTs and other electronics must be treated and shipped as hazardous waste and sent only to a permitted hazardous waste landfill. If the items are to be reused, reconditioned, or recycled, they are not considered hazardous material.

COMPREHENSIVE ENVIRONMENTAL RESPONSE COMPENSATION AND LIABILITY ACT (CERCLA)

This act, better known as the Superfund law, mandates that a business or organization that generates hazardous waste is liable for the proper disposal of the waste. This liability extends throughout the life of the material, no matter who eventually disposes of the material or where it is disposed. It requires the organization that causes environmental damage to clean up whatever environmental mess it made through the dumping of hazardous waste.

What this means for companies disposing of computers and other electronic equipment is that they can be held liable if their disposal vendor disposes of the material improperly. Liability for proper disposal does not go away from the original owner of the material when the material is sold or given to another organization, such as a charity or recycler. If your old equipment is found having been improperly disposed of and can be traced back to you, your organization can be held liable for the entire cost of any cleanup required and also subject to fines.

HEALTH INSURANCE PORTABILITY AND ACCOUNTABILITY ACT (HIPAA)

HIPAA requires that healthcare providers protect confidential information about their patients. Although HIPAA does not address computer disposal directly, its guidelines on the handling of paper-based information can be applied to electronic data. This means ensuring that no data is left on any computers or other electronic devices (e.g., copiers, USB drives, PDAs) at the time of disposal. Healthcare providers should ensure that their disposal vendors use HIPAA-compliant data destruction processes (both electronic and physical), as the healthcare provider is ultimately responsible for any personal protected healthcare information that falls into the wrong hands.

SARBANES-OXLEY ACT (SARBOX OR SOX)

Sarbanes-Oxley requires organizations to make secure all financial information and systems, as well as the IT infrastructure on which these systems operate. It requires that this financial information be kept secure and not be released to the public. Covered financial information includes consumer information, such as financial transactions, credit information, and heath records. The act also requires that all electronic data is erased in such a way that it cannot be retrieved when the device is disposed of. The organization that collected any financial information is ultimately responsible for any personal financial information that falls into the wrong hands.

The Gramm-Leach-Bliley Act makes financial institutions responsible for the security of their customers' information. Section 501 of the Gramm-Leach-Bliley Act requires financial institutions to establish standards relating to administrative, technical, and physical information safeguards to protect customer records and information. This includes ensuring that any personal financial data does not fall into the wrong hands when computer equipment is disposed of. A financial institution is defined as any organization that collects financial information, and includes banks, credit unions, tax preparers, colleges, debt collectors, real estate services, and consumer credit agencies.

Individual State Regulations

While the U.S. government has not been at the forefront of environmental law on e-waste, individual states have begun enacting legislation to address the growing problem. An advantage to this approach is that many different ideas on how to best handle e-waste are implemented and the merits can be compared; the disadvantage is that consumers and, especially, manufacturers have to keep track of a different sets of rules for each state in which they do business. One hopes that at some point the best ideas will sort themselves out and a federal program will be adopted to make compliance easier. Below are details on selected state programs. Figure 2-1 lists all states that have some sort of electronics recycling/reuse legislation currently in effect.

CALIFORNIA ELECTRONIC WASTE RECYCLING ACT

The California legislature passed the Electronic Waste Recycling Act of 2003 to address the growing problem of e-waste from computer and television video display devices. The act requires that an e-waste fee be collected at the time the product is sold to help pay for the safe recycling of what the Department of Toxic Substances Control (DTSC) has determined to be "covered electronic devices" or CEDs. CEDs are defined as display devices that measure more than 4 inches diagonally. These include new or refurbished:

▲ Televisions that use a CRT or LCD for display.

▲ Plasma televisions.

▲ Computer monitors that are either CRT or LCD.

▲ Any other products that contain a CRT.

▲ Laptop computers.

▲ Portable DVD players that have an LCD display.

Several types of products with video displays are exempt from the Act and not subject to an e-waste fee. These include:

▲ Displays that are part of a motor vehicle or a part of any industrial, commercial, or medical equipment.

▲ Displays that are part of household appliances, such as refrigerators, microwaves, ovens, air conditioners, washers and dryers, and so on.

▲ Items that are used and not refurbished.

The fee ranges from $6 to $10 per each CED sold and is based on the size of the screen, measured diagonally. Screens between 4 inches and 15 inches incur a $6 fee; screens larger than 15 inches up to 35 inches incur a $8 fee; and screens 35 inches and larger incur a $10 fee.

An interesting provision of the California law specifically mentions the e-waste laws passed by the European Union by noting that the California Department of Toxic Substance Control "shall adopt regulations, in accordance with this section, that prohibit an electronic device from being sold or offered for sale in this state if the electronic device is prohibited from being sold or offered for sale in the European Union."

MAINE'S HOUSEHOLD TELEVISION AND
COMPUTER MONITOR RECYCLING LAW

In 2003, a comprehensive e-waste law was passed in Maine to create a partnership among local and state governments, the manufacturers of electronic equipment, and consumers to ensure that all e-waste is recycled or properly disposed of. The legislature wrote that "the purpose of this section is to establish a comprehensive electronics recycling system that ensures the safe and environmentally sound handling, recycling and disposal of electronic products and components and encourages the design of electronic products and components that are less toxic and more recyclable."

The law requires that local governments establish a system for their residents to use to ensure that residential e-waste gets to an approved consolidation facility. The local government can operate its own collection center, have special collection days, or have their residents deliver the e-waste directly to a near-by consolidator.

State	Effective Year	Affected Products	Who Pays	Notes	Legislation
Arkansas	2008	Computer and electronic equipment	State	Affects only state-owned equipment.	HB 2115
California	2002/2006	CRTs in 2002; all electronic devices in 2006	Consumer	CRTs are treated as hazardous waste, which makes them ineligible to be sent to normal landfills. Ties regulations to EU RoHS Directive.	Electronic Waste Recycling Act of 2003
Connecticut	2011	TVs, monitors, personal computers, laptops	OEM	Law permits OEMs to establish their own program, but they cannot opt out of the state program.	Public Act 07-189
Illinois	2010	TVs, monitors, personal computers, laptops	OEM	OEMs pay their proportionate share of orphan waste	SB 2313
Maine	2006	Any item containing a CRT	OEM	Uses a consolidation point model. E-waste collected at municipal sites is taken to consolidation points.	Household Television and Computer Monitor Recycling Law
Maryland	2006 Ends 2010	TVs, monitors, personal computers, laptops	OEM	OEMs pay a flat fee into a recycling fund.	Statewide Computer Recycling Pilot Program
Massachusetts	2000	CRTs	State	CRTs prohibited from all solid waste disposal facilities; state-supported recycling.	Massachusetts Department of Environmental Protection regulation
Minnesota	2006	CRTs	OEM	Ties regulations to EU RoHS Directive.	115A.9565 Cathode-Ray Tube Prohibition
Missouri	2009	Computer equipment: computers, monitors, laptops, keyboards, mice; does NOT apply to televisions.	OEM	Requires OEMs to set up recycling programs.	SB 720

State	Year	Covered Devices	State/Consumer	Description	Legislation
Montana	2007	Video, audio, telecommunication equipment, computers, and household appliances	State/Consumer	Establishes a public education program for household hazardous waste recycling.	HB 555 Public Education Program.
New Jersey	2010	Covered electronic devices	OEM	Requires OEMs to set up recycling programs.	Electronic Waste Recycling Act
New Hampshire	2007	CRTs greater than 4 inches.	State	The state department of environmental services monitors the disposal of electronic waste.	HB 1455
North Carolina	2009	Computer equipment: computers, monitors, laptops, keyboards, mice; does NOT apply to televisions.	OEM	Requires OEMs to set up recycling programs.	Solid Waste Management Act 2007
Oklahoma	2009	Computer equipment: computers, monitors, laptops; does NOT apply to televisions.	OEM	Requires OEMs to set up recycling programs.	SB 1631
Oregon	2010	Desktop computer, laptop, TVs and monitors larger than 4 inches.	OEM	OEMs can set up their own recycling plan or join the state's plan.	HB 2626
Rhode Island	2008	Desktop computer, laptop, TVs and monitors larger than 4 inches.	OEM	OEMs can set up their own recycling plan or join the state's plan.	Electronic Waste Prevention, Reuse And Recycling Act
Texas	2008	Computer equipment: computers, monitors, laptops, keyboards, mice; does NOT apply to televisions.	OEM	Requires OEMs to set up recycling programs.	Electronic Waste Recycling Act
Washington	2009	TVs, monitors, personal computers, laptops	OEM	Requires OEMs to set up recycling programs.	SB 6428

Figure 2-1

U.S. STATE ELECTRONICS RECYCLING/REUSE LEGISLATION.

Each manufacturer that sells computers and electronics in Maine is responsible for paying the consolidators for the cost of handling, transporting, and recycling their products, as well as for their share of the costs for products from manufacturers that no longer sell products in the state. They must also provide annual reports to the Maine Department of Environmental Protection on the recycling of their products in the state.

The consolidation facilities are responsible for tracking the e-waste delivered to them by manufacturers and report these numbers to the Maine Department of Environmental Protection. They are also only allowed to ship e-waste to recyclers that are certified to meet the "Environmentally Sound Management Guidelines" developed by the Maine Department of Environmental Protection. The recyclers are then responsible for giving the consolidators a sworn statement that they met these guidelines.

Finally, retailers in Maine can only sell products from manufacturers that have been certified to meet e-waste handling laws. The state maintains a list of approved and unapproved manufacturers and brands on its Web site.

MARYLAND STATEWIDE COMPUTER
RECYCLING PILOT PROGRAM

The "Statewide Computer Recycling Pilot Program" enacted in Maryland in 2005 is designed to encourage computer manufacturers to establish take-back programs to collect and recycle, refurbish, or reuse end-of-life computers. It applies to any computer manufacturer that sells more than 1,000 computers a year in the state. Manufacturers are charged an initial $5,000 registration fee to sell computers in Maryland. Manufacturers that establish such recovery programs are required to pay a $500 annual fee after the initial $5,000 registration. The fees are distributed to local governments to support local e-waste collection efforts. In addition, the law requires the Maryland Department of the Environment to study and compare the impact of cathode-ray tube disposal and to review the effectiveness of the computer recycling pilot program. The law is scheduled to expire at the end of 2010.

MASSACHUSETTS

Massachusetts in April of 2000 became the first state to ban the disposal of CRT displays, mostly because of their high lead content. The law, enforced by the state's Department of Environmental Protection, prohibits the disposal of CRTs in landfills in the state and bans them from waste combustors. The law exempts intact CRTs from hazardous waste regulations to encourage reuse and recycling and works to develop CRT recycling as a viable business by issuing grants and loans. The state also established regional collections centers to feed two statewide processing companies that were awarded contracts to process CRTs. States surrounding Massachusetts have since piggy-backed onto Massachusetts' program by contracting with these same processors.

TEXAS ELECTRONIC WASTE RECYCLING ACT

In 2007, the Texas House passed House Bill 2714, the Electronic Waste Recycling Act, which requires computer manufacturers that sell in Texas to offer consumers free and convenient recycling of the computers sold in the state. The act defines computer equipment as desktop and laptop computers, monitors (display devices without a tuner), and the accompanying keyboard and mouse made by the same manufacturer.

The program is administered by the Texas Commission on Environmental Quality, which maintains a list of computer manufacturers that have been approved to sell in the state. It also requires that all computers sold in Texas be clearly and permanently labeled with a brand owned by a manufacturer that is on the approved list. Retailers can be fined up to $2,000 for each piece of equipment that is not correctly labeled. The law only covers computers that are sold for consumer or home business use and only requires manufacturers to take back their own equipment.

Regulations Adopted Around the World

Many countries have acted sooner and gone much further than the United States in enacting laws and regulations requiring some recycling of materials used in the manufacturing of various products. More densely populated areas, such as Japan and the European Union (EU), are running out of available landfill capacity much quicker than is the United States. As a result, they are mandating recycling to reduce the amount of material going into landfills. Some of these laws affect the computer industry indirectly, such as general restrictions on what can be landfilled, and others directly, such as prohibiting the disposal of CRT monitors.

There are several reasons why you should be aware of recycling regulations in other parts of the world. First, landfill capacity in the United States is not limitless and, sooner rather than later, we will have the same issues as do other areas of the world. Second, many of these regulations impact how products are made by manufacturers that are increasingly global and will, as much as possible, create standard products for all the markets they serve. And third, products made in the United States for sale in these areas will be required to meet increasing strict requirements to support recycling.

VEHICLE TAKE BACK LAWS

In predicting the future of legal mandates for the recycling of computers, it is instructive to look at the recent history of recycling laws in Japan and the EU (the U.S. has no such laws) that apply to motor vehicles. As vehicles are much larger than computer-related waste and because they contain a greater amount of material, it is only natural that lawmakers focused their attention on the recycling of vehicles as landfills began to fill up.

In Japan, the End-of-Life Vehicle (ELV) Recycling Law became effective on January 1, 2005. This law puts the cost of recycling on the vehicle owner. A fee is collected when the vehicle is sold or when it goes through its first required inspection after the law was passed. The collected fees are managed by a not-for-profit organization, which works with manufacturers to ensure that the vehicles are recycled properly. Each manufacturer is required to set up a receiving process to take back its vehicles and is responsible for their proper recycling and disposal. Any surplus fees collected because of exportation of a used vehicle supports local governments in their fight against illegal dumping. The law also establishes a goal to reduce the percentage of a vehicle being landfilled to 30% or less by 2015. It also focuses on the collection and proper disposal of CFCs and the explosives in airbags.

In the EU, Parliament issued a directive in 2007 to harmonize existing national regulations on vehicle recycling. The goal of the directive is to reuse or recycle 95% of each vehicle, with only 5% going to landfill by 2015. Members of the EU are to encourage the reuse of vehicle components and to recycle those parts that cannot be reused. While in Japan user fees fund the recycling effort, in the EU the manufacturers bear all or a significant portion of the costs for the disposal of their vehicles at end of life. Both Japan and the EU avoid having the final user of the vehicle bear the cost of recycling ELVs in order to not encourage illegal dumping of vehicles.

ECO-MANAGEMENT AND AUDIT SCHEME (EMAS)

In 1995, the EU issued Regulation 1836/93 establishing the Eco-Management and Audit Scheme (EMAS) as a voluntary tool for industrial organizations to document their environmental performance. Its aim is to recognize organizations that go beyond the minimum legal requirements. It works much like becoming ISO 9000 compliant in that the organization's environmental performance is independently verified by an outside organization. Starting in 2001, the EMAS was made available to all organizations both public and private.

To receive EMAS registration, an organization must perform the following activities:

1. Conduct an environmental review of all the products, activities, methods, procedures, and so on performed by the organization.

2. Create an environmental management system that ensures that the organization is meeting the objectives defined by its environmental policy. The system should specify the responsibilities, processes, procedures, communications, and so on required to meet the objectives.

3. Perform an environmental audit of the management system performed and approved by an accredited EMAS verifier.

4. Provide a statement of the organization's environmental performance documenting how well it met its environmental objectives. The statement should also outline steps the organization will take to continue to improve its environmental performance.

5. Send all of the above to the EMAS Competent Body for registration and for public review.

Once all of the above steps are completed, the organization receives a registration number and is permitted to use the EMAS logo. The logo can be used on:

▲ Material advertising the organization's participation in EMAS.

▲ The organization's letterhead and other marketing collateral.

▲ Advertising for the organization's products and services.

▲ Environmental statements made by the organization.

RESTRICTION ON HAZARDOUS SUBSTANCES (ROHS)

In July 2006, the EU passed the Directive on the Restriction of the Use of Certain Hazardous Substances in Electrical and Electronic Equipment, commonly referred to as the Restriction on Hazardous Substances (RoHS). The directive bans the sale in the EU of new electrical and electronic equipment containing more than specified levels of six hazardous materials: lead, cadmium, mercury, hexavalent chromium, polybrominated biphenyl (PBB), and polybrominated diphenyl ether (PBDE) flame retardants. It is closely linked with the Waste Electrical and Electronic Equipment Directive (WEEE) (see below), which sets recycling targets for electrical and electronic products.

RoHS defines a manufacturer as any of the following:

▲ Any entity that manufactures electronic equipment that it sells directly to the consumer or through retailers using its own brand.

▲ Any entity that resells under its own brand equipment produced by separate suppliers, regardless of where the product was manufactured.

▲ Any entity that imports or exports electronic equipment commercially into, or from the EU.

Many computer manufacturers, such as Dell and IBM, have standardized the design of computers sold worldwide to meet the RoHS directive.

> **SONY**
> Sony experienced first-hand how serious European countries are about regulations on the use of toxic materials in electronic products. In December 2001, the Dutch government seized over €100 million of Playstation game consoles, when it was discovered that the cables that came with the consoles contained more cadmium than Dutch law allowed.

Waste Electrical and Electronic Equipment (WEEE)

In response to the growing amount of waste from electrical and electronic household and office equipment (e-waste), the EU in early 2003 adopted the Directive on Waste Electrical and Electronic Equipment (WEEE). The directive makes producers of electrical and electronic equipment responsible for what happens to the equipment they manufacture once the equipment reaches its end of life.

Before the passing of WEEE, up to 90 percent of e-waste in the EU ended up as toxic pollution when discarded in landfills or was incinerated. With the large amount of toxic chemicals used in products such as televisions, computers, and refrigerators, these items contribute significantly to the amount of toxic pollution to the environment.

WEEE establishes minimum requirements for reuse, recycling, and recovery of covered items. There are ten categories of products covered by WEEE:

1. Large household appliances – refrigerators, freezers, washers, dryers, stoves, etc.

2. Small household appliances – vacuum cleaners, toasters, clocks, etc.

3. IT and telecommunications equipment – computers of all sizes, printers, faxes, phones, etc.

4. Consumer equipment – televisions, radios, musical instruments, etc.

5. Lighting equipment – Straight fluorescent lamps, compact fluorescent lamps, high-intensity discharge lamps, etc.

6. Electrical and electronic tools (with the exception of large-scale stationary industrial tools) – drills, saws, mowers, etc.

7. Toys, leisure and sports equipment – videogames, electric trains, sports equipment with electrical or electronic components, etc.

8. Medical devices (with the exception of all implanted and infected products) – radiotherapy equipment, cardiology equipment, dialysis equipment, etc.

9. Monitoring and control instruments – thermostats, scales, smoke detectors, etc.

10. Automatic dispensers – All devices that automatically deliver all kind of products, such as coffee, soft drinks, money, etc.

To meet the goal of reducing waste caused by electrical and electronic equipment, the WEEE directive creates the following requirements:

- ▲ Producers (manufacturers or importers) of electrical and electronic equipment are required to register in the countries in which they do business. They will also be monitored on their success in achieving mandated recycling and recovery targets that increase over time.
- ▲ Private households can (but are not required to) return e-waste to collection facilities free of charge. E-waste cannot be thrown in with general waste,
- ▲ Producers will be responsible for financing the e-waste collection facilities.
- ▲ Producers will be required to mark their products with the WEEE symbol (a crossed out wheeled bin, as shown in Figure 2-2) to let consumers know that the product cannot go in with general waste and should be returned to a WEEE collection facility.
- ▲ Member nations must collect and recycle the equivalent of 4kg of "e-waste" for every person living in the country.

Figure 2-2
WEEE PRODUCT IDENTIFICATION SYMBOL

THE ECODESIGN REQUIREMENTS FOR ENERGY USING PRODUCTS (EUP) DIRECTIVE

In 2007, the EU adopted The EcoDesign Requirements for Energy Using Products (EuP) Directive, which sets EcoDesign requirements for any group of products that uses energy. The scope of the directive is deliberately broad so that an increasingly wide range of products can be targeted in the future.

The directive focuses on two areas. First, all electrical equipment must be labeled with the energy rating of the product. Second, it sets standards for energy-efficient product design. The directive initially applies to household electrical products, such as refrigerators, freezers, dishwashers, ovens, washers and dryers, and so on. Consumer electronics and office equipment have been identified as product categories that have ". . . a high potential for cost effective reduction of greenhouse gases" and will soon be a target of this directive.

Just like the EU RoHS and WEEE directives, the EuP directive is expected to influence environmental legislation around the world.

The Bottom Line

Government regulations will increasingly influence how we handle the waste generated from the computers and other IT-related equipment that we depend upon to run our businesses. This will have a growing impact on the cost of disposing of end-of-life equipment, which will affect the total cost of ownership over the entire life of the equipment. Organizations must increasingly take disposal costs into account when determining the overall price of equipment. By taking current and probable future disposal regulations into account when equipment is acquired, you can positively impact your total cost of ownership and your bottom line.

3 BUSINESS CASE FOR GREEN COMPUTING

GREEN COMPUTING is one of those things that many people favor, but few want to work on. The old and familiar ways of purchasing, operating, and disposing of equipment are predictable and proven. Because the concept of "Green IT" is new to many IT people—and potentially adds costs for no perceived business value—anything that injects itself into a process that already works (in the minds of IT executives) introduces another potential for failure. This is very much the "if it ain't broke, don't fix it" approach.

However, nothing around IT or the businesses that it supports stays static—no matter how much anyone wishes it would. Costs go up and down, capabilities change, employees come and go, and the legal environment occasionally bursts forth with expensive mandates. Green computing is not a matter of introducing change into a static work environment. Rather, it is one of addressing the latest variable to the IT business equation.

Not all change is bad. Reduced costs improve the company's financial health and may enable it to expand into new areas, providing new opportunities to the IT staff. Fortunately, Green Computing falls into this category. It reduces a company's cost of computing and the cost of the eventual disposal of obsolete equipment. Imagine the career boost to the IT professional who can demonstrate these benefits to the company's executives!

The potential impact of people on climate change is something that has captured the imagination of many, including lawmakers. Companies that examine their own impact on the environment can choose the actions that align with their business and their desired public image. As more people become concerned, legislators are taking notice and enacting new laws mandating "Green" actions. Those companies that ignore this popular movement are doomed to "crisis" projects to provide last-minute legal compliance. Last-minute solutions are typically an awkward patchwork of processes instead of a smooth-running strategy. This is not an efficient way to run a business.

A business case is developed to educate and persuade company executives to take a specific course of action. It brings together all of the relevant facts about an issue into one story. A business case begins with a problem statement to set the context of the problem (or opportunity) facing the company. Next is a baseline measurement that quantifiably defines the problem. The business case then presents what the desired end result will look like. This details the benefits and how the resulting process will function. Finally, it predicts a timeline for completing the project, an estimate of money and resources required, and concludes with the contact information for the people most knowledgeable about this initiative.

A well-written business case is a high-level view that ties the problem and its solution to published company strategies. In the case of Green Computing, this would be an organization's position on Corporate Social Responsibility. A compelling argument in favor of implementing Green Computing and a demonstration of how it can save money will make any company anxious to be a good neighbor.

Green computing has several components. The primary ones are energy consumption, disposal of surplus equipment, and the purchase of efficient equipment. Companies may wish to break the concept into separate business cases, each based on their own unique requirements. This moves the proposal from all or nothing to picking the ones that make the most sense.

As with any corporate culture change, senior executive sponsorship is essential to success. Culture shifts take time and a belief by the employees that it is good and necessary. Attempts at culture shift that are not sustained over an extended period of time gradually fade away and people slip back into their old habits.

How We Got Here

IT is a service department. It exists solely to serve the needs of the company that pays it. This brings to mind a highly efficient operation with skilled professional working heads-down all day, five days a week. It brings to mind a busy data center full of quiet machines working diligently amid the whirlwind of chilled air rushing between the equipment racks. The reality is much messier.

IT systems are not a single monolithic device. They run on a hodgepodge of hardware, ranging from old servers with upgraded components to storage area networks to equipment from different manufacturers each operating at their own priorities. Applications software is the product of utility programs plus specially coded programs complicated by the operating system and network connections. Application servers depend on the performance of storage area networks and database servers. All of this is further confused by information security constraints. Each of these variables is in flux through software and firmware patches, as well as hardware upgrades.

The Green Computing problem has emerged incrementally. New data systems are carefully planned but then rushed into existence. Most IT projects are over budget and late. They suffer from low involvement of the project sponsor and the people who will be using them. As these systems are installed, they often include extra files and software steps for troubleshooting logic problems. Due to the rush to completion, these files, along with performance tuning, will not be addressed until some future time. Primarily, this is the result of the project team moving on to the next project before this new system is stable. And so, the application development cycle begins anew.

The result is an inefficient system that (somehow) works. If an application seems to run too slowly, it is moved to a more powerful server. Since careers are built on installing new solutions and not on cleaning up existing ones, the inefficiency becomes permanent. The longer an application exists, the less likely it is that anyone knows the reasons why things are set up as they are. Because no one has the time to investigate, the inefficient system struggles on. Given the backlog of work in IT departments, it is cheaper to pay for more electricity than to pay someone to address these issues.

IT systems support many areas of waste. On-line disk storage is an excellent example. A lot of redundant data is stored throughout data centers. This can mean an excessive number of copies of mirrored files, data with excessively long retention times, and so on. Many companies require departments that use disk storage to pay for it through internal funds. This places the responsibility for efficient management in the wrong hands! It adds yet another corporate layer between the people creating the electric bill and those who pay it.

Another cause for storage waste is treating all files equally. Files that are rarely used should be aggregated onto the same drives that can be compressed for more efficient use and then turned off when not needed. This reduces the number of drives required, saves electricity, and reduces cooling requirements, since they will not be generating heat.

Finally, little thought is given to surplus equipment and broken electronic parts. It collects in closets and in the corners of offices until, out of frustration; someone quietly tosses it in the trash bin. This exposes the environment to toxic materials and companies to potential legal sanctions.

IDENTIFY THE PROBLEM

A clearly articulated problem statement is the root of all successful changes. It anchors all future efforts and describes what the final state should look like. There are several problems to solve under the umbrella of "Green Technologies." The problems use the acronym of END (Energy, New equipment, Disposal).

▲ Energy – IT equipment wastes energy.

▲ New equipment – When comparing new equipment for purchase, the acquisition cost must be added to the cost of the energy to operate the device over its useful life and its eventual disposal.

▲ Disposal – Prepare surplus electronic devices for reuse by other organizations or disposal by a licensed recycler.

Problem statements are unique to the company and the specific problem it wishes to solve. Consider these possible statements:

▲ The ABC Company has pledged to its customers, employees, and community that it will operate in a socially responsible manner. To reduce its contributions to Global Warming and decrease its environmental footprint, ABC Company will ensure that its IT systems operate efficiently and with a minimal impact on the waste stream.

▲ The ABC Company is a significant user of electrical power. A portion of this consumption powers essential data processing systems that support company operations. The ABC Company proposes to reduce the environmental impact of its operations by examining the consumption of electrical power by all equipment controlled by the Information Technology department to include the purchase, use, and disposal of all related equipment.

▲ The ABC Company's business processes depend on electronic tools. The proper disposal of this equipment is an essential part of its "good neighbor" program and a corporate responsibility. ABC pledges to use equipment throughout its useful life or to arrange for its use by another organization. Electronic equipment at the end of its useful life will be processed by a licensed recycler.

MEASURE THE PROBLEM

With a problem statement in hand, the next action is to measure the size of the problem. Metrics are the fodder of modern business. They are collected, crunched, charted, reported, reanalyzed and, finally, posted on a wall somewhere to awe the work force. Changing an organization's direction involves determining where you are, identifying where you want to be, and planning a way to bridge the gap between today and tomorrow. The definition of where we are today is known as the baseline. Baseline metrics provide the "how much" description of the problem statement. It is the point from which all progress is measured. It also educates company executives on the magnitude of the issues.

Measurement can be accomplished for the complete population of something. This means every one of what is being counted is counted. So if a measurement was the number of servers in the computer room, they could all be counted. Counting every one of something can be very tedious. It also requires that every item in the population sit still long enough to only be counted once. However, it is the most accurate measurement.

Measurement can also be through inference. Instead of counting every desktop and notebook personal computer in every company facility, we might infer that there is one unit per office worker. Printers can be calculated as a percentage of the desktop units (such as one for every ten people). Inference means that being "close enough" is adequate for the task. Sometimes being 95% accurate is a better value than spending a significant additional amount of time chasing down the final few items to measure 100% of a population.

Measurements require identifying:

▲ What to measure – units, watts, kilowatts, number of entire systems, a unit's useful life, etc. Deciding what to measure determines the answer's units of measure.

▲ How to measure – such as using a wattmeter or a physical count. It is important to ensure that the process for measuring is accurate. Otherwise, all of the work is wasted. For example, if a wattmeter is used to measure the amount of electricity consumed, then it must be validated as accurate before use. If utility bills are used, ensure that all of them pass through the same place and that some are not received and paid by different sections of the organization.

▲ Time period – over what period of time will the measurement occur? It should be long enough to gather an essentially accurate idea of the magnitude and frequency of the issues. The results can be skewed by season of the year or if the measurement period occurs during a company's annual business cycle.

▲ Where to measure – at the wall outlet, at the loading dock for departing salvage materials, or even at the invoices sent over by the electrical utility company. This must be consistent when measuring the same type of thing at different locations.

SAVE ENERGY – SAVE MONEY

At the point where electrical service enters the structure will be a meter of some sort that is used by the electrical company to measure total usage. Executives only see this as a total expense; they do not know how much an individual department consumes.

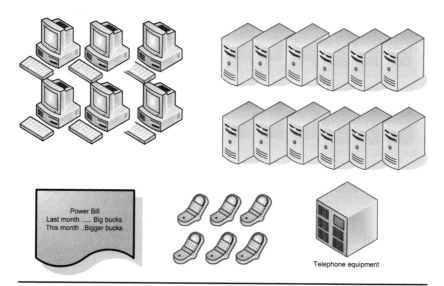

Figure 3-1

METRICS MEASURE THE "HOW MUCH" OF A PROBLEM: HOW MUCH ELECTRICITY IS USED IN A MONTH, HOW MANY SERVERS WE MIGHT VIRTUALIZE, HOW MANY PIECES OF EQUIPMENT WILL REQUIRE DISPOSAL THIS YEAR, AND SO ON

This total number includes all uses of electricity in that structure. Power used for running a coffee pot is mixed in with electricity needed to run a printer. The total electrical usage for a facility is a good baseline number for the company to begin with. If your efforts are successful, this number will decline. If this building only houses the data center, then it alone may be adequate.

Find out how much your company pays per kilowatt-hour of electricity. It is different from what you pay at home. This data is usually found in the Facilities or Accounts Payable departments.

> **ELECTRICAL BILL AS A MEASUREMENT**
> When using the total electrical bill as a measurement, keep in mind seasonally adjusted usage. Using a mild spring for a baseline may not look good when compared to the electricity needed to air condition the offices during a very hot summer.

To estimate the amount of energy used for a company's IT operations, you will need a spreadsheet to crunch the numbers and an accurate count of the equipment in use. There are two significant types of equipment to count. Data center equipment is all of the equipment in the data center, including servers, uninterruptible power supplies (UPS), storage area networks, and so on. Whereas the equipment in the data center is all in one place and easy to count, desktop machines are different. They are more mobile, and the models vary more widely.

Step through this process twice, once for the data center and once for desktop equipment. In most companies, the amount of energy used by data centers and desktop computers is roughly equal.

ACTUAL ENERGY USAGE

The most accurate way to determine the electrical consumption of the company's devices is to place a wattmeter on each one. Then, after several days of operation, collect all of the readings into one place. This would provide a highly (but not 100%) accurate idea, but is more work than necessary. Instead, select a representative desktop unit. Obtain a wattmeter, plug it into the wall, and then plug a power strip with the desktop unit and monitor into the meter. Run the desktop and monitor to obtain three 10-minute long readings:

▲ Idle – where the PC is sitting without power management engaged.

▲ Active – where the unit is running applications, such as the work processor, spreadsheet, and Internet browser. Most people work on their computer intermittently throughout the day.

▲ Sleep or Hibernation – enable power management and place the unit into its lowest power mode. (In sleep mode, a computer uses less power and the system context is maintained in RAM, whereas hibernation uses less power and saves the system context to disk.)

CALCULATING EQUIPMENT ENERGY USAGE
Many free tools are available on-line for calculating computer equipment energy usage:

▲ ENERGY STAR Computer Power Management Savings Calculator. Use this simple calculator (in Microsoft Excel) to estimate typical cash flow opportunity from ENERGY STAR qualified computers and/or power management features. This well-documented spreadsheet explains the data to enter and how to interpret the results. It can be found at www.energystar.gov/ia/business/cfo_calculator.xls - 2006-08-16

▲ Life Cycle Cost Estimate for ENERGY STAR Qualified Desktop/Side Computer(s). This spreadsheet asks a few questions about the local electrical rate and how the computer is used. The results show the lifetime energy expense, as well as the amount of CO_2 created. It can be found at www.energystar.gov/ia/business/bulk_purchasing/bpsavings_calc/Calc_computers.xls

▲ The U.S. EPA provides a spreadsheet for calculating the greenhouse gas equivalent for energy usage. Figures calculated using EPA Greenhouse Gas Equivalencies Calculator available on-line at http://www.epa.gov/cleanenergy/energy-resources/calculator.html.

▲ Calculate how much money you can save each year by using the Energy Saver feature on an Apple Mac, available at http://www.apple.com/environment/resources/calculator.html

---

Typically, a PC is in active use approximately one hour per day. The rest of the time, it is sitting idle. (Adjust the estimate of active use per day to fit your local situation.) If your company does not use power management, then assume the rest of each day, as well as all day on the weekends, holidays, vacation, and sick days, the computers are in Idle mode. If you wish, exclude any of these times when the units are turned off. The result is the amount of energy this typical unit consumes in a year.

The formula is:

1. *Energy consumed per hour.* Measure the power usage while a computer and its monitor are Idle, and while they are Active. Do this for a time period that is a factor of 60, such as 10 minutes. In that case, multiple the watt reading by six to estimate how many watt-hours are consumed in each operational mode. Remember, electricity is sold in increments of thousand watts-hours. Older equipment will likely be significantly less energy efficient than new devices.

2. *Energy consumed per week.* Select an amount of time per day that a typical desktop computer is active. Given telephone interruptions, meetings, breaks, and so on, this is usually about 1 hour per day for office workers and more for workstation intensive jobs, such as computer programmer or Help Desk support technician.

Determine the number of hours in a workday when the workstation is Idle or in Active mode. If the unit is turned off at night, then of course its power consumption is essentially zero (but not quite). Usually the Idle power time is 16 hours per day (24 hours less 8 hours of work time). Add to this 48 hours for the weekend. Of course, if the typical desktop unit is turned off every night, then this number will be significantly less.

▲ Multiply the "Active watts per hour" value by the number of hours in a day the unit is Active by 5 days in a week.

▲ Calculate the "Idle watts" power consumption per week.

▲ This is: Idle watts per week = (7 days times 24 hours) – Active watts (calculated in the previous step)

> **WHAT IS A TYPICAL WORKSTATION?**
> To answer this, walk around and look at the equipment models your company uses. Be sure to check out most departments (not just your own). If possible, walk around about an hour before work normally starts and see how many are running (and likely were running all night long).

3. *Watts consumed per year.* Determine the annual power consumption for the typical workstation. Multiple the number of watt-hours used per week (in step 2) by 48 weeks (52 weeks less two weeks' vacation and less two more weeks for sick days, holidays, off-site meetings, etc.). Add to this four weeks multiplied by the Idle Time rate to account for time off.

Assume that your company's cost for electricity is $.10 per KWH.

Total watts used per year = ((Energy used per week multiplied by 48 weeks) + (Idle watts used per hour multiplied by 24 hours in a day multiplied by 28 days))

Total cost per year = (Total watts used per year divided by 1000 watts per kilowatt) multiplied by the company rate per kilowatt hour.

Total the number of hours per year of active and idle use. Multiple this number by $.10 to see how much this desktop device uses. In this example, assume a 48-week work year, which allows for 10 days of vacation and 10 days of sick or holiday.

(5 hours active per week multiplied by 48) + (163 hours idle multiplied by 48 weeks) + (168 idle hours for vacation, etc. multiplied by 4) = total watts used. The three-year cost to operate this workstation is $394.92. With a five-year useful life, the energy cost is $658.20.

Of course, the most accurate way to determine how much power is used by an electronic device is to measure it. Figure 3-2 shows an inexpensive "Kill A Watt"™ meter manufactured by P3 Inc. with which I measured the amount of electricity used the Gateway notebook PC shown in. Figure 3-3 It uses 48 watts when idling. Figure 3-4 shows a Gateway desktop PC and an LCD monitor. Note that this combination uses 150 watts in idle. This higher consumption may be the result of an additional graphics card with a GPU and video RAM.

HOW MUCH POWER DOES YOUR EQUIPMENT USE?
Imagine that this desktop unit uses 150 watts when idle and 175 watts when active. The total cost is per year is $5 \times 175 \times 48$) + ($163 \times 150 \times 48$) + ($168 \times 4 \times 150$) = 1, 316,400 total watt hours.

Convert to kilowatts by dividing by 1000 = 1316 KWH.

Multiple this by the $.10 KWH rate = $131.60 annual energy cost.

SAVE EFFICIENTLY
Beware of spending dollars to chase nickels. If you only have a few workstations, then set everyone's power management time delays and let people change them as they wish. But if you have hundreds of desktop units or more, then the savings are more obvious.

Figure 3-2

**KILL A WATT METER FOR MEASURING POWER
USAGE AT THE OUTLET**

Figure 3-3

**WATT METER MEASURING THE POWER USED BY A
NOTEBOOK AT IDLE**

Figure 3-4

WATT METER MEASURING THE POWER USED BY A DESKTOP PC AT IDLE

ESTIMATED DESKTOP COMPUTER ENERGY USAGE

Actual power usage is based on what the computer is doing. If the desktop computer operator is deeply enmeshed in Computer Assisted Design programs all day long, then the machine will use considerably more power than one used for occasional e-mail, Internet surfing, or spreadsheet creation.

COUNT THE MACHINES

Determine the number of machines in service. If your company has an accurate inventory of the number and types of equipment, then use that count. If an accurate count is not on file, then state an assumption of the number and type of devices in service. For example, you might estimate one device for every worker, with an estimated 10 percent of those workstations as notebook PCs. Access company inventory records or walk around and take an informal survey of the percentage of desktop computers that are connected to CRT and LCD monitors. Other considerations are the number of laser printers and thin client devices.

Desktop units are typically acquired over time, rather than all at once. In addition, many companies provide equipment to "classes" of workers. Expect to find a number of different models and brands. For example, a team of engineers may be provided with the latest computers filled with RAM and a powerful display adapter with its own Graphical Processing Unit and video RAM. Medium duty users in IT would have a similar computer but without the added graphics adapter. Light duty users might be the receptionist whose applications are less processing intense. Variations among the similar units can be sidestepped unless the add-on consumes a lot of electrical energy.

INCENTIVES

Coordinate your company's Green Initiative with the local utility company. There may be financial incentives available for energy savings in specific areas. These incentives are normally very specific and should be called out separately in your business case report. A list of incentives by state can be found at: http://www.dsireusa.org/

ESTIMATE POWER USAGE

Next, determine how much power each of these typical units use. For simplicity sake, use the Idle mode power rating. For a desktop PC, this is typically 85 watts plus another 25 watts for an LCD monitor (or 75 watts for a CRT) for a total of 110 watts with an LCD monitor (or 160 watts with a CRT) consumed per hour. Although the power consumption rate of desktop units will vary, using a single value to represent all units will provide a reasonable approximation.

To estimate the total amount of power consumed by desktop units, multiply the number of computers by 110 watts, by 24 hours (in a day), and then by 365 days per year. Multiple this product by the number of years between equipment refreshes. Typically this is between three and five years.

Finally, to convert this hours-used figure to money, multiply the cost of a kilowatt-hour by the energy consumed by the desktop unit over its useful life. Together, this indicates the amount of money the company has or will spend on this desktop computer over its useful life.

- ▲ KWH used = Number of units multiplied by the watts used per hour multiplied by 8760 hours in a year multiplied by the years of useful life

- ▲ Cost to power the unit while in the company = KWH used during its useful life multiplied by the company's KWH rate

---

HOW EFFICIENT IS A NOTEBOOK PC?
Notebook PCs are designed to be more energy efficient than desktop units, so that they can run longer on battery power. They consume about one-half the power of a desktop unit when in Active mode. They are typically turned off when not in use and not attached to a "dock." They also spend a portion of their work life powered by a battery instead of a wall outlet. The topic may be worth discussing with company leaders.

Repeat this same exercise of estimating the number of units and their power usage for the many laser printers and inkjet printers sprinkled throughout the company. Laser printers can be big power users, as they must heat their internal fuser to heat the toner so it will adhere to paper. Inkjet printers use much less power. Servers, storage area networks, UPS units, and printers vary widely in power consumption. Some units, such as UPS systems and network firewalls, are always on-line. For those devices present in small number, use the same value as a similarly sized component of a different model.

Finally, double this number. Cooling typically consumes one watt of electricity for every watt used by an electronic device. Computers and printers add to the around-the-clock cooling load of offices. Of course, the cooling in the data centers is more intense and concentrated.

Network devices should be noted but kept separate from the data center and desktop numbers. They are a part of the total cost of powering desktop computing, but their shared nature makes them more difficult to include in power management. However, an understanding of their energy consumption is valuable when comparing energy efficiency of future replacement equipment.

> **SOFTWARE TO MEASURE ENERGY USAGE**
> There are commercial software products that monitor computer energy usage. These tools are normally sold together with network controlled power management software. Working together, they control energy usage and meter both usage and savings. Vendors of these products claim they provide a more accurate picture of energy consumption.

Measuring Data Center Energy Usage

Measuring the energy used in a data center is easier than the desktop approach, as everything is sitting in one place. In contrast, desktop units and printers tend to move around as they are repaired and relocated for temporary projects and other purposes.

To gauge the energy usage of a data center, inventory all of the equipment in it. Then look up the energy rating for each model and variation on the manufacturer's Web site. Because servers may have varying amounts of RAM, select a "typical" unit. Web sites generally do not provide energy usage to the individual upgrade. Equipment to list includes:

▲ Servers (list # by model)

▲ UPS units (list # by model)

▲ Storage area networks

▲ Large data center printers

▲ Other large devices

Unlike desktop units, data center equipment tends to run around the clock every day of the year. This makes calculating energy usage easy. It is 8,760 hours (in a year) multiplied by the hourly electricity usage multiplied by the number of years of its useful life. This can be doubled to estimate the energy used for cooling. The energy used by the air handling equipment can be estimated using the manufacturer's power rating.

Energy savings in the data center can be significant, but it requires careful planning. It involves the purchase of energy-efficient equipment and an understanding of workloads for those servers that are only needed during certain hours and can be moved to a "sleep" state. Equipment maintained in climate-controlled spaces is unlikely to fail if its service is extended for an additional two years.

MEASURING THE DISPOSAL OF SURPLUS EQUIPMENT

A new generation of electronic devices appears about every 18 months. Each new generation brings improved performance and capabilities. Most equipment is sold with a three year parts and labor warranty. When that point is reached, many companies replace the equipment with the latest models. This equipment exchange is primarily driven to reduce downtime for hardware repairs rather than a need for additional capabilities. (So why is everyone so quick to chuck equipment into the trash bin?)

Therefore, the equipment that a company offers for disposal normally has remaining useful life. Rather than tossing equipment into the landfill, it should be offered for sale or donation to other organizations. Few desktop users ever touch the maximum capability of their desktop hardware. It seems the push for faster, higher capacity equipment comes from new versions of the operating system and desktop tools, such as the word processor. Every new version adds more processing requirements to support additional features that few people want. Extending the useful life of equipment reduces the company's capital requirements with little or no loss of service.

Disposal of electronic devices must be properly planned. They should never be thrown into the company trash hopper, as they contain toxic material that may leak back into the environment. This "e-Waste" makes up as much as 2 percent of all solid waste in the United States. It includes everything from computers to cell phones to televisions. Handling and proper disposal of these wastes is regulated by a host of federal, state, and local agencies.

The first step in the disposal process is to identify what is surplus to the organization. Often, this equipment has a lot of useful life remaining, but it must be matched to tasks that need its level of capability. Several years back, when personal computers were considerably more expensive than they are today, many desktop PCs were hand-me-down devices. The most powerful machines went to the front office executives and to the company engineers (who needed the processing capabilities). After several years, these machines were replaced with the latest models and the older machines were moved to the desk of the office staff, where they were used primarily for e-mail, word processing, spreadsheets, and similar functions. Eventually, these desktop machines were moved to the loading dock to support barcode readers that checked in new shipments. The goal was to maximize this expensive asset.

The issues surrounding disposal are Corporate Social Responsibility and legal compliance. Proper disposal is a cost, but it is cheaper than fines and court-ordered landfill remediation. Measuring disposal is the company's cost of adding to the waste stream offset by the revenues from selling surplus equipment.

MEASURE THE AGE AND NUMBER
OF DEVICES DONATED OR SOLD

How old is your company's surplus equipment and can it adequately fulfill existing business requirements? The pressure to make this decision comes from the typical three-year manufacturer's warranty. Many companies with constrained headcounts find it administratively simpler to replace the equipment rather than accept the expense of hiring an external organization to provide on-site service. Another push to change comes from the new operating systems and applications rolled out every several years. In addition, the drop in personal computer prices over the years has made it cheaper to justify the three-year refresh cycle than to purchase extended warranties. Finally, the labor involved in exchanging used equipment within the organization is the same as for exchanging it for a new computer.

To address this, companies adopt a refresh cycle based on the calendar. Notice that this equipment exchange is not based on the business need of obsolete equipment, but rather on the need to keep up with the warranty coverage.

The result of a desktop equipment refresh is that a significant number of devices suddenly become surplus. For a large organization, dumping this many machines into the used equipment market over a short period of time depresses prices. At some point, the equipment's sale price brings in less than the cost to prepare and ship it to a buyer.

The outflow of used equipment should be planned as carefully as are the inflows of new equipment. The first step is to understand types and ages of discarded equipment Use the company's asset inventory (or an analysis of equipment purchase records over the past five years) to count the number of devices and determine their ages and model numbers.

Some companies try to avoid disposal issues by leasing equipment instead of purchasing it. However, the expense for the leasing company to dispose of used equipment is still baked into the price.

Some equipment is not declared surplus even in a scheduled refresh. Examples of these are monitors, printers, and keyboards. They are used as long as they connect to the computer and work. This is an example of how one indicator can hurt one metric and help another. A CRT monitor requires three times the electricity to operate as a similarly sized LCD monitor. However, discarding an operational CRT monitor means that equipment that has not reached the end of its useful life is discarded for reasons other than that it no longer works. The 21st Century Classrooms Act is one solution. It enables large companies to deduct the full price of computers that it donates to a K-12 school within two years of the date of purchase.

MEASURE THE PERCENTAGE OF
EQUIPMENT DONATED OR SOLD

Ideally, 100% of the company's surplus equipment will be sold or donated, but this is not always practical. First, the ability of local or national organizations to absorb all of the available surplus equipment is limited. Second, there are always very old devices inserted into the surplus pile. These devices may not be reusable and must be scrapped. A good example of this would be a five-year old notebook PC. Repair parts for a single problem might cost as much as purchasing a new unit.

The problem with selling used equipment is that the buyer assumes the risk that equipment is broken when sold or is rendered unusable in shipping. Buyers reduce their purchase price to mitigate this risk, making it less desirable for a company to sell.

Another problem is to ensure that the company's data on all fixed disks is rendered unreadable. This reduces the likelihood of company secrets being displayed on the evening news. To accomplish this, the company must either fully erase the fixed disk, require the buyer to certify that they have done so, or the drive must be physically disabled from ever operating again. One tool for erasing data is the standard used by the U.S. Department of Defense. It is found at: http://www.dtic.mil/whs/directives/corres/html/522022m.htm.

MEASURE THE PERCENTAGE OF
DEVICES SENT TO A RECYCLER

The third option is to use a hardware recycling company. These organizations shred the devices to physically separate the materials used to create it. These materials are then recycled for reuse instead of mining fresh material from the earth. The recycler will also ensure the proper disposal of potentially toxic materials that cannot be reused.

Many electronic equipment recycling companies will also prepare used equipment with remaining useful life for sale or donation. Another service available is the total management of IT assets from proposal to disposal, if desired.

MEASURE THE PERCENTAGE OF
DEVICES SENT TO THE LANDFILL

On occasion, it may be cheaper to properly ship equipment to a landfill (as toxic material) than to recycle it. In this case, the wastes must be properly prepared by a qualified waste handler.

> **TAKE BACK PROGRAMS**
>
> Some manufacturers provide a "Take Back" program. Equipment sold by their companies can be shipped to a collection site for proper disposal. A good example of this is Hewlett-Packard's Recycling Services found on-line at www.hp.com/recycle. Dell and IBM are two other major companies that offer similar hardware recovery programs.

MEASURING THE EFFICIENCY OF NEW EQUIPMENT

The single biggest determinant of the cost of disposal of an item is how well it was selected when purchased. Some companies, like Hewlett-Packard, design their new equipment in such a way that it can be more easily disassembled years later when it is recycled. The U.S. EPA has a "Design for Environment (DfE)" standard that minimizes use of toxic materials.

A valuable tool for purchasing energy-efficient and easier-to-recycle computers is the U.S. EPA's Electronic Product Environmental Assessment Tool (EPEAT), available on-line at www.epeat.net. This comprehensive list evaluates the environmental impact of a computer prior to its purchase. EPEAT examines a device's conformance to 23 mandatory and 28 optional criteria, which includes energy efficiency, amount of toxic materials in the device, and even the packing materials used to ship it. This allows companies to purchase computers with the level of compliance that they desire. EPEAT benefits buyers by saving them from technically examining the total environmental impact of a wide range of equipment. It is the basis for IEEE 1680, the "Standard for Environmental Assessment of Personal Computer Products."

MEASURING DISPOSAL

The third leg of the Green Computing strategy is to understand disposal. A quick survey of employees typically finds that the staff is in favor of recycling and protecting the environment but woefully ignorant of how to do this. Many companies have recycling collection points for paper, plastic, and aluminum cans, but no central place for collecting electronic components. If someone replaces a keyboard or mouse, then the old one goes into the trash. If a monitor is replaced and not picked up by the IT department in a reasonable time, it is also likely to be tossed into the local trash hopper. This is the wrong way to dispose of equipment.

Counting the number of devices moved in the waste stream is difficult. The information may come from the asset management manager, who can say how many devices were scrapped in a given year but not if they were donated or thrown away without reference to the asset manager. Also, spare parts, such as broken keyboards and computer mice, tend to be difficult to count. If the company's desktop support team keeps a work ticket database, it may provide some idea of the number of broken parts for the past year and where they went.

Ideally, surplus electronic equipment is collected at one central location for disposal. Equipment can be can be sold, donated, or scrapped. Aggregating everything into one place facilitates counting, inspecting, and data erasure prior to its departure. Part of the employee education program must include educating staff on what is included, such as batteries, cellular telephones, broken keyboards, cables, and so on. The central control of electronic equipment disposal also ensures that equipment is properly removed from the company's asset inventory. This is significant for companies that pay a property tax on assets.

In each device with onboard storage, the equipment's fixed disk (computers) or static RAM (cellular telephones) storage must be completely erased. Disks require a special disk management tool that performs repeated passes over the entire disk storage surface writing zeros and then the number one at every location. This repeated process is not foolproof, but it will require a laboratory and considerable expense to extract any of the original data from the disk.

Once the equipment is prepared for disposal, it must be removed by a company licensed to handle hazardous wastes. It is your company's responsibility to ensure that the recycler is actually recycling and properly handling the equipment. Laws that protect the environment hold the company that purchases hazardous material liable for its proper disposal. If someone shows up and offers to handle it without a visible and verifiable process, the company may find itself liable for a very expensive dump clean-up.

AUDITING DISPOSALS

Have you ever been audited to demonstrate where your company's old terminals went? Does someone have the receipts to show their proper disposal? Companies have a cradle-to-grave responsibility to properly handle and dispose of material they use. Visit the recy-

cler's facility to verify that they are properly handling and disposing of these toxic materials as promised. These visits should be
unannounced and be made throughout the year.

In your business case, go as deep as you feel is necessary to describe the
problem. The key points are to identify the breadth of the issue (there are
more electronics to throw away than just desktop PCs) and the potential
legal liabilities for improper disposal. Most companies mitigate these issues by contracting with a qualified recycling company and requiring that
they address all of the issues.

CREATE YOUR VISION FOR THE SOLUTION

So far, your business case has a problem statement and a baseline of measurements that provide some indication of the extent of the issue. The next
step is to develop what the solution should look like. This should be described in sufficient detail so that everyone can understand it, especially
the executives reading the business case. It should explain what the final
state will be for each of the three Green Computing END challenges:

- ▲ Energy – reduce use on desktop units and in data center by 30%
  (or whatever you feel is achievable).

- ▲ New equipment – reduce lifetime operating and disposal costs of
  new equipment by some percentage, perhaps 20 percent would be
  realistic.

- ▲ Disposal – ensure all company electronic components are properly
  disposed of in a legal and cost effective manner.

"Green" as a Competitive Strategy

With apologies to Mr. Shakespeare, "To Green or not to Green," is not the
question. Changes in the legal landscape have already forced companies to
change their business practices. The trick is to identify these changes early,
so they can be eased into the organization's business processes without the
sudden shock of a last-minute requirement.

Once the problem statement has been approved, and a baseline metric
has been determined, the next step is to select a strategy for achieving organizational goals. The company's Green Computing strategy must align
with its Corporate Social Responsibility strategy. It must also reflect its
sense of urgency, such as "to do as much as possible right now" or "from
here on out." In addition, the Green Computing strategy should only be
one component of a company's overall Green efforts, which may extend to

its building, water management minimizing emissions, and managing its waste stream to minimize its environmental footprint.

There are three primary strategies to pick from:

▲ The Looking Ahead strategy says that the company wants to be Green but lacks the time, money, and management will to convert everything at once. Instead, it says that all future purchases and disposals will be based on the company's Green principles. Further, power management of all sorts of electronic equipment will be enabled. However, this approach takes the longest to show appreciable gains. Companies choose this approach because:

    ▲ It is the least disruptive to the normal flow of work.

    ▲ It maximizes existing assets and gradually replaces them with more efficient ones. This minimizes the flow of usable equipment into the waste stream.

    ▲ It is the easiest to implement, as it is primarily executed by the IT, Facilities, and Purchasing departments. Focusing on three departments minimizes management oversight requirements. IT sets up power management, Facilities provides information on energy usage along with implementing its own efficiencies, and Purchasing ensures that incoming equipment is energy efficient.

        △ This strategy targets the "low-hanging fruit" results that have high visibility for a low price.

        △ This approach can be quietly implemented by a single department with minimal executive approval.

▲ The Competitive Advantage strategy says that this is a way for the company to stand out from its competitors. The company's Green initiatives become selling points for a company's good citizenship and stewardship of the environment. With this strategy, the company immediately begins a wall-to-wall Green strategy that includes educating all employees and establishing baseline metrics with target goals for all departments. A midlevel manager is appointed as the "Green Champion" to administer the program and promote it throughout the organization. The Competitive Advantage strategy includes all of the elements of the "Looking Ahead" strategy, as well as:

    ▲ All departments are required to comply, so executive attention is needed to minimize the disruption to ongoing company operations.

▲ The company incurs expense as it proactively purchases more efficient equipment and disposes of less efficient devices. This equipment is likely not at the end of its useful life, so a program is needed to prepare it for sale or donation.

▲ This is a company-wide effort. All employees must be educated as to their role is moving to Green and for sustaining its gains. Old work habits die hard. To make Green a permanent part of the company's culture, someone must create the program and constantly promote it.

▲ This effort scrutinizes all energy consuming devices and packing materials used by the company and received from its suppliers, as well as paper recycling, waste water treatment, and so on.

▲ The Thoroughly Green strategy includes the previous Green strategies, as well as the remodeling or replacement of company buildings to include the capture and use of rainwater and on-site renewable, nonpolluting energy sources. The environmental impact of every action has equal footing to the financial issues of making a decision. The company's "Green Champion" is a top level executive, who personally ensures understanding and compliance with the company's Green policies. Thoroughly Green is more than just a program; it is a way of thinking and approaching business issues. This strategy:

▲ Is a multiyear plan that touches everything and everyone in the company.

▲ Is a consideration in all of the company's short- and long-range plans.

▲ Requires that new facilities be acquired to replace existing buildings. Business processes are reengineered to be completely Green before moving into the new facility.

▲ Requires that the company select suppliers who are also Thoroughly Green as a way to encourage and reward other companies to adopt this philosophy.

▲ Will initially be an expensive shift. Over time, operating expenses will be reduced.

GREEN TECHNOLOGY POLICIES

To make strategies a reality, the company must create policies to guide employees' actions. A Green Technology policy explains to all employees the value of this effort to the company and to the community. It is the formal executive guidance on what is expected to translate the strategy into action. It must include the metrics for measuring results, a reporting cycle, and who is responsible for what actions. An example of this is Western Digital's(TM) Global Citizenship policy found at http://wdc.com/en/company/globalcitizenship/environment.asp?language=en

ACTIONS FOR EXECUTING THE STRATEGY

So far, your business case has kept the executive reader's attention with its adequate (but not too deep) level of detail and statements of fact. Now it is time to explain how this change in the company will be accomplished. Fortunately, introducing a corporate culture change is a widely studied theme. For Green Computing, your approach might include these steps:

▲ Obtain an executive sponsor with enough internal political clout to break down internal barriers to change and to encourage employees to follow the strategy.

▲ Select a test area that would have the greatest likelihood of significant and visible gains. Erect visual aids so that everyone can see the before and after.

▲ Appoint a midlevel company executive to provide long-term promotion of Green Computing. This person's responsibility is to ensure everyone knows about the company's Green strategy and their role in its success. The "Green Champion" conducts periodic campaigns to remind everyone over and over again about the policy.

▲ Develop an information campaign to reach all levels of the organization. People get information from a wide range of sources. Some of the common ones are posters, newsletter articles, mass e-mail blasts, and contests that promote compliance. One the most effective methods of persuasion is the personal appeal in meetings with small groups of employees.

Green Computing is an easy sell. Most people are will to help if you show them how. An important part of this information campaign is to ensure that well-intentioned people do not take it upon themselves to do things they think will help but that actually hinder the company's efforts.

PULLING IT ALL TOGETHER

Once the Corporate Vision for Green Computing has been developed, the business case must detail the milestones for achieving this goal, the estimated time to get there, and the estimated cost in money and resources. Everyone has experienced a desire to achieve a goal, but lacked the resources to accomplish it. Therefore, no matter how good the business case sounds or how attractive the potential results, the executive readers will want to know how much it is going to cost.

Sometimes, this information is not available until after the strategy is selected. Sometimes, the executive sponsoring the business case selects the most likely strategy to be approved, and the estimates are based on that. Fortunately, Green Computing is primarily a cost savings for energy, and the disposal costs should already be in place. Some efficiency from centrally collecting surplus equipment may reduce overall disposal fees.

In terms of benefits, always watch for financial incentives from local government and utilities. These may be short term but significant to the approval of the proposal. As in any business decision, the plan with the greatest benefits at the least cost to the company always wins.

The Bottom Line

An IT department that decides to "Go Green" has the opportunity to save money for the company. To gain executive support for the time and expense to roll out this program, someone must build the business case for consideration. The compelling part of the business case will be the metrics – the measurements of how big an issue is.

A business case is a succinct picture of the challenge facing the company. It must contain a description of the problem and any relevant metrics that quantify it. If a solution is offered, it must include the expected benefits, the timeline for completing the solution, ad a budget for cash and other resources. For a business case to persuade executive leaders, it must demonstrate how it aligns with the company's strategies and how it helps the organization achieve it business goals. A properly assembled business case will enable a company to launch its Green Computing program with the appropriate level of executive support.

Once the magnitude of the energy issue is determined, people will be able to see the potential for a 10 or 20 percent reduction. These savings will always be welcome in an organization. The business case for keeping equipment for five years instead of three years provides additional savings. Finally, the cost avoidance for proper disposal is also important. Although proper disposal is more expensive than tossing surplus equipment in the trash bin, it also reduces the chances that the company will be fined (and publically embarrassed) by equipment that is disposed of improperly.

Implementing a Green Strategy takes time. Many companies adopt process improvements that quietly fade away. In the beginning, everyone is enthusiastic about the potential savings. They change their processes to conform to the current management climate, and everything is great. Then, after a few months, they begin sliding back into their old habits, and gains are gradually lost.

Therefore, Green Computing must become a part of the company culture. To do this, a Green Champion must be appointed to promote the program and to monitor the critical metrics used by management to approve the project. Company posters and newsletter articles are useful tools for reaching a large number of people. However, persuasion must be accomplished at the personal level. For this, departmental meetings addressing Green IT issues are more effective at changing behaviors. The Green actions must become an integral part of business processes.

Green computing requires a change in thinking and the values applied by companies toward areas of their business. It is not difficult to force employees to comply with the company's Green strategy – so long as the executive is present. The trick is to shift the employees and their managers' business decision process to always consider the impact on the company's Green program.

4 ENERGY USAGE

MOST GREEN initiatives focus on the energy savings of turning off equipment when it is not needed. However, significant savings can also be realized by improving its efficiency while in full operation. Everyone hears about how computers use a lot of electricity. Statistics are cited about how some units are more efficient than others. However, what are these differences and what should someone look for in new equipment and replacement parts? When salespeople chat on about new advances, what sorts of problems are they trying to solve?

Unlike oil or natural gas, electricity is not easily stored. It must be generated and delivered at the moment it is needed. To reach consumers, electricity must travel from a power plant through hundreds of miles of transmission and distribution lines until it reaches the final destination at which it will be used. Electrical power, as it comes from a wall outlet, is optimized for the efficient transmission of energy. To minimize line losses, long-distance power distribution lines typically operate at 110,000 volts or more.

As it gets closer to the consumer's wall outlet, this high voltage is gradually reduced to the 120 volt alternating current (AC).

Everything in the computer uses some slice of this incoming energy. However, some of the significant users are power supplies, CPUs, GPUs, RAM, and disk drives. An understanding of how these devices use power will make it easier for IT professionals to appreciate the significance (or lack of significance) of product improvement claims by major manufacturers.

A power supply transforms the electrical energy as it comes from a wall outlet to the level needed by a device. Where some devices, such as refrigerators, welcome a 120-volt power feed, solid-state electronics prefer lower voltages. The lower voltages enable use of smaller components, saving space on the desktop, and reducing heat losses. (Remember how much space the old CRT mainframe terminals hogged on your desktop?)

The Central Processing Unit (CPU) and its close relative, the Graphical Processing Unit (GPU), consume a lot of energy. Consequently, they give off a lot of heat. An indication of this is the large heat sinks and fans attached to them. For most desktop computers running typical office and e-mail programs, heat is not a factor. However, in computing intense and graphical intense applications (such as 3D CAD), these devices can become quite toasty. Desktop CPUs can consume upward of 45 watts, while a graphics acceleration card (with a dedicated GPU and RAM) can consume another 30 watts.

Other significant power users are fixed disk drives (always spinning at high speeds) and RAM. Like the CPUs, disk drives and RAM get hotter the more they are exercised. All of the energy used to create this heat must be counteracted by more energy used for cooling.

In many companies, computers are a significant consumer of electricity. Given the steady rise in energy prices and potential limitations on the use of certain inexpensive fuels sources, this expense will continue to rise. Reducing energy consumption saves both the environment and the company's wallet. This chapter will enable IT professionals to make informed decisions on green improvements for existing computers, as well as understand what features to investigate when acquiring new machines.

Power Supplies

A power supply receives electrical energy from a source (usually a wall outlet or a battery). It reformats this electricity for use by a computer, monitor, printer, or similar device. It also provides a secondary function of "cleaning" the incoming AC power by smoothing noise on the line, such as short-term voltage spikes or sags. Screening these line variations is important, so that the cleanest and most consistent power is provided to the equipment.

Power supplies can be internal or external. An internal power supply is attached to the inside of the unit. An example of this is the power supply in a personal computer. An external power supply sits outside of the unit, such as the "brick" power supply commonly used with notebook PCs. Using an external power supply unit allows the computer or peripheral device to be physically smaller, since there is no longer a reason to leave space for it inside of the cabinet. An example is the thick power adapter, such as those provided with a cell phone charger or external speakers. Power adapters are very high-efficiency power supplies. Although they may sometimes get warm, they remain cool without a fan.

Power supply design is tuned to the equipment that it supports. Server power supplies are unique to the manufacturer and are designed specifically for a particular model of server. Most data center servers are supported by dual power supply units. Desktop computer assemblers usually use an ATX sized power supply, so that it will fit into most computer chassis. ATX is an industry standard chassis size; it also standardizes the color code for output connectors.

POWER SUPPLY INEFFICIENCY COMES FROM ITS DESIGN

A power supply is a multistep operation. The first step is to reduce the voltage from 120 volts wall power to the level required by the device. The device's plug that you push into the wall receptacle connects the power lines to the computer's power supply transformer.

A transformer is a set of coils. The primary coil is connected to the incoming power, and the secondary coil is connected to the next step in the power supply. Based on the number of windings in the coils, the voltage can be stepped down (in the case of the computer) to the lower level required by solid-state electronics. The amount of reduction is based on the number of turns in the coil.

The alternating current leaves the transformer and is passed to the rectifier. The rectifier uses a switching transistor (and a few other components) to produce unregulated direct current. This output is then filtered by capacitors and other circuitry to minimize electromagnetic interference (EMI) emissions.

There are other components that further shape the power and filter out line noise, but the important thing to understand is that the lowly power supply is a significant user of energy within your computer. Because of the heat it generates, a fan is required to keep it cool.

The typical mean time between failures for a power supply is 100,000 watt hours. The higher the power supply efficiency, the longer the life. Heat is the number one killer of power supplies, and the primary compo-

nent to fail is the cooling fan. Once the fan stops turning, the power supply components will fail soon thereafter. This is why a computer with a
loud fan (which indicates that the fan's ball bearings are failing) needs to
be promptly addressed. Often the smell of something burnt signals an imminent power supply failure.

Refer to Figure 4-1 which illustrates a 60 cycles per second wave form.
The unused portions of the wave (anything above the dotted line or anything below 0) can be stored briefly in capacitors and/or inductors and released during the down cycle periods. The result is the value at the dashed
line – a smooth voltage and current.

The output cables from the power supply are color coded and may vary.
However, they are generally 5 and 12 volts. The motherboard and the circuit cards that attach to it are powered by the 5-volt line. The CD drive,
fixed disk drives, and cooling fans use the 12-volt feed.

HEAT LOSSES: A TRIPLE WHAMMY

Heat in a power supply is the result of the electrical resistance on the components. The balance to strike is between the use of energy efficient materials and the cost to the consumer.

Most computers do not approach the maximum potential of their power
supplies and operate at around a 30% load. Computer power supplies are

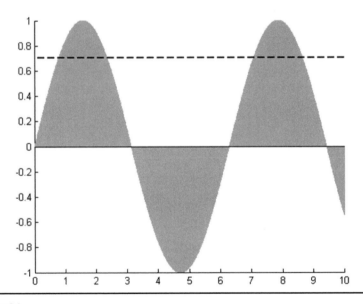

Figure 4-1
60 CYCLES PER SECOND WAVE FORM

typically between 70 and 90 percent efficient. However, a 500-watt power supply with 70 percent efficiency that is running at full load wastes 150 watts as heat. Of course, it is rarely drawing all of the 500 watts for which it is rated, but all that it does draw results in wasted energy. This heat causes multiple problems.

Figure 4-2 illustrates the problem. Any energy not used by the computer is given off as heat. The industry standard for power supplies is to run at an internal temperature lower than 40 °C (104 °F). The higher the operating temperature, the greater its impact on the equipment. High-efficiency units typically run cooler than this.

Energy cannot be created or destroyed. As no power supply is 100 percent efficient, the energy not leading to power components is emitted as heat. This represents wasted money in three ways:

▲ Energy "lost" to heat: In some of the less efficient power supplies, this can be up to 50% of the total power received from the wall outlet. Money is lost buying something that is not used as intended. Even the 80PLUS power supplies, some of the most efficient on the market, lose 20 cents of every dollar's energy that passes through it.

▲ Energy spent cooling the computer: Heat dumped out of the power supply raises the computer's internal temperature and that of the surrounding air space. This requires that more energy be put into cooling the computer and the room in which it is located.

▲ Increased likelihood of component failure: In general, the hotter that the power supply and computer run, the greater the thermal expansion damage to the devices. Eventually, this expansion and contraction due to heating and cooling will cause these parts to fail.

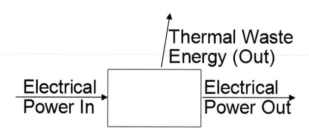

Figure 4-2
CONSERVATION OF ENERGY

HOW EFFICIENT IS YOUR POWER SUPPLY?

An initiative to improve the efficiency of power supplies is known as the 80PLUS program (www.80plus.org). If your new equipment is ENERGY STAR compliant, then it already has an 80PLUS unit inside of it.

Companies fixate on the initial purchase cost of equipment and not the cost of operating a device over its useful life. Therefore, manufacturers cater to this desire by using less efficient and more inexpensive power supply units to win sale. However, as more companies insist on ENERGY STAR compliance, they will begin to benefit from the greater efficiency.

An 80PLUS unit runs with about one-third more efficiency than a "legacy" power supply. It uses less power and generates less heat. This results in diminished thermal stresses on the equipment, greater reliability, and a longer service life.

Central Processing Units

The Central Processing Unit (CPU) is a little thing that consumes a lot of power. Once a computer is powered on, the CPU is running, and it burns a lot of energy. It runs hot enough to require a dedicated heat sink and a fan to cool it down. This signifies the double waste of energy in simultaneously powering (which heats it up) and cooling down the CPU. How it is built and how it is configured have a significant impact on its power consumption. In the case of servers, the CPU can consume up to 35 percent of the power used by the machine, so using the appropriate sized CPU in a server could lead to substantial energy savings. Random Access Memory (RAM) to support the CPU can consume another 15 percent of the computers total power (depending on how much RAM is loaded).

For many years, manufacturers have promoted processors by how much faster the clock's speed is for this unit over its predecessor. The downside of this is that higher clock speeds require greater power. Processors were touted by the instructions per second that they could execute or the number of floating point operations in a second.

The power consumed by the processor speed is calculated as $P = CV^2f$, where P is power, C is the capacitance, V is the voltage, and f is the frequency. Lowering the speed at which the CPU executes allows both the voltage and frequency to be reduced, which in turn generates significant power savings for the processor.

Processor manufacturers usually release two power consumption numbers for a CPU: the typical thermal power, which is measured under normal load, and the maximum thermal power, which is measured under a worst-case set of instructions. However, it is of little value to estimate power consumption by looking at the specification sheets. They typically report only the maximum power consumption. This scenario is like the car with a speedometer that tells you the maximum speed is 120 mph. It can go that fast, but it is never driven that hard.

Over time, heating and cooling weakens a CPU, thereby increasing the likelihood of a failure. When a CPU becomes too hot, it throttles down to protect itself and to reduce the power required to cool it. If a computer is regularly heating up to the point where this kicks in, and it is not being used for graphical design or intense data processing, then the machine is likely not properly ventilated.

Some of the recent industry improvements include:

▲ Notebook computers, in an effort to extend battery life, utilize processors that reduce their speed if they are not being used intensely. This is also available in more recent CPUs for desktops. Intel's version of the technology is called "Speed Step," and AMD has a similar system known as "Power Now!"

▲ Core Scheduling – Multicore machines that are not able to task every core enough to merit keeping them running will now shut down cores until they are needed.

▲ Deep Sleep – Processors that are idling for a certain period of time can go into a sleep mode.

▲ Some implementations of CPUs use very little power, for example, the CPUs in mobile phones and artificial pacemakers often use just a few microwatts of electricity.

▲ AMD CoolCore Technology evaluates which parts of the die – the cores, the memory, or both – are needed to support currently running applications. It can cut power to unused transistor areas to reduce power consumption and lower heat generation.

COMPARING COMPUTING POWER
TO CPU ENERGY USAGE

Comparing processors is a problem, as different manufacturers use different metrics. Some present the theoretical maximum power; others present the average power consumed. This makes it difficult to compare. Another consideration is the need – if workloads can be planned or are predictable and controllable, then low power solutions will be just fine. However, computers with a substantially fluctuating workload and with high computation power demands will still need a higher power supply – in this case, get a CPU that is optimized for higher loads.

The Average CPU Power (ACP) metric is used by AMD to give customers a more accurate idea of the power consumed by the processor. It rates energy usage while running the sorts of programs that a typical desktop might use. ACP allows customers to more realistically forecast their power budget assessments to estimate how much power might actually be consumed at the wall and, more accurately, plan their data center power and cooling infrastructure. This tool will be handy when estimating power requirements for data centers

Intel Corp. rates their processors by the Thermal Design Power (TDP). This indicates the maximum amount of power the cooling system in a computer must dissipate from the CPU for it to operate properly. The TDP rating indicates the maximum power that it would draw when running real applications. This is a more realistic and cost effective measurement, so customers are not expected to provide cooling to meet the maximum processor power draw. Otherwise, excess cooling capacity would be provided by the customer and never used by the device.

For example, consider a processor with a TDP rating of 75. This means the computer must dissipate 75 watts of heat without exceeding the maximum junction temperature for the chip.

TDP is measured at the geometric center on the topside of the processor integrated heat spreader. If no heat spreader is in use, then the rating is the same as the junction temperature. This is measured by the processor's thermal monitor function. A processor's ACP rating is roughly 12% less than its TDP rating. This is due, in part, to the differences in measurement methodologies.

EASY FIXES TO CURRENT CPUS

For those who do not have the luxury of replacing all of their current processors, several things can be done with the current machine. If you are using AMD processors, enable Cool 'n' Quiet in the BIOS (activated by default). Windows XP users will need a driver, available from AMD's Web site, to enable Cool 'n' Quiet to function. If you are using Intel processors, enable "Speed Step" (activated by default), which also controls processor clock speeds.

Disk Drives

Even though the CPU is necessary to accomplish much of anything on a computer, most of the data will ultimately be stored on and recalled from a disk drive. In a data storage center, depending on how data is stored, many disk drives may be simultaneously running. Each drive draws power. Done incorrectly, it wastes a large amount of power and costs the company a large amount of money.

Disk drives work by storing data on a set of flat rotating surfaces called a disk or platter. Spinning these platters is the main source of energy consumption. The disks spin at a very high speed. However, the speed at which the disks spin, as well as the other functions of the drive, can all be regulated to reduce power consumption with a relatively small, if any, degradation in read/write speed.

Because a data center stores so much information, it needs a large volume of storage media. If the data is simply being stored and seldom referenced, and it is OK to have a slow access time, then tape drives will suffice. Idle tape drives consume little power. However, when the data is expected to be needed relatively quickly and will be accessed often, it should be stored on a disk drive. If all disk drives in the center are spinning all the time, a large amount of power is constantly consumed. This activity also generates heat that must be dissipated or cooled. A rule of thumb in the data center is that one watt of power for equipment means one watt of power for cooling.

Many companies have introduced new products to reduce the amount of energy consumed and heat generated by their products. This has been a challenge given that it must accompany their materials changes to accommodate RoHS and other regulatory guidelines.

For example, Western Digital introduced three power saving improvements for its disk drives, with a power reduction of up to 40%. The more efficient use of power indicates that these hard drives will also run cooler.

▲ IntelliPower – By balancing spin speed and transfer rate, as well as by utilizing special caching algorithms, the hard drives reduce energy usage while maintaining "solid performance."

▲ IntelliPark – By unloading the recording heads while the drive is idle, drag is reduced on the disk, requiring less energy to maintain its minimum rotation speed. Also, it disables some of the internal electronics during these rest periods to save additional energy.

Technology to watch includes the Solid-State RAM Disk. With advances in RAM technology, it is now possible to provide the quantity of storage space by using nonvolatile memory instead of a spinning disk platter. This would require less energy to operate, as it has no moving parts. As prices drop, these will be more common in notebook PCs.

The Bottom Line

The amount of energy used by a computer depends on the efficiency of its internal components. Like anything else engineered by humans, there are sloppy designs and there are efficient designs that both work. To evaluate the various options available, IT professionals must educate themselves on what is in the marketplace and what is about to emerge. In this way, they can make a more informed purchasing decision.

One of the important labels to look for is an Energy Star declaration. This is a self-declaration that the product meets the program's criteria. A piece of that criterion is an 80PLUS rated power supply. This device will save money in reduced electrical consumption and extend the life of the equipment by emitting less heat (which is the bane of electronic components).

More efficient CPUs and GPUs are also emerging. They consume less power, provide comparable performance to their energy hungry predecessors, and ease cooling requirements.

Of course, if you want a computer that tends to already have all of these energy saving features, you need to purchase a notebook computer. Notebook design with its limited battery life has long demanded that it be light weight, require less power and, more recently, offer comparable computing power.

ENERGY SAVING INITIATIVES

THE ENERGY STAR, EPEAT, and 80Plus are complementary programs designed to improve the quality of computing equipment. Their goal is to reduce costs through reduced energy consumption without reducing performance. These government supported initiatives have transformed the design of computers and how they are used.

ENERGY STAR is a program developed by the U.S. Environmental Protection Agency (EPA) to promote the use of efficient technologies to reduce the amount of energy wasted through inefficient design. It encompasses more than 50 areas, ranging from construction to office appliances. An ENERGY STAR certified computer uses between 30 and 75% less power to perform the same work as one that is not ENERGY STAR certified.

80Plus focuses on the design and manufacture of more efficient power supplies (a significant source of wasted energy). Power supplies certified under 80Plus are at least 80% efficient, with a power transfer factor of 0.9. The 80Plus program encourages manufacturers to continually improve efficiency of their products through its multilevel grading approach.

The Electronic Product Environmental Assessment Tool (EPEAT) provides a comprehensive environmental impact rating for computers. EPEAT, a U.S. government funded program, describes a device's conformance to 23 mandatory and 28 optional criteria, which include energy efficiency, amount of toxic materials in the device, and even the packing materials used to ship it. This allows companies to specify environmentally efficient equipment with the level of compliance that they desire. EPEAT benefits buyers by saving them from technically examining the total environmental impact of a wide range of equipment. EPEAT is the basis for IEEE standard 1680, the "Standard for Environmental Assessment of Personal Computer Products."

Background

Car owners eventually make comparisons about performance and fuel efficiency among their vehicles. It is common knowledge that a Sport Utility Vehicle travels fewer miles on a gallon of fuel than a subcompact car. This is based on the vehicle's weight, efficiency of the vehicle's engine, and other factors. Using the larger vehicle to haul large loads makes sense. However, using it for a single person to drive back and forth to work is not an efficient choice. We have all used equipment that we considered to be efficient energy users, as well as similar devices that seemed to burn through fuel quickly and provide less service.

However, whereas many of us have personal experience purchasing fuel for our cars and know the cost, we do not have personal knowledge of the amount of energy used by a specific piece of office equipment. Without the appropriate measurement equipment, none of us can readily determine the amount of energy a device uses. Until the recent rise in energy costs, few IT professionals even bothered to ask.

People rarely stop to consider the complexities of powering their computers. They just turn it on and use it as needed. How it works or its efficiencies of power usage compared to other units is not a concern. So long as it is available when needed, the operator is content. Yet just as cars have different levels of energy usage, so do electronic devices.

So how does someone who purchases electronic equipment know which units are efficient and which ones are wasteful? The ENERGY STAR program determines this for them. It was created to assist consumers in identifying the units that cost the least to operate.

ENERGY STAR'S GOVERNMENT ROOTS

ENERGY STAR began as a 1991 U.S. Department of Energy "Green Lights" program. This was an effort to persuade businesses to convert to the use of efficient lighting. In 1992, the U.S. Environmental Protection Agency (EPA) created "ENERGY STAR" as a voluntary labeling program for manufacturers of energy-efficient devices. It promoted energy efficiency among home and commercial users, thereby reducing greenhouse gas emissions.

ENERGY STAR's initial focus was on computers and monitors. In 1996, the ENERGY STAR program became a joint effort of the U.S. EPA and the U.S. Department of Energy.

Each year, the ENERGY STAR program has expanded into new areas. Currently, it encompasses more than 50 categories, including home and commercial construction and consumer and commercial electronic office appliances. Each area has its own energy waste issues, and each offers an opportunity to become part of the solution. The ENERGY STAR program encourages energy efficient designs and the automatic switching to a low power option when the device has been idle for a period of time. Over the years, ENERGY STAR has contributed to the adoption of LED traffic lights, power management for office equipment, and electrical efficiencies improvements for a wide range of electronic devices.

A measure of ENERGY STAR's success is its recognition as an international standard by the European Union (EU), Canada, Australia, Japan, and Taiwan. In 2006, the EU renewed its cooperation agreement with the United States for another five years. North of the border in Canada, the ENERGY STAR program is managed by the Natural Resources Canada's Office of Energy Efficiency. In Australia, ENERGY STAR efficiencies are supported by the Australian Government and State and Territory Governments. Obtain the latest information about ENERGY STAR at: http://www.energystar.gov and www.energystar.gov/powermanagement.

The Challenge of Energy Efficiencies

ENERGY STAR relies on the voluntary compliance of manufacturers. Each manufacturer certifies that its devices meet the ENERGY STAR criteria. These criteria extend beyond certification for the individual item to how the sponsoring manufacturing company itself uses energy. It also requires that a company seeking an ENERGY STAR certification for its products include in the shipping container information about energy management features of that device and encouragement for the customer to use it. This includes:

▲ Potential energy (and cost) savings over devices that are not power managed.

▲ An explanation of how these energy savings translate into environmental benefits for everyone.

POWER SUPPLIES

Electronic devices do not directly use electricity as it comes from a wall outlet. To protect the equipment from power fluctuations and to convert 120-volt line power to the various low direct current levels that a device requires, a "power supply" module is used. Sometimes this power supply sits inside the device; other times, it is an external "power adapter." How serious is this problem of conversion?

Power supply efficiency addresses the issue of how much of the power that is supplied to a device's power supply is actually converted to power the device. This amount of efficiency varies according to the power supply design, the quality and types of materials used, and related factors. A power supply that approached 100% efficiency at its rated load may be much less efficient at a lower power setting. Usually, the lower the load on the power supply, the less efficiently the power supply performs.

Power supplies waste energy in several ways:

▲ Power lost to heat – During operation, some of the internal computer components become quite warm. This heat comes from the movement of electrical current through the components. Electrical energy that is converted to heat during the device's operation represents money spent without generating any income.

▲ Power lost when idle – For as long as an electronic device is energized, it draws electrical power. If no one is using it, then this is all wasted money. Think of it as the price paid for something to be ready the moment you reach for it. Think about computers that are never turned off. How much electricity is used to run equipment that no one is using overnight, over weekends, during vacation?

▲ Power when plugged in – Even when the device is switched to the "off" position, it continues to draw a small amount of electrical power. Again, the equipment is consuming resources and providing no useful result. The U.S. Department of Energy estimates that 75% of the energy used by home electronics occurs when the device has been powered off.

Now look around your office. How many monitors, computers, printers, and other devices are left running around the clock every day of the week? A typical office worker is on the job around 1900 hours per year (40 hours per week, times 52 weeks, less vacation, holiday, sick leave, and other days off). However, there are 8736 hours in a year. So why pay to power something 6836 hours per year more than it is needed?

An ENERGY STAR certified computer uses approximately 70% less electricity than a computer that is left running all of the time. The energy lost is all waste – sort of like buying a tank of gas for your car and throwing away 70% of it – every day. Imagine running your family car around the clock – just so that you could hop in and drive it away on short notice. True, electricity is cheaper than gas, but the price for all types of energy has risen over the last few years and is expected to continue to rise in future years.

This is why the ENERGY STAR program is so relevant to businesses. It saves money without reducing service to anyone. There is no loss of performance as the reduced power is only applied after the device has been idle for longer than a period of time set by the operator. It simply requires purchasing ENERGY STAR certified efficient equipment and ensuring the power management features are enabled.

In mid-2007, ENERGY STAR version 4.0 further tightened requirements to improve energy savings from approved equipment. The introduction of the new standard eliminated all previous ENERGY STAR certifications. To carry the ENERGY STAR logo today, devices must be retested to the new standard. A key requirement is that the power supply in new computers be at least 80% efficient when operating at its rated power.

ENERGY STAR 4.0 recognizes advances in the use of new materials, techniques, and designs. It challenges manufacturers to apply these advances to their product lines. As equipment provides ever greater performance in smaller spaces, its power usage continues to rise without improved power supplies. Also, improved power efficiencies result in reduced heat, thereby reducing residential and office space cooling requirements.

ENERGY STAR version 4.0 for computers looks at three primary areas: computers, monitors, and power adapters. ENERGY STAR is an ongoing program. The next and even more stringent version of the program, version 5.0, is due to take effect in July 2009. This program is still under development, but it will include additional areas of computing, such as thin client computers. Version 5.0 will examine a computer as a unit and its electrical performance across the range of operation (active use, idle time, sleep time, and standby). Like version 4 of this standard, it will exclude servers.

COMPUTERS

Computers are significant users of energy. In most businesses, there is one unit for each person – sometimes more. As computers became less expensive, they proliferated throughout organizations. This has lead to a slow but steady increase in the amount of electrical power consumed by businesses.

Computers consume power through several significant operations. First, the power supply loses energy (through heat) as it converts power from a wall outlet to the lower direct current levels needed by the electronic components. Second, the CPU is a significant user of electrical power, which is why it requires its own cooling fan to counteract the heat it generates. RAM and hard drives both get a workout and also generate heat. All of this heat becomes an additional burden on an office's air conditioning requirements. Again if equipment is powered on when no one is around to use it, additional energy is wasted running office air conditioning equipment to cool it.

The ENERGY STAR program talks a lot about "power management." Power management of a computer has two components:

1. The hardware component provides linkages into the hardware elements unique to that device. This is provides by the equipment's manufacturer. Power Management for computers and their monitors is a function of both the hardware and the operating system. The hardware manufacturer provides a set of standard interfaces into the major sub assemblies and USB attached devices through the hardware's Basic Input Output System (BIOS) chip.

2. The software component is a utility program provided by the operating system. It enables changing the time delay for shifting to low power. All of this is explained in Chapter 6, "Advanced Configuration and Power Interface" (ACPI). The interface is a user-friendly way to select options such as "never sleep" or the timer for when to switch to sleep mode. The operating system component also provides a pathway for the keyboard, mouse, and other devices to "wake up" the equipment.

To be ENERGY STAR compliant, computers must be shipped from the manufacturer configured to switch to sleep mode after 30 minutes. The packaging must alert the purchaser about this sleep mode setting and explain how to return the computer to "active" mode.

In addition to the power management setting for plugged into a wall outlet, a notebook PC also has power management for its battery power. Notebook PCs are purchased to be portable and often depend on their limited battery power. There is a separate value for when to place the display and the computer into sleep mode when on battery power. If the unit is left idle too long, the battery will run down and the unit will not be available when needed.

POWER MANAGEMENT MODES
Many people leave their desktop computer running until something forces them to reboot it. They would prefer that it draw electricity around the

clock, every day of every week, than be inconvenienced by a few minutes delay in starting the machine every day. The key to implementing power management is to demonstrate to everyone that delays will be minimal and that the company's power savings significant. These delays are minimized by placing idle computers in a "sleep" mode.

ENERGY STAR's power management for computers recognizes two dimensions of power management: computer controlled and network controlled. Computer-controlled power management has five states:

1. *Active* – The equipment is performing useful work. Although this varies with the type of work performed, it may be as little as five percent of the workday.

2. *Idle* – The computer is powered on but not performing useful work. The operating system, applications, and utility programs are all loaded in memory, with some of them running unseen in the background. The unit remains in this mode drawing 100 watts or less until the operator activates an input or pointer device.

3. *Sleeping* – The computer is in a reduced power state drawing 4 watts or less. The work in progress is still resident in RAM, but the RAM is drawing low power for a slow refresh rate. No power is provided to the CPU. With these reduced requirements, the power supply switches to drawing a small amount of electricity. The computer is "awakened" by pressing on a key or moving the mouse. The transition from sleep mode to fully operational takes less than a few seconds.

> **SLEEP MODE WARNING**
> If power is lost while in sleep mode, it is the same as pulling the plug while using the machine. Everything stored in RAM is lost and files in process of writing to the disk may become corrupted.

4. *Standby* – The machine has been powered "off" by the operator. Power is withdrawn from the CPU, RAM, disk drive, and other components. The computer continues to draw less than 2 watts of power for as long as it is plugged into the electrical outlet. Part of this power is used to operate the network card at low power as it listens for the Wake On LAN signal. The best way to cut even this small flow of electricity is to plug the unit into a power strip and turn off the power strip.

5. *Hard Off* – A device that is not receiving any electrical power at all. This may be the result of physically unplugging it from an outlet or connecting to the power source through a power strip that has been turned off.

Network Controlled Power Management addresses one of the significant objections to deenergizing computers. Most companies push software patches and antivirus updates to company machines after normal working hours. This minimizes disruption to the operators and allows plenty of time for long downloads and mandatory restarts. ENERGY STAR certified computers do not lose their network connection when in a low power (Standby) state.

Network Controlled Power Management includes the hardware and software that connects the computer to the organization's network. This is the network card, connection, driver software for the card, and so on.

▲ Wake Event – Moving a device from stand-by or sleep to powered mode. This is the receipt of a signal over the network to wake up.

▲ Wake On LAN – A capability of the computer to return to a fully powered state from a Sleep or Standby state on receipt of the proper command. This requires that the unit's network security configuration is set to permit Wake On LAN. Usually this is a combination of an operating system setting and a logical switch in the hardware.

▲ While in Standby mode, the computer listens on the network connection for a command to wake up, known as a "magic packet." This signal is sent on a LAN's broadcast address and uses port 0, 7, or 9. The computer examines the packet to see if holds its MAC address (actual format is hexadecimal FF 6 times followed by the target unit's MAC address repeated 16 times). If the NIC uses password protection for this feature, then it is appended to the packet.

Computers shipped to commercial customers must be set for Wake On LAN. Units shipped to consumers should have this capability turned off. However, Windows users can activate this through the network device's properties under the Device Manager.

Companies that use Microsoft's Active Directory supporting Windows XP operating system can download a free utility for controlling workstation power management. "EZ GPO" enables power management using Group Policy Objects (GPOs). Windows Vista already has this function and an extra utility program is not required. EZ GPO is offered as open source and does not charge licensing fees.

VOICE OVER IP
Computer Power Management requirements are sometimes adjusted to address how people use the technology. Some use their computers for Voice Over IP (VOIP) to provide telephone service.

This saves on long distance charges. However, what happens if the
computer is in sleep or standby mode when a call comes in? In 2008,
Intel introduced a Remote Wake capability on its motherboards so
when a call is received, the computer is moved from standby or sleep
mode to full operation.

MONITORS

Computer monitors have come a long way. From modified televisions displaying text and basic graphics they have evolved into devices with the
ability to display an infinite number of colors with great clarity. However,
monitors have always been significant consumers of electricity. The high
energy usage of monitors was one of ENERGY STAR's original challenges.

Older monitors used cathode ray tubes (picture tubes) to display images.
This technology requires high voltages to paint the picture on the screen.
A 17-inch display might require 70 watts or more of power under normal
use. Since the display was operational as long as the computer was running,
this amounted to a lot of electricity. Screen saver software was popular to
prevent the same image from burning into the screen of a computer that sat
idle over time. Unfortunately, running a screen saver program is the same
as running a computer and its monitor for other tasks, so the unit consumed as much electricity as if it was performing useful work.

Most monitor manufacturers today use liquid crystal technology to display information. In full operation, these monitors consume about one-
third as much power as a CRT-based device. However, to be ENERGY STAR
compliant, they must also switch to sleep mode if they are idle for more
than 15 minutes. Turning a monitor off and on multiple times a day will
not hurt it. The voltage surge from a "power on" only wears on the components a small amount. The cumulative effect would take many more
years to become apparent than the device will be in service.

Monitors seeking an ENERGY STAR rating must meet three criteria:

1. Power on mode (displaying an image) – The maximum power allowed
for ENERGY STAR certification is 28 times the number of megapixels. So
if the display resolution was rated at 1280 by 1024, the maximum allowed
power would be 1.31 megapixels multiplied by 28 watts or 37 watts.

2. Sleep mode (i.e., a blank screen that is initiated by a command from
the computer) uses 2 watts or less. The monitor returns to full operation
on command from the computer. Manufacturers must ship monitors with
a switch setting for the monitor to change to sleep mode if idle for 30 minutes. However, the device's operator may change this setting as desired,

such as for a monitor that must always display the status of a particular operation. Monitor sleep mode is controlled by both the computer and the internal monitor logic. The monitor may act independently of the computer to enter sleep mode. However, its wake up comes from the computer's operating system.

3. Off mode – When the user has turned the power switch off, the monitor cannot use more than 1 watt of power. To ensure a monitor is completely powered off, it must be plugged into a power strip that is turned off to stop the flow of all electricity to the device. The ENERGY STAR program requirements for computer monitors version 4.1 refer to this as "Hard Off" mode.

EXTERNAL POWER ADAPTERS

Portable devices are designed to be as small and light as possible. ENERGY STAR recognizes two classes of external power adapters: battery chargers and external power supplies.

An excellent example of this is a cell phone. It is designed to fit in a pocket but still provide the maximum number of services. One way this is done is to power the cell phone from a battery that is reenergized by a battery charger. This removes the power supply from the unit and places it in an external adapter. Other non-portable devices, such as desktop speakers, use a similar arrangement. In this case, by moving the bulky power supply module out of the speaker casing, space is saved on the desktop.

According to the ENERGY STAR Web site, 1.5 billion power adapters are in use throughout the United States. "The total electricity flowing through all types of power supplies is about 300 billion kWh/year, or 11% of the national electric bill." See http://www.energystar.gov/index.cfm?c=ext_power_supplies.power_supplies_consumers

The amount of energy consumed by these many small adapters is so large that ENERGY STAR has a special program to improve their performance. This program uses its own ENERGY STAR logo. Adapters with the ENERGY STAR adapter logo are usually 30 percent more efficient and smaller than less efficient units. To qualify for an ENERGY STAR certification, the external adapter must meet efficiency thresholds when it is providing power to the device and when it is idle.

PRINTERS

It is a rare business that does not have printers sprinkled throughout the office. Usually these are networked and shared laser printers, although occasionally a desktop may have an inkjet printer for convenience or to make

Powered by an
ENERGY STAR®
qualified adapter
for a better
environment

Figure 5-1
ENERGY STAR ADAPTER LABEL

color images. These devices also represent a significant energy drain on the company.

The ENERGY STAR requirements for desktop or office printers are somewhat complex because of the many technologies that can be used. Monochrome laser printers, color laser printers, inkjet printers, and many points in between make it difficult to determine the standby power level and when an idle printer should shift to standby mode. In times past, printers printed whatever was sent their way. Now, they may use internal hard drives and extensive RAM arrays; they may also print complex graphics.

ENERGY STAR's goal is efficiency of operation. How efficient a device is depends on its underlying technology. It is up to the purchaser to select the particular technology that fits his or her application. Laser printers use significantly more power and cost less in supplies per printed page than inkjet printers. However, inkjet printers consume less energy while being used and while in idle mode.

Some technologies are more energy intensive than others. Laser printers use around 350 watts of power when printing, whereas a fast inkjet printer may use about 50 watts. A laser printer sitting idle power may still use 50 watts waiting for its next print job, whereas an inkjet printer may consume as little as 5 watts. To ensure that the company is purchasing the most efficient technology available, look for an ENERGY STAR certified logo.

ENERGY STAR certified printers must automatically switch to Sleep mode after 4 hours of idle time. This can only be changed by the manufacturer. However, most are shipped with a much shorter setting that can be modified by the purchaser. Based on the print volume capability of the printer, it is shipped to move to sleep mode within 5 minutes for small printers to one hour for high-speed office printers. This time delay (up to four hours) can be adjusted by the operator.

PEOPLE PLAY AN IMPORTANT PART

People play an important role in power management. Their actions can bypass the power management timers or disable them entirely. The software controlling power management for a device is accessible to the device's operator. Companies installing ENERGY STAR compliant devices must consider the human factor in all energy efficiency programs.

Most organizations manage this as they do any other cultural change.

▲ Begin with a powerful executive sponsor.

▲ Inform everyone what will happen, and why.

▲ Engage representatives from around the company to advise employees about the installation, such as how long before a unit is moved to a Sleep state.

▲ Inform everyone before the change is made.

▲ Provide a process for someone to opt-out of power management.

Successfully implementing power management in an organization requires paying close attention to the people side of the issue. Not every computer is suitable for power management. Some are used to display the status of something or to monitor if something changes. Others must be available for remote access. The "P" in PC stands for personal, and many people take literally. Consequently, they become disturbed whenever someone adds something to their machine (such as mandatory timers for switching to sleep mode) without any way to override the change. After all, in their eyes, this new inconvenience benefits someone far away and not them (since they likely do not pay the electric bill).

Each exception should be approved by the IT staff on an individual basis. (The higher the executive that must grant the approval, the fewer the number of requests that will be received.)

Computers are shipped with a 30-minute delay before switching to sleep mode, and a 15-minute timer before they command monitors to switch to sleep mode. Both of these settings can be changed by the unit's operator. (On a computer using the Windows operating system, this is found under the Power Options on the Control Panel.)

> **WAKE ON LAN**
> Computers shipped to home users are delivered with the Wake On LAN feature disabled. Machines sold to commercial users (usually sold in bulk or built to a special configuration) are shipped with Wake On LAN enabled.

Computers sold to consumers can easily be configured to bypass all of the power management features. ENERGY STAR addresses this by requiring that the equipment manufacturer provide information to the buyer about the value of allowing equipment to switch to sleep mode automatically. However, they must also provide information on the timer settings and how to turn them off.

Equipment delivered to commercial operations is a different matter. These devices are often centrally managed for the benefit of the company. Once the operating system configuration settings are loaded, they are locked so that only the system administrator can change them. This includes the power savings options.

However, ENERGY STAR compliant computers sold to a commercial customer with a custom software image may no longer meet ENERGY STAR criteria if the customer image changes or eliminates the settings.

80Plus Program

The 80Plus Program encourages the manufacture of power supplies that are at least 80% efficient. It funded by electric utility companies interested in electrical efficiency across North America. When the ENERGY STAR 4.0 standard was issued for computers in July 2007, it included a requirement for 80Plus power supplies in all certified units. ENERGY STAR version 5.0, anticipated in July 2009, is likely to raise the bar even higher.

Power supplies are typically most efficient when delivering about 75% of their rated load. This is another argument again delivering computers with oversized power supplies as a "system feature." The power supply will waste energy unless it is further loaded after delivery, such as with the addition of disk drives, more RAM, additional circuit cards, and so on.

To be certified under this program, the power supply must be at least 80% efficient under 20%, 50%, and 100% of its rated load. It must also perform at these loads with a true power factor of 0.9. True Power Factor is a ratio of how efficiently power is used in the device. It ranges from 0 (poor) to 1.0 (efficient). A low rating means that more power is applied to circuits than is needed. This excess is converted to heat, which weakens components and wastes energy.

Everyone has felt how warm some electronic equipment becomes when it runs. Some devices run much hotter than others. This heat represents wasted electricity – much of it from the power supply. The amount of heat created by computer power supplies is why they have their own cooling fans. A typical power supply is about 70% efficient. For example, it takes 100 watts of incoming power to provide 70 watts of usable power in the device. The remaining 30% of the energy is lost as heat.

An 80Plus power supply has many other benefits (The latest information on this program can be found at www.80plus.org.). More efficient power transfer reduces the amount of heat the power supply generates. An 80Plus power supply costs slightly more to build than a standard power supply, but the EPA estimates that this cost difference is repaid through efficient operation within the first year. Given that computer equipment is purchased with a three- or five-year useful life, the savings may be significant.

This permits the use of smaller and quieter cooling fans. Heat is the enemy of electronic parts, so cooler running devices suffer fewer mechanical breakdowns. Finally, with less air forced over the power supply, less dust is pulled into the unit.

Plan to spend a bit more money. 80Plus power supplies cost a few more dollars to make. This improved efficiency is the result of improved design, newer materials, and careful assembly. In the price competitive market for computers and monitors, they are offered as options or in specially build "green" devices. However, within a year, they will have saved more than the extra expense and will continue to save the purchaser on their power expenses for the rest of the useful life of the device.

In 2008, the 80Plus program added three additional ratings: Bronze, Silver, and Gold. Each higher level raises the amount of required power supply efficiency. At present, Gold rated power supplies are few.

▲ 80Plus – 80% efficiency at 20%, 50%, and 100% load, and a power factor of 0.9 at 100% load.

▲ 80Plus Bronze – 82% efficiency at 20%, 85% at 50%, and 82% at 100% load, and a power factor of 0.9 at 50% load.

▲ 80Plus Silver – 85% efficiency at 20%, 88% at 50%, and 85% at 100% load, and a power factor of 0.9 at 50% load.

▲ 80Plus Gold – 87% efficiency at 20%, 90% at 50%, and 87% at 100% load, and a power factor of 0.9 at 50% load.

Electronic Product Environmental Assessment Tool (EPEAT)

The Electronic Product Environmental Assessment Tool (EPEAT) gages the environmental impact of purchasing a product. EPEAT was created by the Zero Waste Alliance (www.zerowaste.org) through funding provided by the U.S. EPA; it is currently administered by the Green Electronics Council (www.greenelectronicscouncil.org).

EPEAT is the result of advice from manufactures, buyers, and environmental groups. The goal was to examine computers, notebook computers, and monitor from initial design through to final disposal, including all points in between. This includes the equipment's manufacture, shipment, installation, use, decommissioning and, finally, recycling. EPEAT measurements meet or exceed all known U.S. and international environmental statutes. An advantage is that equipment that meets EPEAT criteria will also comply with most international export criteria, such as the EU's RoHs (Restriction of Hazardous Substances Directive).

EPEAT examines a product in eight different categories and against 51 different criteria. This holistic approach provides concerned purchasers with a "score" for how environmentally friendly something is.

EPEAT ratings are based on the manufacturer's self-declaration of equipment conformance to the standard. The standard details are what to measure and how to measure it. These claims are randomly audited.

EPEAT benefits both buyers and manufacturers. It provides manufacturers with a well-recognized standard to use when designing new products. It results in fairer competition because everyone knows in advance how their product will be measured and how it stacks up against the competition. EPEAT also benefits society, as it identifies weaknesses in a manufacturer's products for improvement. It is also an indicator that products will meet EU environmental standards.

Purchasers like EPEAT, particularly since they lack the technical expertise and time to examine so many products. The EPEAT rating not only indicates what criteria the product meets, but which ones it does not. When soliciting equipment bids, purchasers should require that all equipment be certified as EPEAT Bronze level or higher. Companies seeking to improve their "green credentials" can purchase equipment with EPEAT Silver or Gold ratings. Individual buyers benefit since it provides them with an environmental friendliness rating system for their personal purchases.

EPEAT is an ANSI approved standard and has been adopted by the Institute of Electrical and Electronic Engineers (IEEE) as standard number 1680 (Standard for Environmental Assessment of Personal Computer Products). For the full details about each criteria, measurement processes, and other data, manufacturers should purchase a copy of this standard. This will ensure that a self-declaration of an EPEAT rating for a product will survive an audit. For the latest information on EPEAT, check out www.epeat.net.

EPEAT RATING SYSTEM

Trying to describe everything about a computer's environmental impact from beginning to end is complex. To accomplish this, EPEAT's eligibility criteria is broken into eight categories. Each category includes mandatory criteria that a device must meet to earn the lowest level of EPEAT certification. There are also optional criteria that a manufacturer can meet to demonstrate their higher commitment to a clean environment.

The EPEAT is aimed squarely at large commercial and government purchasers. Individuals may use EPEAT to guide their own purchases, but some of the criteria may not be met. For example, under the category of "Packaging," an optional criteria is the "Provision of take-back program for packaging." A large commercial purchase of equipment would spread this expense among many units, so the time and transportation expense to move the packing materials (boxes, packing foam, etc.) to a recycler is easily covered. Sales of an individual unit would likely not include this feature or the expense might be significantly higher.

> **TAIWAN'S GREENMARK PROGRAM**
> Taiwan's Greenmark program is similar to EPEAT. Unlike EPEAT, Greenmark performs on-site compliance inspections to validate a company's compliance. Greenmark certification is important when purchasing or selling Green products in the Asian market.

EPEAT certifies electronic products according to three tiers of environmental performance – Bronze, Silver, and Gold. A product must meet all the required criteria in order to qualify for EPEAT bronze. Manufacturers may pick and choose among the optional criteria to boost their EPEAT "score" to achieve a higher level. Some of optional criteria may not apply to the device in question, based on its design and materials content.

- ▲ Bronze - Meets all 23 required criteria.

- ▲ Silver - Meets all required criteria plus any 14 optional criteria.

- ▲ Gold - Meets all required criteria plus any 21 optional criteria.

Like all rules, there are some caveats. For example, where elimination of some hazardous substances is mandated, a very low level may be permitted if they are due to use of recycled materials.

- ▲ Reduction/Elimination of Environmentally Sensitive Materials

  - ▲ Mandatory

    - △ Compliance with provisions of European RoHS (Restriction on the Use of Certain Hazardous Substances in Electrical and Electronic Equipment) Directive 2002/95/EC.

    - △ Reporting on amount of mercury used in light sources (mg) for flat-panel displays.

    △ Elimination of intentionally added Short Chain Chlorinated Paraffins (SCCP) flame retardants and plasticizers.

▲ Optional

    △ Elimination of intentionally added cadmium in videoscreens.

    △ Low threshold for amount of mercury used in light sources for flat-panel video displays.

    △ Elimination of intentionally added mercury used in light sources for flat-panel video displays.

    △ Elimination of intentionally added lead in video displays.

    △ Elimination of intentionally added hexavalent chromium.

    △ Large plastic parts free of certain flame retardants classified under European Council Directive 67/548/EEC.

    △ Batteries free of lead, cadmium, and mercury.

    △ Large plastic parts free of PVC.

▲ Material Selection

  ▲ Mandatory

    △ Declaration of postconsumer recycled plastic content (%).

    △ Declaration of renewable/biobased plastic materials content (%).

    △ Declaration of product weight (lbs).

  ▲ Optional

    △ Minimum content of postconsumer recycled plastic.

    △ Higher content of postconsumer recycled plastic.

    △ Minimum content of renewable/biobased plastic material.

▲ Design for End of Life

  ▲ Mandatory

    △ Identification of materials with special handling needs, particularly for items not common with recycling companies.

    △ Elimination of paints or coatings that are not compatible with recycling or reuse.

    △ Easy disassembly of external enclosure.

- △ Marking of plastic components.

- △ Identification and removal of components containing hazardous materials.

- △ Minimum 65 percent reusable/recyclable.

- ▲ Optional

  - △ Reduced number of plastic material types.

  - △ Molded/glued in metal eliminated or removable.

  - △ Minimum 90 percent reusable/recyclable.

  - △ Manual separation of plastics.

  - △ Marking of plastics.

- ▲ Product Longevity/ Life Extension

  - ▲ Mandatory

    - △ Availability of additional three-year warranty or service agreement.

    - △ Upgradeable with common tools.

  - ▲ Optional

    - △ Modular design.

    - △ Availability of replacement parts.

- ▲ Energy Conservation

  - ▲ Mandatory

    - △ Conform to the current version of the U.S. EPA ENERGY STAR® program.

  - ▲ Optional

    - △ Early adoption of new ENERGY STAR® specification.

    - △ Renewable energy accessory available.

    - △ Renewable energy accessory standard.

- ▲ End-of-Life Management

  - ▲ Mandatory

    - △ Provision of product take-back service.

    - △ Provision of rechargeable battery take-back service.

▲ Optional

△ Auditing of recycling vendors.

▲ Corporate Performance

▲ Mandatory

△ Demonstration of corporate environmental policy consistent with ISO 14001.

△ Self-certified environmental management system for design and manufacturing organizations.

△ Corporate report consistent with Performance Track or GRI.

▲ Optional

△ Third-party certified environmental management system for design and manufacturing organizations.

△ Corporate report based on GRI.

▲ Packaging

▲ Mandatory

△ Reduction/elimination of intentionally added toxics in packaging.

△ Separable packing materials.

△ Declaration of recycled content.

▲ Optional

△ Packaging 90% recyclable and plastics labeled.

△ Minimum postconsumer content guidelines.

△ Provision of take-back program for packaging.

△ Documentation of reusable packaging.

EPEAT of the future is already in progress. The Zero Waste Alliance has been hired by the U.S. EPA to develop EPEAT-SDR (EPEAT-Standards Development Roadmap). This program expands the scope of EPEAT from computers to a wide range of electronic equipment. The roadmap recommends modifying IEEE 1620 to a range of standards, each with their own focus (just as EPEAT in its original form focused on personal computers). The next four areas of concentration are:

▲ Imaging devices

▲ Televisions and television monitors

▲ Computer servers

▲ Mobile devices

EPEAT-SDR is still in its early stages and changes may be approved as it progresses. However, it builds on the success of the original EPEAT ratings and, as it expands into new areas, it will be easier for buyers to purchase products that are friendlier to the environment.

GOVERNMENT ORDER

Executive Order 13423 (Strengthening Federal Environmental, Energy, and Transportation Management) requires all U.S. federal agencies to use EPEAT when purchasing computer systems. Signed by President George W. Bush in January 2007, this order mandates that 95 percent of electronic products procured by all federal agencies meet EPEAT standards, as long a standard exists for the product.

In terms of purchasing power, the U.S. Government is gigantic. Every year it purchases approximately $10 billion of energy-consuming products. In addition, its purchasing of energy usage is likewise huge. By focusing such a large market on the purchase of energy-efficient equipment, it is hoped that manufacturing costs will decrease to the point where these worthwhile products become affordable for everyone. It also demonstrates that the government is following its own advice about purchasing energy-efficient equipment.

Along with this comes the savings in tax dollars that results from energy savings. Because the government offers such a large market for electronics, it also has a large appetite for energy. Reduced energy usage translates into reduced operating costs and a reduction in pollution.

Along with EPEAT and ENERGY STAR, the Department of Energy's Federal Energy Management Program (FEMP) helps to identify those devices in the top 25% of energy efficiency. Electronic devices not covered by any of these standards can still be purchased if they meet one of three criteria:

1. If the product is not cost effective over its expected useful life.

2. If ENERGY STAR or FEMP-designated product is not reasonably available to meet functional requirement.

3. The product is for combat or combat-related missions.

The Bottom Line

These three certifying programs form a hierarchy of excellence for manufacturers of computer equipment to strive toward and for purchasers of equipment to look out for. ENERGY STAR addresses power usage and efficient use of equipment, putting it to "sleep" when it is not needed. 80Plus power supplies efficiently provide energy to equipment. Together, these two programs save companies money without reducing the level of service to the equipment operators

EPEAT provides a benchmark with which to gage the environmental impact of a purchase. This is a significant advantage to manufacturers because they no longer need to guess what to focus on, and how much they must improve. This program enables them to focus on specific improvements which help to contain their costs. In addition, an electronic device that fulfills the requirements for EPEAT certification will also pass European requirements, thereby making it easier to export the devices.

Buyers appreciate EPEAT since it provides information by which they can ensure conformance with the company's environmental objectives. Of course, government buyers depend on EPEAT certification when purchasing electronic equipment.

There are significant issues with these three programs. First they are all self-certifying. Given the financial rewards, someone is bound to cheat, and the chance they will be caught is slim (unless their action is very blatant). Second, equipment operators can defeat ENERGY STAR's power management if they are able to completely override the sleep mode timer. This means that companies must regularly reeducate everyone on the value of leaving the times set as delivered.

ADVANCED CONFIGURATION
AND POWER INTERFACE

IN CHAPTER 5, we discussed Energy Star's use of power management to reduce the amount of electricity used by idle equipment. Now that we understand the "what" and "why" of power management, we can delve into the "how" of it. While Energy Star deals with managing people and equipment, this chapter describes the technical details of how power management controls a computer to minimize its electrical consumption while idle. It reviews the history of two power management approaches and how they are implemented in Microsoft Windows and Linux workstations.

Power management has two important parts. The first is the hardware component, which is supplied by the equipment manufacturers. This is stored as parameter information about the basic computer equipment that is stored in the Basic Input Output System (BIOS) chip on the motherboard. It also comes from the driver software accompanying add-on devices. The second part is the software side, which is now controlled by the operating system. It contains software that reads this information and controls the power management for the unit based on the idle timer set by the operator.

Advanced Power Management (APM) initially brought power management to the personal work space. Driven by the need to conserve battery power in the newly developed notebook PCs, its acceptance by desktop PC users was tepid. Several years later, the Advanced Configuration and Power Interface (ACPI) open standard built on APM's successes and shortcomings to create the power management solution used in most of today's computers. The key difference was in the system design – APM is hardware centric, and ACPI is software centric.

Advanced Power Management (APM)

The initial push for power management came from the old "portable" PCs. Early portable units were the size of a sewing machine, with considerably more weight. If they ran on battery power, it would not be for long. Most of the time, these bulky, power-hungry units were plugged into an electrical outlet. It was the advent of the notebook PC that pressed the need for power management. Notebook PCs considerably shrank the size of portable units by replacing their small CRT based monitor with a liquid crystal display. This made them considerable lighter and much more popular. The problem was the limited battery power.

Batteries are composed of chemicals that combine to create electrical current. There is a limit as to how long they can supply this current before this chemical reaction is exhausted. Power management on these notebook PCs was originally intended to conserve battery power.

Shift for a moment to desktop computers. In the beginning, personal computers were thought of as desktop appliances, much like a computer terminal. You turned it on at the beginning of the day and, if you thought about, you turned it off before leaving for home. A major concern was the monitor. If the same image was displayed without change for an extended period, it might be permanently burned into the screen. This would blur the latest information displayed under it. So, wherever possible, screens were turned off or a screen-saver program was started. The focus was on saving the screen, not on saving electricity. The power management issue was how to turn off the display when the operator neglected to do so.

Added to all of this was the gradual lowering of the price of computers and their increased capabilities. It did not take long to realize the impact of these machines that were proliferating throughout companies. First, came the call for more electrical outlets (one for the large CRT, one for the PC, one for the personal printer, one for the external modem, etc.). The company's electric bills slowly rose, as each new device incrementally added to the overall load. Leaving PCs turned on overnight seemed normal, since mainframe terminals were commonly left with the power on and many companies installed one on every desk. Eventually, it became obvious that something needed to be done.

THE APM STANDARD

The first serious attempt at an industry-wide solution to the power management of personal computers began in 1992. Intel, IBM, and Microsoft worked together to develop a standard solution. The result was the Advanced Power Management (APM) standard. APM first appeared in Windows 3.11, and then in an upgraded form in Windows 95.

APM is a hardware centric solution. Its key components are:

▲ BIOS - The central control for switching power states is managed by the motherboard's Basic Input Output System (BIOS) which is burned into an integrated circuit chip.

▲ Hardware devices – Each hardware device has its own power management code in its device driver. However, not all devices chose to provide a power management aware driver to work together with APM.

▲ Power management subroutines in software applications enable them to communicate with the BIOS to prepare for transition into or out of a power management mode.

▲ APM recognizes five power states:

   ▲ ON – Normal operations.

   ▲ APM enabled – The computer is operating, but some of the idle hardware devices may be powered off.

   ▲ APM Standby – The computer is not working, as many devices are in a reduced power state. The CPU clock is slowed or stopped. Upon command, the computer quickly returns to service.

   ▲ APM Suspend – Minimum power level, long recovery time. The CPU clock is stopped ,and the CPU is at minimal power.

   ▲ Off – All power is removed from system devices.

HOW APM WORKS

Devices are installed with APM-aware drivers and communicated to the BIOS through them. When a device has been idle for a set period, these drivers notify the BIOS and put themselves into a low power mode (or sleep). APM also controls the sleep control on individual devices and may also command a device to switch to low power.

APM manages power to the overall computer system. It defines activity as movement of interrupts and data through the input/output port. If the computer was idle for more than the timer value, then APM uses separate idle times for individual devices and for the entire system.

Similarly, application software communicate with the BIOS when it needs something to stay active even if it has been idle for extended periods of time. When the BIOS decides to shift the computer to low power, it notifies the software that has communicated with it that a shutdown is imminent. This allows time for the software to save its content. However, if the software does not communicate with APM, then the sudden loss of power results in data loss.

LINUX APM

Some Linux users still prefer to use APM over ACPI simply because they are already familiar with its use and limitations. However, only one (APM or ACPI) can provide a computer's power management at a time. Linux users start APM using the apmd command. This is a daemon that is typically run at system boot. The apmd command also monitors notebook or attached Uninterruptible Power Supply (UPS) batteries. If the remaining battery power level falls below a defined threshold, then APM puts the computer to sleep to conserve power.

APM SHORTCOMINGS

It did not take long after its introduction before APM was panned by the trade press. People using it felt that it would abruptly shut down in the middle an application and result in lost data. The only way to wake the system up was to reboot it. Consequently, most people avoided it, and the technical trade press regularly hammered its shortcomings.

APM's primary limitation was its hardware centric architecture. Computer manufacturers sometimes implemented it slightly differently from the standard to accommodate peculiarities in their system's design. A well-designed computer, in which everything worked well together when it left the factory, might become APM unstable through the addition of peripherals and circuit cards from other manufacturers after the machine was delivered. Even the APM BIOS code might vary among models from the same manufacturer.

Some of the architectural issues with APM include:

▲ A computer's BIOS might command APM to enter power saving mode without notifying the operating system. This caused a loss of data residing in RAM. The same could occur with the system components, such as the hard drive shifting to suspend mode without informing the operating system. Likewise, the operating system may reduce power to the system without first checking with APM.

▲ APM monitored the state of the hardware and could not tell what the applications were doing unless they included APM interaction code. It could be that the screen did not move for a good reason, but was cut off by APM for inactivity, such as during a long team discussion about a single PowerPoint slide.

▲ APM could only detect devices on the motherboard. Externally attached components were not monitored, so the computer may appear to APM to be idle when the add-ons were quite active.

▲ APM lacked an adequate capability for monitoring network activity. If the system appeared to be idle, there may have been network traffic (such as waiting for the distant site to respond) that was disrupted by APM.

▲ APM required a reboot if the power management settings were changed.

▲ APM support in computer motherboard's BIOS was not universally available.

APM was a good first try at energy management. However, it was too simplistic an approach to adequately determine if it was safe for a device or for the entire computer to go to sleep. A computer needs to track a large number of statuses, requires logic to determine when it is safe to move into and out of power management, and must provide a full-featured user interface. The standard was too loose for manufacturers to implement consistently, thereby causing enough system failures for most operators to disable it. Besides, during the mid to late 1990s, most desktop users did not see a need for it.

APM FUTURES

APM is still supported by most manufacturers as a legacy system. Most developers and system designers have converted to ACPI because of its flexibility, many features, and general industry acceptance. It is never a good idea to use both APM and ACPI to manage power usage on the same equipment. However, some components of APM are included and managed by ACPI.

APM is still supported in older equipment and in some operating systems, such as Linux. Design engineers and software developers tend to stick with what is familiar to them, even if it is not optimal. Every shortcoming is another opportunity for a patch that results in a product with more features and better stability. However, most new power management work is done in ACPI, which offers greater flexibility and has earned industry-wide acceptance.

The Advanced Configuration and Power Interface (ACPI) Standard

The IT industry profited greatly from its experience with APM. In 1996, five major companies joined together to design a replacement to APM that addressed its shortcomings and improved its capabilities. Hewlett-Packard, Intel, Microsoft, Phoenix, and Toshiba drafted an open standard that also encompassed mobile systems and servers.

The primary architectural difference between APM and ACPI is that where APM was BIOS based, the Advanced Configuration and Power Interface (ACPI) standard is based in the operating system. Moving control to the operating system provides space for extensive logic to support immediate and future requirements. In addition, there are fewer operating systems than there are computer manufacturers. This provides the entire industry with a more consistent interface for hardware and software designers.

An open standard is very important. It reduces the amount of redundant investment in power management throughout the industry. As an open standard, it benefits from the sharing of many different perspectives across hardware and software development industries. Manufacturers are free to focus their efforts and investments on innovation rather than on arguing over variations in interpreting some other company's technical approach.

ACPI hit the streets with Windows 98. Currently, it is found in notebook, server, desktop, and special purpose computers—and for good reason. It is simple to implement. For the technical details of ACPI, download the standard from http://www.acpi.info/spec.htm.

HOW ACPI WORKS

The ACPI architecture places control of all of the power management functions (APM, Plug and Play, legacy, device controlled, etc.) into one place. It is broken into two major components. The hardware devices provide information about their power requirements and status, and the operating system provides the software logic for managing power. Separating hard-

ware and software components frees the manufacturers of each to cre-
atively focus on what they know best, with an assurance that their product will work with the other. An open source model prevents one company
or another from gaining a marketplace advantage by modifying the standard to the advantage of its product and the detriment of its competitors.

When a computer boots, the hardware information table (along with its
associated ACPI controls) is read from the BIOS into the ACPI work space.
This information is called the Discrete System Descriptor Table (DSDT).
Added to this table, is device information about attached peripherals connected via Plug and Play, PCI, IEEE 1394, and USB. These data tables are
used by power management software to control individual devices. It also
establishes a table of information on their power level in a central location.
The ACPI tables describe the power planes and clock sources used by a
specific device, as well as the controls for turning them off. An example
would be the different device requirements between device state "D0" (full
power) and state "D1" (reduced power).

The current ACPI specifications version is 3.0b and was last updated in
August 2006. Some of the design requirements include:

▲ Every component in the system or attached to it must be capable
of power management. The standardization of interfaces enables
support of a wide range of equipment, both known and which may
be created in the future.

▲ Power management is handled by the operating system for flexibility and consistency across computer manufacturers.

▲ The operating system interfaces with the ACPI data tables that describe the power characteristics of each device, along with the
ACPI Machine Language (AML) commands to control it.

▲ Wake On LAN is required for remote management of computers.

USER ADMINISTERED POWER PLANNING

Energy Star standards require that default values be placed into the idle
times. Equipment should ship to commercial customers with a 15-minute
idle time-out for the monitor and a 30-minute idle time-out for the computer. If the defaults do not suit the work environment, they can be adjusted by the operator.

Someone must decide how long a computer or its monitor can sit idle
before it should be placed in a reduced power sleep mode. Power planning
begins with the computer operator selecting a sleep timer value for both
the display and the computer system.

Notebook users will also set a shutdown timer for when the battery gets too low. UPS users have a similar problem for the times they are running on battery power. The computer's power status function indicates the amount of power remaining. At some point, the system must save its context and force a shutdown before all power is exhausted.

ACPI supports two types of battery power level-monitoring software. Basic battery information controls in the ACPI description table report the total and remaining capacity. If loaded, the operating system uses the Smart Battery System Implementers Forum (SBF-IF) to monitor remaining battery (notebook and UPS) power.

When in operation, the operating system compares the idle timer times to the length of time that either the display or computer have been idle. If the time has been exceeded, then that device will be placed in a sleep state. However, an application can request that ACPI temporarily suspend movement to sleep if it needs that device and expects that the system may transition it to sleep.

Companies that wish to maintain control over equipment power usage will do so through their domain or local group policies. They will set the idle times and lock out the user from changing them. There will always be devices somewhere that must always stay on. Anyone wishing an exemption should request it from the technology management. The higher the authority needed for an exemption, the fewer the number of requests that will be made.

Some of the most significant savings can come from the power management of servers. They tend to have the largest configuration of RAM, disk, and CPU(s). In most data centers, once they are energized, they stay that way until turned off to add even more components or until the day they are unplugged for scrap.

Servers can still benefit from ACPI power management. During normal operation, they can put unused devices to sleep for short periods of time. Even individual CPUs or disks can be switched to low power for short periods when demand slacks. In the evening, after the daily batch processing is completed, they can sleep more deeply and still wake when traffic to it comes in over the LAN. There is a delay as it starts back up, but the power savings can be significant. This would be particularly beneficial over weekends and holidays when no one is around to use the server. Power management idle timers for individual servers must be set according to their workloads and patterns of usage.

AML CONTROL LANGUAGE

ACPI Machine Language (AML) is a pseudocode language used by the operating system's ACPI interpreter to control ACPI compliant components.

These commands, along with a description of a component's power modes, are provided by the device at boot time to the ACPI tables.

The challenge was to develop a way for devices from a wide range of manufacturers to request services from the operating system. For example, a video display program might signal the operating system to ignore the idle computer time-out for as long as a particular program is running even if there is no user input. The same program would cancel this request as it gracefully shuts down.

AML is based on a series of macrocommands called "controls." Each control passes one or more parameters to the operating system's AML interpreter. For example, a command may be issued to see if the device is running on batteries or to read a CPU's temperature.

ACPI uses a series of controls to manage communications, hardware, and software. For example, the control "SetThreadExecutionState" is used to set status for devices that should not be put to sleep, such as a communications monitoring routine awaiting inbound traffic. The device or application later clears their status when no longer needed. This is only needed if the ACPI control software cannot detect activity from user input.

AML controls are created through the ACPI Source Language (ASL). ASL is used by device manufacturers and BIOS chip developers as the source code for controls. This human readable code is then compiled into AML. ACPI Component Architecture (ACPICA) project provides an OS-independent version of ACPI at: www.acpica.org/

ACPI STATES

ACPI describes power management by "states" – what something is ordered to do at a particular time. There are different power management states. The Global states apply to everything in the system and, usually, the attached peripherals. Sleeping states are reduced power levels for individual devices or for the complete machine. Device power states apply to individual devices that may be running on minimal (or no) power even when the main system is running (such as an idle scan gun that puts itself in a low power mode when not needed). As a major consumer of the computer's electricity, CPUs have their own power, performance, and thermal monitor states.

ACPI standard version 3.0b recognizes four power modes, based on the amount of energy used by the computer:

▲ On – Full power operation.

▲ Off – No power applied to the unit.

▲ Sleep (or Standby) – The system state (operating system, applications, data) are kept in RAM supported by a few watts of electricity.

▲ Hibernation – The data and operating system context are saved to disk and power is stopped for most components.

GLOBAL STATES

The ACPI Global states (prefixed by a "G") apply to everything in the computer. This is the highest level of abstraction for power management and represents what the person operating the computer can see.

▲ G0 – Working State is when the computer is in normal operation and is consuming the most power. Individual devices, such as an attached printer, may move to a reduced power state if they are not needed. The ACPI software may adjust power usage if battery power is detected.

▲ G1 – Sleeping State is when the computer is idle and the system context is cached in RAM or the hard disk. Power consumption is a few watts. Restarting the system back to G0 takes a few seconds. The deepest sleep state that uses the least power is called "hibernation."

▲ G2 – Soft Off means the entire system is powered off except for the small amount of power used for Wake On LAN (if enabled). The G2 state is reached when the power switch is moved to the "off" position. The computer must be rebooted to start. The computer is not safe to disassemble as there is still a small amount of power running through the system.

▲ G3 – Mechanical Off is when all electricity has been removed from the computer, including unplugging it from the wall outlet. The mechanical part is pulling the plug or turning off the power strip.

SLEEP STATES

When it is time to transition the computer to Sleep power mode, ACPI broadcasts a notice to all hardware and applications. If none object, it then notifies hardware devices to switch to low power. The exception is when it detects a critically low battery and the system is turned off. In that case, the warning broadcast is followed by a forced shutdown. To prevent an idle system from moving to sleep mode, certain applications will notify the ACPI system to stay on even if it appears to be idle. Examples of this might be presentation software or communications software monitoring inbound traffic.

Once the sleep command is used, applications have two seconds to save their context and complete processing. The applications context includes closing open files and applications registers in RAM, as well as saving data in transient working storage.

ACPI Sleep states (prefixed by a "S") describe the depth of sleep. The less power used during sleep mode, the more time that is required to restore service. When the device "awakens" from sleep, it resumes where it left off. The ACPI software selects the lowest power usage sleep state that is supported by the installed equipment. S1 through S3 are referred to as "sleep" state because of their quick "wake up" time. S4 is commonly referred to as "hibernation," or deep sleep, which requires a longer restart cycle.

Sleep (or Standby) – The system state (operating system, applications, data) is kept in RAM and is supported by a few watts of electricity. Full service can be quickly restarted. However, if total power is lost, so is everything stored in RAM – similar to pulling the plug on a running computer.

Hibernation - The data and operating system context are saved to a special hibernation file on the hard disk, and power is stopped for most components. Restarting from Hibernation takes longer than from Sleep mode, as the hardware must be reenergized, after which then the operating system and application context must be reloaded from the disk. The computer system resumes within the application where it left off when it went into hibernation. If a computer is low on disk space, it may be a good idea to disable Hibernation mode, as it needs disk space to save the system context.

▲ S0 is normal system operation

▲ S1 (Sleep) is the lowest level of sleep. No system context is lost. The CPU input clock is stopped and return to full operation is quick.

▲ S2 (Sleep) includes all of S1 plus the CPU; its caches lose power.

▲ S3 (Sleep) removes electrical service from everything in the computer except RAM and selected other devices that maintain the system context.

▲ S4 (Hibernation) turns off everything, including RAM. Less than 3 watts are used. Restarting computer service from hibernation is essentially the same as a cold boot.

▲ S5 (Soft Off) uses very little power but can be restored to normal operation by the keyboard, another input device, or the Wake On LAN feature. Computer must be rebooted.

Waking from a sleep state may be initiated by the computer operator. Using an input device (pressing a keyboard button or moving a mouse) is sufficient to begin the "wake up" process. Another way to wake up computers is through the Wake On LAN process. Remember that even when a computer appears to be in full operation one or more components may be in a sleep state until they are needed.

DEVICE STATES

ACPI manages the power state of the entire computer system, as well as its individual components. This permits saving power even while the machine is in full operation. It is this attention to detail that provides ongoing power savings without negatively impacting the operator.

It is not unusual for some components to be on no or low power while the computer appears to the operator to be in full power operation. For example, if the computer is connected to a high speed network through an Ethernet connect, there is no need for an internal modem to be on. Running the modem in this example is the same as leaving a light bulb turned on in a closed closet when no one is at home.

ACPI data tables are read into the ACPI work space at boot time. They store information on each device in the computer or attached to it. This information includes:

▲ The amount of power the device consumes.

▲ The amount of "context" retained by the device when it shifts to low or no power.

▲ How the device driver restores the device to full operation.

▲ How long it takes to restore the device to full operation.

ACPI Device states (prefixed by a "D") describe the power management state of an individual device. The operating system controls movement of devices between power states.

▲ D0 – The device is operating at full power.

▲ D1 – Reduced power consumption where the device may lose its context.

▲ D2 – Reduced power management and the bus has a degree of control over power management.

▲ D3 – Maximum power savings as the device powered off.

CPU POWER STATES

A significant user of a computer's electrical power is the Central Processing Unit (CPU). In older machines, this might be 85 watts; in newer processors, it may be as low as 50 watts. The power used is determined by the chip design, as well as its clock speed. In general, the faster the clock speed, the more power it uses.

For many years, CPU manufacturers competed on speed. However, faster processors are difficult to effectively cool (which uses even more energy). Today, the manufacturing emphasis is on performance per watt. Whenever the CPU detects an idle time, it can reduce its own power usage (and temperature) until it is needed again. These "idle times" may be as short as fractions of as second. Power states for CPU models can vary greatly, but, in general, the higher the clock speed, the more "C" code options are available.

Another CPU power control is a heat sensor. CPU temperature may be managed by the CPU or by the motherboard chipset. If the chip becomes too hot, then the clock speed can be reduced so the CPU can run cooler. The slower the clock speed, the less heat is generated by the CPU chip. Some units also use CPU temperature to adjust the speed of the CPU cooling fan.

ACPI powers states for CPU Power is prefixed by a "C."

▲ C0 – The CPU is in normal operation.

▲ C1 – The CPU power mode changes to this state when it receives a Halt command from software. CPU power savings are significant with a very quick restart.

▲ C2 – In addition to C1, the processor's core clock and I/O buffers are gated.

▲ C3 – The bus clock is gated, and wake up time is a bit longer.

▲ C4 – The CPU core voltage drops to one volt, and the L2 cache contents slowly shrinks.

▲ C5 – Level 2 cache is empty.

▲ C6 – CPU context is lost, as power usage is reduced to near zero.

Multicore processors manage CPU power differently from single–core processors. Each core can have its own power level state, depending on its design. In this case, the processor is considered to be in the highest C state being used by any core. The ability to move one or both of the dual core processors to a lower power setting is determined by its physical design. Quad processor CPUs are essentially two dual core CPUs in a single package. Each core pair is separate and may be in its own C state at any given time.

"C" code power states are also applicable to Graphical Processing Units, which are just special purpose CPUs. They range from simple to complex

CPUs. As with the computer's CPU, they have heat issues, use a dedicated fan for cooling, and draw a significant amount of power. As the CPU architecture migrates to multiple cores for cooler and more powerful operation, so will the GPUs. This may open opportunities for placing portions of their capability in sleep mode during text (nongraphical) operation.

ACPI APPLICATION INTERFACE

One of the important components of the ACPI architecture is the connection between software applications and ACPI control in the operating system. Most applications do not need to do anything when ACPI transitions the computer to sleep. However, if an application anticipates long delays between operator interactions with the software, the application can request that ACPI ignore the idle times until the program removes the prohibition when it closes.

Applications are expected to check the operating system's battery power level (if the computer is running on batteries) before beginning a routine that could be deferred to later, such as an automatic saving of a word-processing document. A similar battery signal may be issued by an attached Uninterruptible Power Supply (UPS) if the unit is on battery power.

Another check is to see if the hard drive is powered up. This ensures it is ready when issuing a read or write command. Where practical, applications should avoid cycling the hard drive in and out of sleep mode, as this reduces power savings.

An issue when using battery power is what must be done when the battery is critically low? Applications must check for battery activity and monitor usage. This provides time to force an orderly shutdown of the application and save all data prior to completely losing power. Typically, an application will be allowed advance notice before a forced shutdown.

Sometimes, an application takes action when ACPI issues an alert that it is about to transition to sleep. For example, an Instant Messaging program might notify other users that that person is "away."

When a "wake up" transition is executed, applications must first reconnect to the network. This can be a challenge if a notebook PC went to sleep in one place and "awoke" far away in a different wireless network that it may not be able to access.

Next, the application tries to restart from where it stopped. If it cannot, then it prompts the operator for instructions. If the program is peer-to-peer, it signals that the operator has returned. If multiple programs awake at the same time, there may be momentary contention for the same resources.

LINUX ACPI

ACPI is not confined to desktop and notebook computers running Microsoft Windows. It is also available in Linux and FreeBSD. The ACPI4Linux project began in 1999 and works to ensure that Linux benefits from all features described in the ACPI standard. This includes kernel modifications and software tools.

The ACPI subsystem integrates with Linux and is licensed under the GNU public license. The BIOS of most computers is tuned toward the Microsoft implementation of ACPI, so you should verify that a unit works well with a particular implementation of Linux. In some cases, you must recompile the device description tables that are embedded in the BIOS. Many changes to Linux ACPI also require kernel changes and a reboot.

Linux starts ACPI using the acpid daemon command, usually at system boot. That program is controlled by the contents of /etc/acpi/events. Every file whose name does not begin with a ."" is an event for ACPI. If that event occurs, then ACPI reads this file and executes the action indicated. The contents for each file are a two-line format. The first line begins with "event=" and the second line begins with the "action=." The "action" is the command to execute. Linux support for ACPI can be found on-line at: www.lesswatts.org/projects/acpi/.

ACPI SHORTCOMINGS

The ACPI standard is complex. It provides a full range of features to address many possible situations, but this range of choices makes it confusing for developers. The 600-page ACPI standard version 3.0 describes a lot of code, which increases the likelihood of bugs. The complexity is compounded by first writing code in ASL, which is then turned into AML.

An issue of significant security concern is that ACPI controls must execute with full privileges. This leaves the system open to compromise through controls that maliciously shutdown devices or that are poorly written.

Another concern is that manufacturers write their code to fulfill Microsoft's specifications, not the ACPI specification. This slight difference makes implementation of a UNIX ACPI difficult and requires local tuning on each manufacturer's machine (which violates the idea of a standard).

ACPI FUTURES

ACPI's architecture was designed to accommodate future and unknown equipment. Future devices can develop in many directions, so AML building blocks may need to be combined in a variety of ways. For example, as computers move into the a home living room or media room, they can be attached to televisions, video recorders, and other devices. These devices may have little operator interaction, but the ACPI code must be intelligent enough to know the difference between playing a long movie and safely going to sleep when no one is around. In addition, computers running Voice Over IP (VOIP), which provide fax and answering machine services, are beginning to replace telephone. They must wake when detecting incoming calls.

ACPI is now working on version 4.0 of its standard. This is the first significant upgrade since version 3.0b was issued in October 2006. Information about ACPI version 4.0 is available at: www.acpi.info/spec40.htm.

The Bottom Line

APM was the original industry standard for workstation power management. It was created originally to support notebook PCs. APM gained a reputation as something that destabilized a computer's predictable performance. This was often the result of adding components to the computer after it was delivered to the customer.

APM lives on in legacy computing systems and is currently offered as part of Linux. However, most hardware manufacturers and software developers have moved on to ACPI because of its flexibility and widespread acceptance.

ACPI, which was introduced to the marketplace in 1996, has grown steadily more stable and robust. It is available on today's computers (notebooks, servers, and desktops) as they come out of the box. The operating system of these new machines is delivered preconfigured with default sleep timer values. Almost all new hardware and common commercial software install their ACPI configuration information into the operating system when they are added to the unit. To ensure their equipment is operating efficiently, companies set the time values in group policies and then lock them so that individuals cannot change them.

Power management is the control of the idle timers to ensure that unused equipment is powered off. To manage their power usage, companies must set the idle timers to suit their environment and then lock them under secured group policies. Exemptions can be made for special circumstances.

A significant shortcoming of ACPI is that its controls must run with full administrator privileges. This is an invitation for a malicious person to use this opening for harmful purposes.

Finally, given that ACPI is a common interface, it is important that companies train their developers and hardware designers on how it works. Properly designed and coded devices and software will ensure that power management will not cause their customers to lose application data and context during transition to a sleep session.

7 DOCUMENT MANAGEMENT

IT CAN have a positive impact on the environment by reducing the amount of paper an organization uses. While we are still not yet ready to eliminate the use of paper, available document management solutions take a big step in that direction. An effective document management system will not only reduce the number of trees killed to support your business, but will also help you meet legal requirements, such as those stipulated in Sarbanes/ Oxley and HIPPA, and support your disaster recovery plan.

Among the many advantages to storing and working with an electronic document versus using a printed piece of paper are:

▲ No trees are killed in the production of an electronic document.

▲ The document can be accessed by more than one person at a time without the need to physically make copies.

▲ Back-ups of the document are easy to create and retrieve if needed.

▲ Electronic documents cannot be easily lost by placing them in the wrong file.

▲ They can be found using computerized search technologies.

▲ They be processed by a workflow system and quickly routed to the appropriate person.

▲ Versioning of the document is much easier than when using paper.

▲ Electronic documents are much cheaper to store than paper.

Document management systems come in many different flavors, but all are used to capture, store, manage, and print documents. These documents can originate physically on paper or can be created using document creation software, such as Microsoft Office. This can also include the storage of paper or microfiche in file cabinets, as well as the storing of documents in electronic formats on a computer system.

The Problem with Paper

According to the Paper Industry Association Council, more than 99 million tons of paper and paperboard were used in the United States in 2005. InfoTrends estimates that the average white collar worker used 130 pounds of paper in 2008. The U.S. EPA reports that in 2006, paper and paperboard were the largest components of municipal solid waste, representing 34% of all waste generated. No matter how you look at it, a lot of paper is generated and wasted in the modern office, causing a number of costs, such as:

▲ Cost of the paper.

▲ Supplies and maintenance of printers and copiers.

▲ Energy to power printers and copiers.

▲ Storage space for management and storage of documents.

▲ Cost to dispose of the used paper if not recycled.

Reducing the use of paper, like most green activities, can save you money as well as reduce IT's impact on the environment. Benefits to the environment include:

▲ Reducing the number of trees and the amount of water needed for the production of paper.

▲ Reducing air and water emissions.

▲ Reducing the amount of material added to the municipal waste stream.

Reducing Paper Usage

While ideally we would eliminate paper entirely from the modern office, the fact remains that paper is still being used for many different reasons. Paper is still an effective, portable way to share information. The portable computing devices available today, such as tablet PCs, PDAs, and cell phones, are still not easy enough to use to totally replace paper. The older generation of workers has an almost emotional attachment to paper, as it is what they grew up with. As better electronic devices become available and the workforce shifts to a generation raised with electronic devices, the need for paper is sure to decrease. Until that day comes, a number of practices can be encouraged to dramatically reduce the amount of paper used in the modern office.

DUPLEX PRINTERS

Duplex printers can print on both sides of the sheet of paper, which can reduce your paper usage by almost 50%. It also reduces the amount of paper that ends up in a file cabinet, reducing physical storage costs. If possible, configure all printers to default to duplex printing and provide instructions to users for those rare situations where single-sided printing is required.

NEVER PRINT E-MAILS

While not as common as a few years ago, some people still insist on printing e-mails. Sometimes this is done in order to file a copy; other times it's so the email can be transported and read later. Many companies will restrict the amount of storage available for archiving e-mails to save disk storage space, which forces users in some cases to print hardcopies for long-term storage.

FORMAT DOCUMENTS FOR PRINTING

Most document creation programs allow you to alter the format of the document for printing, which potentially can save paper. For example, Microsoft Excel has a "Fit to Page" feature that allows you to print a large spreadsheet to a single page. Microsoft Word allows you to print multiple pages of a document on each sheet of paper, which can be used for printing drafts if need. Of course, the ultimate saving of paper comes when all editing and sharing of documents is done electronically.

USE PRINT PREVIEW

Many times documents are reprinted due to slight variations in how the document looks on the screen versus how the final product looks when printed. To avoid reprinting documents just to make small editorial or layout changes, make use of the "Print Preview" feature found in almost every document creation program. "Print Preview" allows you to see exactly how your pages will look when they are printed. You can save paper right up until the final printing by using this function. Print Preview is easy to use and, in most applications, you can print directly from the Print Preview page by clicking on the print button or the printer icon. This feature is especially handy for applications such as Excel or Visio that may have a small section of a document bleeding onto another page or pages. Sometimes a simple layout adjustment will save several sheets of paper at print time.

ONLY PRINT WHAT YOU NEED

Many times when printing a document you only need a small section printed; if so, don't print the entire document just to get the part you need. This is especially true when printing Web pages, as many will have extraneous information or ads toward the bottom that you probably don't really want or need. For Web pages, it is easy to use the browser's "Print Preview" feature to see exactly what will be printed. You can then scroll through the pages to find exactly what you need. In most cases, the first page is all you

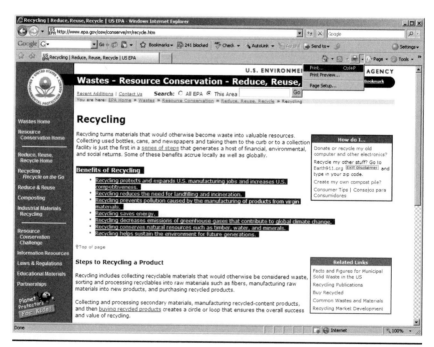

Figure 7-1

HIGHLIGHTING JUST WHAT YOU NEED TO PRINT IN INTERNET EXPLORER

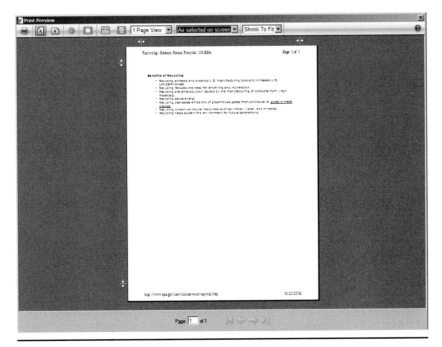

Figure 7-2
PRINTING JUST WHAT YOU SELECTED IN INTERNET EXPLORER

need; in other cases, you might need to print only a specific range of pages. Most browsers will also allow you to select and print a particular portion of the text.

For example, if you are using Microsoft Internet Explorer, highlight the section you want by clicking and dragging the mouse over the text you need. Click on the down arrow beside the Printer icon, and select "Print Preview," followed by "As selected on screen" (See Figures 7-1 and 7-2).

Electronic Document Management

Although reducing paper usage through smart practices is good, eliminating the use of paper via electronic document management is even better. A well-designed document management system will eliminate the need for paper for documents used within the organization and can reduce the need to send hardcopy outside the organization.

CAPTURING DOCUMENTS

To be effective, a document management system must make it easy for documents to be captured and stored electronically. For paper-based documents, the capture process must be fast, simple, and reliable. It must be able to handle the many different source formats that exist, as well as the different electronic document creation tools in use. To be most effective, your document management system should support the ability to scan all paper-based documents as they arrive at the organization and route the documents electronically to the intended recipient. This makes it much more likely that the paper will end up in the recycling bin rather than the trash bin.

PAPER FORMATS

Paper documents come in many different sizes, including (in inches) 8.5 × 11, 11 × 17, 17 × 22, 22 × 34, and 34 × 44. The International Organization for Standards (ISO) has created a standard paper size system specifying a number of formats. The most common formats and their uses are:

▲ A0, A1 – technical drawings, posters.

▲ A1, A2 – flip charts.

▲ A2, A3 - drawings, diagrams, large tables.

▲ A4 - letters, magazines, forms, catalogs, laser printer and copying machine output.

▲ A5 - note pads.

▲ A6 - postcards.

▲ B5, A5, B6, A6 – books.

▲ B4, A3 - newspapers, supported by most copying machines in addition to A4

ELECTRONIC FORMATS.

Of course many documents created in the modern office start out as an electronic file and many never see physical paper. Popular electronic file formats include:

▲ .doc – Microsoft Word 2003 and earlier.

▲ .docx – Microsoft Word 2007.

▲ .html – Web page.

▲ .pdf – Adobe portable document format.

▲ .rtf – rich text format.

▲ .tiff (or .tif) – used for images.

▲ .txt – plain text file.

▲ .xml – eXtensible Markup Language; a standard for creating markup languages which describe the structure of data.

Documents can also arrive at the organization as e-mail attachments or through a network fax server. The system should support forwarding these documents electronically rather than having to print them before distribution.

SYSTEM CONSIDERATIONS

When reviewing document capture options, consider the following:

▲ How many paper documents do you receive in a day?

▲ How many electronic documents are created each day?

▲ Does the condition of the documents allow them to be scanned using an automatic document feeder? Older or worn documents may have to be scanned by hand on a flatbed scanner.

▲ What size documents need to be scanned? Larger documents, such as blueprints or architectural drawings, may require a large flatbed device.

▲ Can the system be administered from a central location? Centralized administration can lessen the burden on the help desk by reducing configuration errors caused by users in remote locations.

▲ How well does the system scale? As your needs change and increase, will the system be able to handle future volumes?

▲ Does the system support batch processing of documents? Batch input of documents is important when source documents arrive in batches.

Most organizations will want to consider using a scanner with an automatic document feeder. This allows a stack of documents to be scanned at one time rather than having to place each page by hand on a flatbed scanner. The most important consideration is that the scanner be able to handle the size and condition of the majority of paper documents to be scanned by the organization.

STORING DOCUMENTS

Whether a document is scanned or not, it has to be stored somewhere if someone will need to access it. The type of storage method selected can have a big impact on the cost to the organization and to the environment.

ORIGINAL DOCUMENTS

There are several options for dealing with the original documents once they have been scanned:

▲ Shred the documents after scanning. If the original is no longer needed, this is the most environmentally friendly way to deal with the paper, as it can then easily be recycled. The vast majority of documents can be shredded and recycled after they are scanned.

▲ Store in file cabinets. Do this only for documents where you need quick access to the original, as you will incur the cost of file cabinets and storage space required.

▲ Use a professional document storage company. This option eliminates the need for on-site storage, but can be more expensive. Access to the physical document may require several hours for the document to be retrieved and delivered.

ELECTRONIC STORAGE

There are several options for the storage of digital documents:

▲ On-line storage, usually in the form of magnetic media such as hard drives. This type of storage is becoming increasingly less expensive and allows for fast access to digital documents. Technologies, such as storage area networks (SANs) and network attached storage (NASs), support the scaling of storage requirements to whatever is needed. Its major drawbacks are that a hard drive contains a large number of moving parts that are subject to failure and that it requires energy to keep the disk running in case access is needed.

▲ Compact disks (CDs). These are small disks used to store digital information. Its main advantages are low cost, durability, and ubiquitousness. Its main disadvantage is the limited amount of storage available per disk (650 MB).

▲ Digital video disk (DVDs). A DVD is essentially a larger CD. Like a CD, it is very durable and ubiquitous, but holds up to eight times as much information as a CD.

A major long-term concern with an electronic document management system is that it must be flexible enough to support new technologies as they are developed. This includes both storage technologies and the technologies that create and read documents. Users should be encouraged to use nonproprietary open file formats whenever possible to ensure that documents saved today can be read in the future. The two most common and oldest standard file formats are ASCII for text and TIFF (TIF) for images. It is a good bet that future systems will continue to support these formats.

INDEXING

Once documents are saved in a document management system, they must be indexed so that they can be easily found when needed. Common indexing processes include:

▲ Creating electronic file folders to reduce search time by only having to search specific folders. This also allows users to browse a folder that contains documents of the type they seek. A flexible electronic folder system also eases the transition from a paper-based file system to an electronic one by having the electronic folders mimic the paper-based system.

▲ Metadata is the use of index field information stored about a document that makes search quick and easy. For example, you might enter metadata to store the date the document was created, the author, the subject, and so on. You can then use this metadata index to "quick find" the document. This is especially helpful if the metadata does not occur within the text of the document.

▲ Optical character recognition (OCR) translates printed characters into the alphanumeric characters recognized by a computer. This allows the document to be stored not just as a picture but as the words in the document. OCR cannot usually translate handwriting or characters created with ornamental fonts.

▲ Full-text indexing is used in conjunction with OCR to allow the entire text of a document to be searched. The usefulness of full-text indexing depends on the accuracy of the OCR process and the power of the search logic. There are several search options that make full-text indexes more useful:

    ▲ Soundex – This is a phonetic algorithm for indexing names by their sound when pronounced in English. This allows for words with the same pronunciation to be encoded to the same string so that matching can occur despite minor differences in spelling.

    ▲ Fuzzy logic – Allows for minor differences in spelling of words to still return a match during a search. This helps compensates for words that were either misspelled in the source document or for errors in the OCR process.

▲ Wildcards – Allows for the use of special characters in a search to match portions of a word. Common wildcard characters are the asterisk (*), used to match any character or characters (e.g., "comp*" would find the words "computer" and "company") and question mark (?) for matching any single character (e.g., "d?g" would find the words "dig", "dog" and "dug").

▲ Proximity – Finds occurrences of words used within a specified number of characters or words from each other.

COMPLIANCE, RETENTION, AND LEGAL ISSUES

While we might like to think our documents have everlasting value, the truth is that most documents have value only for a short period of time. Whether on paper or in electronic storage, storing a document has a definite cost that should be eliminated once there is no value in keeping the document. On the other hand, some documents have a definite legal lifespan that requires that they not be destroyed too soon. It is important to have a document retention plan that ensures that documents are kept only as long as necessary. In addition, federal and state laws dictate how certain documents should be handled and stored, as well as the method of destruction to be used.

Your document retention plan should consider the following questions:

▲ What type of documents will be stored?

▲ How long should each type of document be kept?

▲ What process should be used to destroy each type of document?

▲ Who is ultimately responsible for retention activities?

▲ When and how are retention policies to be tested?

▲ How is the destruction of documents to be tracked?

There are several types of documents that should be covered in your document retention plan:

▲ Accounting documents, such as invoices, purchase orders, and other business transactions.

▲ Business records, such as articles of incorporation, bylaws, capital stock, copyrights, and trademark registration and patents.

▲ Tax records, any documentation to support deductions, and federal, state, and local tax returns.

▲ Employment records, such as resumes, applications, performance reviews, and employment contracts.

▲ Legal documents, such as customer and supplier contracts, intellectual property, and corporate records.

▲ Electronic records, such as e-mail and instant messages. These items are subject to discovery in legal proceedings.

Figure 7-3 lists the generally recommended retention period for different types of documents. These are only guidelines; please consult your organization's legal and accounting advisers for specifics that may apply to your type of business and your legal jurisdiction.

All paper documents should be destroyed at the end of the retention period on-site either by supervised personnel or by a licensed and bonded third-party document destruction company. In either case, the destruction of the documents should be monitored to ensure all documents are destroyed. The latest information on tax record retention can be found at the IRS Web site at www.irs.gov.

SECURITY

Your important documents can be a rich source of valuable information for hackers and others who want to harm your organization and/or your customers. Your document management system must ensure that your

Type of Document	Retention Period
Annual financial statements	Permanent
Auditor's reports	Permanent
Business records	Permanent
E-mails	Depends on subject
Financial records	4 years
Insurance records	6 years
Legal documents	10 years
Payroll records	6 years
Pension and profit sharing records	Permanent
Personnel records	6 years
Press releases	Permanent
Sales and marketing documents	3 years
Tax records	Permanent

Figure 7-3
RECOMMENDED DOCUMENT RETENTION PERIODS

documents cannot fall into the wrong hands. In addition, the system's security should ensure that legitimate users are able to do their jobs without compromising the integrity of the underlying database, file system, and network. The document management system should provide multiple levels of security, including the authentication of users, the proper assignment of what the user is authorized to do, and the logging of activity in an audit trial.

The system must balance access and security through the control of access to the system and control over what each user is able to do once in the system. Access to the system is done through some sort of authentication process, which might include any combination of the following:

▲ The user gains access by providing a user name and password.

▲ Access to certain features and functions based on the user's login level.

▲ Access controlled by some biometric process, such as scanning a fingerprint or by voice recognition.

Once authenticated into the system, the user is allowed to perform activities based on the rights setup by the system administrator. There are several basic types of rights that the system should support:

▲ Rights can be assigned to each user individually or as a member of a group.

▲ Rights are assigned to specific objects in the system, such as folders and document.

▲ Right are determine by what features a user has access to, such as view or read/write.

The security system should also support the logging of all system activity and the generation of audit trails. It should include who used the system and when and what actions were performed. Especially important is logging unsuccessful attempts to access content or to make unauthorized changes to documents.

RETRIEVING DOCUMENTS

While the capturing of documents is important, retrieving documents is where most users interact with a document management system. Ease of use in document retrieval is critical for user acceptance.

DOCUMENT ACCESS

A well-designed document management system allows access to the right information stored in the right document by the right person at the right time. The system should support the following processing for getting documents into user's hands:

▲ Easy to use search, and quick access to documents.

▲ Access documents using a Web browser on the organization's Intranet or via the public Internet.

▲ Support for common printers and fax systems.

▲ Ability to easily create CDs and DVDs for archival or delivery of large volumes of documents that might be too much for other methods, such as e-mail.

▲ Interface with popular e-mail systems as e-mail has become the most common form of communication. E-mail also makes it possible to distribute documents widely at a very low cost.

▲ Portable folders that allow users to synchronize important documents between their laptops and the document management system. This allows users access to documents on their laptops when they are not connected to the system.

ANNOTATION AND REDACTION

Annotation is the ability to add comments to a document without altering the original document. It also includes adding "stamps," such as "draft" or "secret," to a document to warn readers of its special status or simply highlighting specific portions of the text.

Redaction is the ability to hide selected portions of the text using "blackout" or "whiteout." This is commonly done in documents that must be released to the public, but require that certain information, such as social security numbers, be hidden.

A document management system should allow you to control who has the ability to annotate or redact a document and to guarantee that the original document is not affected in any way so that users with the proper permission can still see the original.

WORKFLOW

Workflow is the ability to route a document from one person to another. Most of the work in a modern office involves the movement of documents within an organization. A document management system allows this to happen electronically, which has several benefits over routing documents manually:

▲ The status of a document is available at all times.

▲ A document cannot get lost or left under a pile of papers.

▲ The document is less likely to be misfiled and is more easily found if misfiled.

▲ Productivity based on the length of time a document is in a particular step in the process is easier to calculate.

▲ Alerts can be generated if a document is in a given step for too long.

Workflow can be of two different types:

▲ Serial or Linear. The document flows in a single path from one person or department to another until the workflow is complete. As a single step, only one person can route the document to the next task.

▲ Parallel or Group. The document can routed to the next step by more than one person. For example, a wire transfer is approved if any one of two different financial managers approves it for transfer. Or a proposal may require the approval of two different managers in a single step before going on to the next step.

Workflow can significantly improve productivity if implemented and used correctly. It can also eliminate the need to make copies of a document along its work path, resulting in a tremendous savings of paper.

ARCHIVING DOCUMENTS

LONG-TERM STORAGE

Archiving is the long-term storage of documents. Many important records must be kept for the life of the organization (and its successors) and must be in a format that can be accessed 50 or 100 years from when they were first produced. These documents most likely will never be accessed, but must nevertheless be available if needed. There are several issues to consider that can affect your ability to access documents that have been archived:

▲ All media will eventually fail. Hard drives, CDs, DVDs, and magnetic tape do not last forever. The only way to avoid media failure is to periodically read and refresh the data to new media. This may require that you maintain obsolete equipment until all documents are moved to a more current storage format.

▲ All software has bugs, so it is possible that a bug in the software could damage a document and make it unreadable.

▲ As software for creating documents gets updated to "new and improved" file formats, document created earlier may at some point be no longer readable.

▲ If all your documents are stored in one place, will they survive a fire or natural disaster?

▲ If an organization ceases to exist, what happens to the important documents being stored?

LEGAL REQUIREMENTS

Well-publicized incidents of organizational misconduct, such as those of Enron, Tyco, and WorldCom, have resulted in an increase in regulations concerning the handling of documents at the local, state, and federal levels. A properly implemented system can help ensure compliance by enforcing the consistent application of document policies and procedures and by providing a verifiable audit trail of all actions taken surrounding a document.

While legal requirements will differ in the details, two major features must be supported to fulfill the basic requirements of most regulations:

▲ Storage media cannot be altered. All activities performed on a document from creation to destruction must be tracked in a way that cannot be altered.

▲ Information must be set in time. All activities performed on a document from creation to destruction must be time stamped in a way that cannot be altered.

In addition to the items above, additional features that the document management system should support to meet legal requirements include:

▲ Documents can be retrieved and printed as needed.

▲ Indexes should be used to allow for quick retrieval.

▲ Documents are stored on appropriate media.

▲ Documentation on how the system works must be available and up to date.

▲ Allow for cross-referencing of other systems.

▲ Controls should be in place to detect and prevent the deterioration of documents.

While following the processes listed above should keep you in compliance with most legal requirements, an attorney should be consulted for any specific local requirements.

DISASTER RECOVERY

One major advantage of storing documents electronically is the ability to easily back up and store the documents off-site. This makes planning for recovery from a disaster much easier than with paper documents. The entire document repository can be stored off-site on backup media such as tape or DVDs or on a live "hot" backup system that is updated in real-time by the production system.

DESIGNING A SYSTEM

Designing a document management system is much like any other new IT system. You must start with clearly defined business requirements and design or select the new system with these requirements in mind.

DEFINE BUSINESS REQUIREMENTS

As with any new business system, the first step in implementing a document management system is to define the business requirements for the system. Being "green" may not be the main business driver for implementing the system; it may just be a happy side benefit. Other business requirements that may drive such a project include:

▲ Regulatory compliance.

▲ Office space considerations.

▲ Workflow efficiencies.

▲ Disaster recovery.

▲ Better document tracking.

All of these business needs occur in every type of business, whether your business is one person in your basement or a Fortune 500 corporation with operations in several countries. Everyone deals with paper, filing paper, and the problems that paper generates.

So the issue here is that one of these needs or maybe several of these needs are the reason why we want to or need to implement a document management solution. Defining the most critical needs is to define our business objectives.

While there are usually many objectives for a project, the primary business objective is often the only reason for purchasing and implementing a document management solution. Once the primary objective is met then—and only then—will you be able to move on to secondary and ancillary business objectives. However, often we find that multiple objectives are met because of the overlapping nature of documents. Financial benefit is determined by the value of the data on the paper and what goes into storing the ever growing amount of paper. Here are some items to consider when evaluating the financial benefit of a document management solution.

▲ What is the current cost to store paper?

▲ What are the long-term storage requirements?

▲ What is the relative value of the data on the paper?

▲ Can the paper documents be easily recreated by other means?

▲ Does someone else own a copy of the paper document?

▲ Is there some regulation forcing the preservation of the data?

DEFINE TECHNICAL REQUIREMENTS

Once the business requirements are understood, they can be compared with available hardware and software to design a solution that fits the organization. Many elements need to be considered, such as:

▲ How much on-line storage space is required?

▲ What are the server requirements and their effect on the data center?

▲ Will multiple monitors be required for some power users?

▲ What are the access requirements inside and outside the organization?

▲ Is color required?

▲ What are the source systems for the documents, both hardware and software?

The quality of the network infrastructure is vitally important to the end users who are using the document management system. A well-designed infrastructure is necessary to move the large amounts of data that are found within a document management system. If the network infrastructure is not adequate, then scanning a large number of documents will cause the entire system to run slower, thereby impacting business productivity.

Workstation and server hardware should be fairly new and robust. Many document management systems require the use of a thick client. A thick client is software loaded on the local workstation that connects with the server component. Other document management systems will store the documents on an Internet connected server and only require a Web browser to attach to the server. This will allow older equipment at the workstation or even appliance terminals to be used as the client workstation. However, with newer software it is best advised to stay current on the workstation hardware. Upgrades to hardware and software should be considered every year and completed when productivity begins to decrease because of old or outdated hardware and software.

The discussion about the workstation is also true of the server. Servers purchased from most hardware suppliers and manufacturers usually carry a three-year warranty. The hard drives in the server may have a five-year warranty. The technology is upgraded so fast that more often than not the server will need to be upgraded every three years, and it is advisable to upgrade at least within five years of purchase.

Of equal importance with the computer hardware is the scanning hardware used to convert paper documents into digital ones. Devices used to scan paper documents fall into the following categories:

▲ Scanner only: Scanning is the only function the device performs.

▲ Multifunction devices: The device performs functions besides scanning, such as copying and printing documents.

▲ Desktop scanners: A small device sits on a desktop and is used by a single user at a single workstation.

▲ Workgroup scanners: A larger device that is connected to multiple users through the local area network. Many organizations will use one or more large workgroup scanners to scan each document as it is received by the organization.

PLAN FOR IMPLEMENTATION

Implementing a document management solution is similar to any other IT project. An internal project leader must be assigned to see the project through to completion. The project leader will also be responsible for managing the activities of any outside vendors used, especially the selected document management solution vendor. Planning is critical for the success of the project and should include the following:

▲ Organize the project team: The team should include representatives from the user community as well as IT.

▲ Develop a detailed work plan: Break the project down into manageable phases with clear deliverables at the end of each phase.

▲ Hold regular status meetings: Review project progress on a regular basis.

▲ Develop a communication plan: Be sure to keep all important stakeholders informed of progress, as well as any issues that come up.

▲ Develop a support plan: The long-term success of the project will depend on the quality and level of support available to users. The plan should include service level agreements and how issues are to be handled.

End-user training is critical for the success of a document management solution. Training should be performed on-site if possible so that the users' training experience is as close to what they will experience on the job as possible. Make sure that all end-users understand the following:

▲ How does a user get access?

▲ What are the scanning procedures?

▲ How are documents retrieved?

▲ How is tech support supplied?

    ▲ Via Web site

    ▲ Telephone

▲ Who is the on-site expert?

▲ What follow up training is available?

The Bottom Line

IT can have an enormous impact on the amount of paper used by an organization. By designing procedures, systems, and processes, and selecting equipment with paper reduction in mind, users can have increased flexibility and improve productivity while simultaneously helping the environment. Wherever possible, replace paper file systems with electronic document management systems and encourage employees not to print a hardcopy unless absolutely necessary.

MANUFACTURER PROGRAMS

ALL PRODUCTS go through a life cycle that starts with an idea and ends when the product is no longer useful or wanted. Many factors considered and decisions made along this path from idea to the end of product life affect the impact of the product on the environment. In this chapter, we look at how manufacturers are making changes to how they design and build their products, and increasing the available options for disposing of end-of-life (EOL) computer equipment in an environmentally friendly way.

All electronics eventually become obsolete and are no longer wanted by the original owner. According to a 2007 U.S. EPA report, about 1.3 million tons of computer equipment (desktops, laptops, printers, keyboards, etc.) reached their end of life in 2005. Of that, only about 17 percent was recycled.

The term "recycle" is defined by dictionary.com as "to treat or process (used or waste materials) so as to make suitable for reuse." We normally think of recycling as taking a product back to its raw material form and then using the reclaimed raw material to make a new product (such as the recycling of paper). However, when many people apply the term recycling to computer equipment, it can also mean giving the equipment to others who can use it (such as donating it to a school or charity) or reusing still functional parts to make a new system (technically remanufacturing). All of these options are preferable to dumping the equipment into a landfill, but this chapter focuses on how design affects the feasibility of breaking down equipment so that the raw materials can be recovered.

PRODUCT LIFE CYCLE

Every product has a life cycle that consists of three major phases. The first begins with the idea for the product and ends with a completed design for its manufacture. The second consists of manufacturing the product. The third is the delivery to and use of the product by the ultimate user until the product is ready for disposal. During each phase of the life cycle, decisions are made that affect the product's environmental impact.

An increasingly significant factor is the impact the product has on the environment. This has become important in recent years for two major reasons: (1) government rules and regulations and (2) increased public concern about how products they use impact the environment.

When creating a new product, the designer has to consider several factors. Among the most important are the product's appeal to the end user, the cost to manufacturer, durability, safety, and ease of use. Until recently, computers and related products were designed with no consideration given to the product's impact on the environment. Motherboards are covered with heavy metals and toxic materials and CRT monitors are full of lead, mercury, and other toxic materials. Cost and performance have been the major concerns of computer designers since the beginning of the industry.

GOVERNMENT REGULATIONS

Over the years, the U.S. Congress has passed several environmental laws that affect the products used in the computer industry. Most are not targeted specifically at the computer industry, such as the Clean Air Act, the Solid Waste Disposal Act, and the Resource Conservation and Recovery Act, but they do affect how products (including computers) are manufactured and disposed of at end of life. In recent years, an increasing number of state and local regulations have affected the disposal of computer equipment, specifically the banning of CRT displays from landfills in many localities.

An example of a state on the leading edge of this issue is California, where the Electronic Waste Recycling Act of 2003 limits the amount of cadmium, hexavalent chromium, lead, and mercury in displays used with electronic equipment to 0.1% or less. The act also requires retailers to collect an Electronic Waste Recycling Fee from consumers that is paid to the state for distribution to organizations that collect and recycle electronic waste. The act also encourages state agencies to purchase environmentally friendly electronic equipment. There are stiff penalties for not complying with the Act – retailers who sell electronic devices covered by the act and do not pay the recycling fee are liable in civil court for up to $5,000 per offense, and manufacturers that do not comply face fines of up to $25,000.

In the European Union (EU), the Waste Electrical and Electronic Equipment (WEEE) directive places restrictions on the use of many of the chemicals that are found in electronic equipment. It also requires producers to take back and recycle the electronic equipment, including computers that they sell in the EU. This gives manufacturers a huge incentive to design and build products that are easier to recycle.

IT'S GOOD TO BE GREEN

In response to pressures from government regulations and from customers, all major computer equipment manufacturers have developed programs to address the environmental issues surrounding the manufacture, use, and disposal of their products. These programs range from changing manufacturing processes so that fewer toxic materials are used to consumer takeback programs that allow customers to return end-of-life products to the manufacturer for remanufacturing or proper recycling. This has created a virtuous circle, as requirements for taking back the equipment have caused manufacturers to make their products easier to recycle. This, in turn, encourages consumers to recycle old equipment and purchase new devices. Manufacturers have also found that many "green" processes can also save them money, as they improve their manufacturing processes to meet green objectives. This chapter looks at some of the green programs from various manufacturers and how they benefit the environment, the consumer, and manufacturers themselves.

Hewlett Packard

Hewlett-Packard (HP) has been very active in trying to be a Green company. HP started its recycling program in 1987 and, throughout the 1990s, added ink recycling programs. As of 2007, management reached its goal of recycling 1 billion pounds of computer hardware and printer supplies. The company currently offers Trade In services that even cover non-HP products. It also has Return for Cash services for businesses, allowing companies to receive cash for unneeded equipment. This equipment is then refurbished and resold. HP offers to recycle HP inkjet and LaserJet cartridges for free. It offers to recycle any brand of computer hardware and also offers drop-off locations for rechargeable batteries in the United States and Canada. HP has partnered with the National Cristina Foundation to place donated computer equipment that can be reused.

MANUFACTURING PROCESSES

HP has made top priorities of reducing its energy consumption and limiting the solid and hazardous waste it produces. Management monitors and manages other areas of environmental impact, such as water use by its facilities, chemicals used in manufacturing (such as PFCs, air emissions, chemical releases), and even the fuel used by HP-owned vehicles. According to company records, HP's energy consumption in 2006 dropped 16% from its level in 2005. An Environmental, Health, and Safety management system is used to change and maintain efforts in environmental protection. HP has reported that using such processes has saved a great deal of money; in 2007, a waste diversion strategy saved the company $7.5 million in landfill and incineration fees.

GLOBAL CITIZENSHIP

Responsible use of world resources and protection of the environment is one of the top objectives of HP. One of HP's seven corporate objects is Global Citizenship, an objective that has HP aiming to be environmentally, socially, and economically responsible. HP's stated environmental, health, and safety policy goals include meeting or exceeding all laws and regulations of the communities in which the company does business, and to reduce pollution, waste, and energy use in the production of its products. It will also require suppliers to do the same. For a complete list of HP's objectives for being a good environmental citizen, see its environmental policy objectives at its Web Site at http://www.hp.com/hpinfo/global citizenship/environment/envprogram/envpolicy.html.

PAPER WASTE

One of the major areas HP has focused on is reducing the amount of paper waste, as paper and paper products make up the largest percentage by volume of global solid waste streams. Steps taken include reducing the number, size, and weight of manuals, printing double-sided, using addendums and revisions for updating manuals, and using recycled paper as much as possible. In 1999 HP restricted its paper suppliers from providing products from nonsustainable forest sources.

Apple

Apple first started taking environmentalism seriously in 1990, when the company first released and implemented a corporate environmental policy. The next year management phased lead out of its batteries, and, the year after that, phased out the use of chlorofluorocarbons (CFCs) in its manufacturing processes. Since then, Apple has taken further steps, such as cessation of the use of polyvinyl chlorides (PVCs) in packing materials and restricting the use of lead and cadmium in cables. In 2006, Apple became the first computer manufacturer to entirely replace CRT displays with LCDs, which are more energy and material efficient. In 2008 Apple introduced the MacBook Air, which is made without many of the environmentally harmful chemical compounds used in older PCs. Apple says the new MacBook Air is made from "brominated flame retardant–free material for the majority of circuit boards as well as PVC-free internal cables." It also has a recyclable aluminum enclosure and Apple's first mercury-free LCD display with arsenic-free glass. Apple was also one of the founding members of the U.S. Environmental Protection Agency's (EPA) ENERGY STAR® program.

MANUFACTURING PROCESSES

Apple focuses much of its attention on making sure its products are environmentally friendly. Company studies have concluded that 95% of its carbon footprint comes from its manufactured products. As such, even in the earliest stages of product design, it tries to limit the environmental impact of its products. Management tries to make products from materials that can be easily recycled and goes to great lengths to remove hazardous chemicals from created products. Apple's recent focus has been trying to reduce the amount of mercury and arsenic in its displays and the amount of brominated flame retardants (BFRs) and PVC used in manufacturing internal components. Even with its latest products, you can see advances: the iPhone 3G shipped with PVC-free handsets, headphones, USB cables, BFR free printed circuit boards, and a mercury-free LCD display. Apple has also focused heavily on wireless technologies, such as AirPort, Bluetooth, and wireless Internet connections to reduce the amount of cabling manufactured.

ENERGY USAGE

As part of trying to reduce the impact of their products, Apple makes its products as energy efficient as possible, since a device's largest contribution to greenhouse gas emissions comes from its consumption of energy over time. Apple tries to minimize energy use a couple of ways: using power supplies that are more efficient and using components that require less power. Apple claims that it has reduced the off-mode power consumption of its portable computer power adapters by 82% when the computer is not in operation. Also, many Apple products have an automatic shut-off feature to conserve energy, and the Mac OS X operating system has an Energy Saver feature that allows consumers to manage the power consumption of their computers. All of Apple's products ship with power management measures enabled by default. Since 2001, Apple computers, laptops, and displays have earned the ENERGY STAR® rating.

Apple has also made improvements in CPU power management, which has dramatically reduced the power required of all of its computers. For example, Apple claims that the Mac mini consumes as little as 25 watts, while the MacBook Air uses only 13 watts when on. These numbers make the Apple computers among the most energy efficient available. Apple has also worked hard to reduce the power usage of its monitors. By using energy efficient LCD displays instead of CRTs the current generation of Apple computers use less than one-quarter of the power used by the CRT monitors supplied with the first generation Mac.

Apple has also tried to reduce the amount of energy it consumes as a corporation. Management has set up an employee transit program that provides up to a $100 monthly subsidy for all U.S. employees as an incentive for using public transportation and carpooling. They have even provided a free bus service from metropolitan areas and train stations to its headquarters in Cupertino, California. Apple has also purchased 25% of the total energy demand for the company's Cork, Ireland, facility from renewable sources, predominantly wind power.

RECYCLING

Apple also considers recycling to be a top priority. The company first introduced a take-back initiative in Germany in 1994. Since then, Apple has instituted recycling programs in 95 percent of the countries where its products are sold. So far, it has kept 53 million pounds of electronic equipment from landfills worldwide. In the United States, Apple offers a free recycling program for old computers and displays with the purchase of a new Mac. Apple also offers a free recycling program for other electronics, taking back iPod players or any cell phone (regardless of manufacturer or model). The company will even offer a 10% discount on the purchase of a new iPod for bringing in an iPod for recycling at an Apple stores.

IBM

IBM has been working on being green since it issued its first corporate policy on environmental affairs in 1971. IBM heavily focuses on reducing emissions, as the corporation feels that climate change is one of the most critical global environmental challenges facing the planet. IBM's strategy for reducing emissions centers on conserving energy, reducing PFC emissions, using renewable energy, supporting alternate employee commute options, and increasing the efficiency of the company's logistics. Management also tries to develop energy efficient products and provide diverse solutions for energy efficient data centers. The company also collaborates with clients and others on innovations that help protect the climate.

ENERGY USAGE

IBM's Web site details what the company has achieved in energy conservation: "From 1990–2007, IBM avoided nearly 3.1 million metric tons of carbon dioxide (CO_2) emissions, equal to 45 percent of the company's 1990 global CO_2 emissions, and saved over $310 million through its annual energy conservation actions."

IBM, like Apple, tries to encourage its employees to reduce emissions by offering alternatives to normal commutes. IBM has been running a work-at-home program and a mobile employees program for nearly two decades. The company reports that more than 100,000 employees participate in these programs. Also, many of its locations provide support for the use of public transit systems, including shuttles from locations to mass transit stations and alternate transportation or "loaner" cars for business trips during the workday.

ENVIRONMENTAL OUTREACH

IBM has also done a significant amount of environmental outreach, trying to help other companies become and stay green. IBM has partnered with several governmental and nongovernmental organizations focused on the environment, such as the U.S. EPA's ENERGY STAR, Climate Leaders and Green Power Partnership programs, the World Wildlife Fund's Climate Savers Program, The Green Grid, and The Climate Group.

IBM is also careful in choosing its suppliers by only doing business with suppliers that also try to be green. In 1972, IBM started evaluating suppliers of hazardous waste services, and in 1980, management started evaluating production related suppliers. In 1991, the company did even more, expanding its environmental evaluations of suppliers by adding a requirement that its product recycling and product disposal suppliers be evaluated. The main reason for pushing these evaluations was to ensure that IBM was not inadvertently funding companies that did not take environmental protection seriously. IBM also joined the U.S. EPA's SmartWay Transport Partnership, an initiative to improve fuel efficiency and reduce emissions associated with logistics. Last year, 85% of its shipping in the United States, Canada, and Mexico was done with SmartWay carriers.

Dell

Dell is yet another manufacturer that has taken great strides to reduce its effect on the environment. In 2008, Dell committed to making itself the greenest technology company on the planet. Management also pledged to make its operations carbon neutral beginning in 2008. Dell has already made its headquarters in Round Rock, Texas, carbon neutral by using less energy, using green energy where available and economical, and offsetting the remaining impact.

RECYCLING

Dell offers multiple recycling methods. Much like Hewlett-Packard, Dell has partnered with the National Cristina Foundation to refurbish machines and then donate them to disabled and economically disadvantaged children and adults. For actual recycling of personal computers, Dell will come to your home and pick up any brand of computer, keyboard, mouse, or printer. For a fee, Dell will come and take care of any obsolete hardware from businesses.

MANUFACTURING PROCESSES

Dell has recently committed to making its manufacturing processes even more green. It is working on making products more energy efficient, as well as using fewer toxic chemicals in manufacturing. One of the major plans in this regard is the elimination of BFRs from all of its new products. Dell has also put green manufacturing into the hands of the customers, allowing customers to choose if they would like Dell to offset the carbon footprint of their purchases by planting a tree. Through the "Plant a Tree for Me" program, you can purchase trees to offset monitors, desktops, laptops, servers, or even to offset yourself! Dell has even set up a separate program (named "Plant a Forest for Me") to help companies with which it works offset their carbon footprints.

GLOBAL CITIZENSHIP

Along with its donation services in partnership with National Cristina Foundation, Dell has set up a community site where concerned people or companies can share green tips and tricks. If you visit http://www

.regeneration.org/, you can find a blog discussing green ideas, videos with people discussing the benefits of going green, inspirational stories, and plenty of tips on how to be more green.

ASUS

ASUS, a leading manufacturer of motherboards, has recently started implementing several policies designed to make the company more green. The company has developed a comprehensive set of policies covering how it designs its products by considering how its products affect the environment during manufacturing, while in use, and how they are disposed of at end of life. It has also developed a green design procedure to ensure all of the products meet the company's environmental objectives. The company also works to reduce the environmental impact of the packaging materials it uses to ship its products, and aggressively looks for sources of renewable energy for its manufacturing and corporate facilities, such as wind, solar, and bio-energy sources.

MANUFACTURING PROCESSES

ASUS strives to design all its products to be environmentally friendly from the ground up. At each stage of the design process, a product goes through an optimization process to reduce waste, reduce the use of toxic materials, and use recycled materials where possible. Another innovative idea ASUS is incorporating into its designs is to try and make its products as easy to disassemble as possible, the idea being that they could then easily be refurbished, reused, or recycled.

ENERGY USAGE

At the beginning of every fiscal year, ASUS reviews its energy saving objectives from the previous year and sets targets for the coming year. Management's main approach to energy saving is replacing existing equipment with more energy efficient devices. The company also combats energy waste through routine equipment maintenance. On a regular basis the company looks at how it heats and cools its buildings, how it uses energy for lighting, and how it piece of equipment uses energy.

Equipment End of Life

ASUS supports the idea that the manufacturer is responsibile for the environment impact of its products from initial manufacture through disposal at end of life. It prohibits its disposal vendors from using prison labor for the recycling of its products, or from using incineration as a disposal method. It also only works with vendors that support the Basel Action Network's "Electronics Recycler's Pledge of True Stewardship."

The Bottom Line

Whether due to their concern for the environment or simply to follow the letter of the law, manufacturers of computer equipment are becoming more responsible for the impact their products have on the environment. Computer technology is moving beyond just being a solution to a business problem with no thought to the environment to being a part of the solution for improving our environment. Look for technology vendors that design and build their equipment to environmentally friendly, so that you are less likely to end up with the bill for disposal of equipment that's bad for the environment.

IT ASSET DISPOSAL

GREEN IT is more than the impact on the environment of equipment that is in service; it is also about the impact on the environment of IT equipment that has reached its end-of-life (EOL). Many organizations have focused on reducing the cost of powering the computer equipment to run their businesses. Whether intentionally or not, this has reduced their impact on the environment. What has been of less concern is the impact on the environment of equipment once it is no longer needed.

For some time management has recognized the cost of disposing of EOL equipment, but, until recently, management's only concern was the cost. Because no one was ever arrested for tossing EOL equipment into the regular trash, little concern was paid to the method of disposal.

The U.S. EPA estimates that 53 million computers became obsolete in 2007, along with 35 million monitors and 82 million mice and keyboards. Governments are now beginning to pass laws and regulations at a rapid pace that will result in a penalty if EOL equipment is not handled properly from an environmental perspective. Companies will pay a penalty if their EOL equipment contains sensitive data about their customers that is not properly erased. And businesses are starting to realize that asset disposal is less costly if considered as part of the complete asset management life cycle.

Disposal Issues

Computers are filled with toxic materials that are used to create the cases, displays, storage devices, cables, and circuit boards. And, with so many becoming obsolete every year, the disposal of this equipment becomes a major environmental issue. As discussed in Chapter 2, governments around the world are passing ever stricter laws and regulations to prevent these obsolete machines from ending up in a landfill or being incinerated. Organizations face several penalties if their end-of-life equipment is not disposed of in a responsible manner.

Hazards of IT Material Recovery

While not putting end-of-life equipment directly into the waste stream to be landfilled or incinerated is a good first step, if the equipment is not re-cycled properly more environmental and health damage can be caused than if the equipment was just thrown in the trash. Some of the toxic ma-terials that can cause environmental and health damage include:

▲ Lead, which can cause severe damage to the blood-forming, nerv-ous, urinary, and reproductive systems in the body, is used in large amounts in CRT displays and is also found in the solder used to assemble the circuit boards.

▲ Cadmium, which is a carcinogen and can cause kidney damage, is used in semiconductors and printed circuit boards.

▲ Mercury, which is more toxic than lead, cadmium, and even ar-senic, is found in batteries and switches.

▲ Polybrominated flame retardants that can cause nervous system problems are used in the plastics in the case and keyboard.

While none of these materials are hazardous to the user during normal use, the problems occur when these materials leach out of landfills or are re-leased into the air when incinerated. See Figure 9-1 to see where these haz-ards exist in a typical computer.

RECYCLING OVERSEAS

The good news is that numerous recycling laws and regulations in the United States have greatly decreased the amount of e-waste going into land-

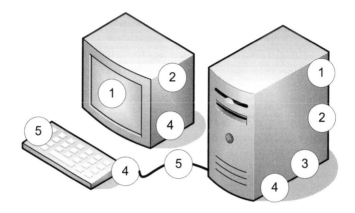

1 – Lead in CRT and solder

2 – Cadmium in printed circuit boards, semiconductors

3 – Mercury in batteries and switches

4 – Hexavalent chromium, polybrominated biphenyl (PBB) and polybrominated diphenyl ether (PBDE) flame retardants

5 - PVC plastics used in cables and housings

Figure 9-1

HAZARDOUS MATERIALS IN A TYPICAL DESKTOP COMPUTER

fills or being incinerated. The bad news is that much of this e-waste ends up in Africa or Asia to be stripped for usable materials in techniques that are hazardous to the environment and to the health of people living in the area. Although China has banned the import of e-waste, much of the e-waste from the United States ends up there. The local governments receive a significant amount of tax revenue from these operations and are not eager to shut them down.

The e-waste "recycling" industry in China is centered around the city of Guiyu, which is a few hours north of Hong Kong. We put "recycling" in quotes because the process used is more like a salvage operation than true recycling. Some of the techniques used in the "recycling" of electronic equipment include:

▲ Open-air burning of wire to recover copper.

▲ Open acid baths for separating metals, such as lead, silver, and gold.

▲ Washing the acid residues directly into nearby rivers and other water bodies.

▲ Using the smell of burning plastics to determine what type they are.

▲ Sending components that cannot be recycled to landfills or burning them in the open.

Africa has its share of e-waste environmental disasters, mostly located on the Ivory Coast and in Kenya. While a portion of the computers and other electronics sent to these areas are repaired and sold locally, much of it is not repairable and ends up as scrap. Local laws are ineffective in keeping this material out of the local landfill or in keeping it from being incinerated.

Figure 9-2
LABORER HEATING AQUA REGIA—A MIXTURE OF 5% PURE NITRIC ACID AND 75% PURE HYDROCHLORIC ACID—A MIXTURE THAT WILL DISSOLVE GOLD. WITHOUT ANY RESPIRATORY PROTECTION, WORKERS INHALE ACID FUMES, CHLORINE, AND SULFUR DIOXIDE GAS ALL DAY AS THEY SWIRL COMPUTER CHIPS REMOVED FROM CIRCUIT BOARDS IN ACID TO COLLECT TINY AMOUNTS OF GOLD. THE SLUDGES FROM THE PROCESS ARE DUMPED DIRECTLY INTO THE RIVER. (GUIYU, CHINA. DECEMBER 2001. (© BASEL ACTION NETWORK 2006)

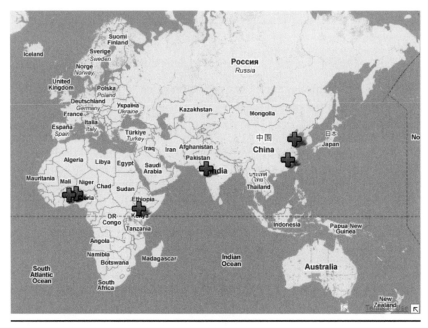

Figure 9-3
MAJOR E-WASTE "RECYCLING" LOCATIONS

NIGERIA: THE DIGITAL DUMP
Forty-five percent of the e-waste that is imported into Nigeria comes from the United States, 45 percent comes from Europe, and the remaining 10 percent from Japan and Israel, according to a report entitled "The Digital Dump" from the Basel Action Network.

LEGAL LIABILITY

There are also legal hazards for an organization if IT assets are disposed of improperly. Accountability and privacy laws, such as the Gramm-Leach-Bliley Act, the Health Insurance Portability and Accountability Act, and the Sarbanes-Oxley Act, can impose fines of $100,000 or more per violation if consumer data falls into the wrong hands. If material that is dumped illegally can be traced back to the original owner through asset tags or serial numbers, the original owner could be liable for any cleanup costs.

ADDED COSTS

Several costs are associated with the disposal of IT assets. Unlike some other manufactured items, such as aluminum cans, steel (which is easily

Figure 9-4
ONE OF THOUSANDS OF NIGERIANS INVOLVED IN REPAIRING
AND RESELLING IMPORTED USED ELECTRONIC EQUIPMENT.
UNFORTUNATELY MUCH OF THE IMPORTED ELECTRONIC EQUIPMENT
CANNOT BE REPAIRED AND IS INSTEAD DUMPED. (© BASEL ACTION
NETWORK 2006)

separated from other waste with magnets), paper, glass, and certain plastics, e-waste is a complicated mixture of many different materials that can
be difficult and, therefore, expensive to separate. While most household or
business waste can be recycled with no cost to the end consumer, e-waste
is often not profitable to recycle unless there is a fee or some other sub-
sidy. The reasons for this include:

▲ Labor intensiveness. Because the equipment must be separated into its many different components, computer recycling can be very labor intensive. Parts that are more easily resold as is, such as hard drives, network cards, and CD-ROM drives, must be removed before further processing. Many other parts must be separated because the recycling process is different for each type of part; this includes cables, metal cases, plastic parts, and circuit boards.

▲ Expensive processing. To process the metal and plastic scrap into raw materials that can be resold requires expensive machinery for each type of material.

▲ Toxic materials. Many pieces contain toxic materials that must be handled carefully to avoid environmental contamination. There are also added costs in disposing of any toxic material that cannot be resold for use in other processes.

These costs can tempt some recyclers to cheat by exporting the material they take in for recycling rather than recycling it themselves. The EPA reports that the vast majority of used electronics donated for reuse or recycling end up being exported outside of the United States.

Figure 9-5

E-WASTE DUMP SITE. (IMAGE COURTESY OF SILICON VALLEY TOXICS COALITION)

EXPORTING RECYCLABLES
A General Accounting Office investigation found 43 electronics recyclers in the United States that were willing to export broken,
untested, or nonworking CRTs under conditions that would appear
to violate the EPA's CRT rule against exporting nonfunctional CRTs.

Figure 9-6
WOMAN ABOUT TO SMASH A CATHODE RAY TUBE FROM A
COMPUTER MONITOR IN ORDER TO REMOVE THE COPPER LADEN
YOKE AT THE END OF THE FUNNEL. THE GLASS IS LADEN WITH LEAD,
BUT THE BIGGEST HAZARD IS THE INHALATION OF THE HIGHLY
TOXIC PHOSPHOR DUST COATING INSIDE. MONITOR GLASS IS LATER
DUMPED IN IRRIGATION CANALS AND ALONG THE RIVER, WHERE IT
LEACHES LEAD INTO THE GROUNDWATER. THE GROUNDWATER IN
GUIYU IS COMPLETELY CONTAMINATED TO THE POINT WHERE FRESH
WATER IS TRUCKED IN CONSTANTLY FOR DRINKING PURPOSES.
(GUIYU, CHINA. DECEMBER 2001. (© BASEL ACTION NETWORK 2006)

Environmentally Friendly Recycling

While we are not aware of any recycling process that is 100% environmentally friendly, recycling done correctly can dramatically reduce the impact that the use of computers and other electronic equipment have on the environment. Several organizations are working to ensure that recycling and the handling of e-waste are done in a responsible manner, with minimal impact on the environment. It is also your responsibility as a consumer to ensure that the vendor you use to recycle your end-of-life equipment does what you expect them to do and does not simply transfer the problem somewhere else.

SILICON VALLEY TOXICS COALITION

The Silicon Valley Toxics Coalition (SVTC) was founded in the early 1980s in response to the discovery of contamination in the ground water near high-tech manufacturing facilities in Silicon Valley. Its mission is to promote human health and protect the environment through research, advocacy, and grassroots organizing. SVTC led the effort to bring in the U.S. EPA to identify 29 Superfund sites throughout Silicon Valley for immediate clean up. More recently, it has exposed health and environmental problems caused by e-waste all over the world and has pushed for the elimination of toxic materials in electronic equipment. SVTC, in partnership with the Basel Action Network and the Computer TakeBack Campaign, maintains a list of electronics recyclers that meet its standards.

BASEL CONVENTION

The Basel Convention, more formally known at the Basel Convention on the Control of Transboundary Movements of Hazardous Wastes and their Disposal, is an international treaty regulating the shipment and disposal of toxic waste. It is designed to protect human health and the environment from damage caused by the generation, management, transportation, and disposal of toxic waste. It began in the 1980s, when ships loaded with toxic waste made headlines when they could not find a port at which to unload their toxic cargo. The tightening of environmental regulations in industrialized countries led to a dramatic rise in the cost of hazardous waste disposal. To reduce costs, producers of hazardous waste began shipping their waste to developing countries in Africa and Asia, as well as to Eastern Europe. Outrage over these practices led to the drafting and adoption of the Basel Convention.

Created by the United Nations, it was ratified in 1989 and became effective in 1992. The Basel Convention has been signed by 170 countries and ratified by all but three (Afghanistan, Haiti, and the United States). Waste from electronics and computers is covered under the Basel Convention and is a growing source of toxic waste. The organization's stated current areas of focus are:

▲ Active promotion and use of cleaner technologies and production methods.

▲ Further reduction of the movement of hazardous and other wastes.

▲ The prevention and monitoring of illegal traffic.

▲ Improvement of institutional and technical capabilities – through technology when appropriate – especially for developing countries and countries with economies in transition.

▲ Further development of regional and subregional centers for training and technology transfer.

BASEL ACTION NETWORK

The Basel Action Network (BAN), based in Seattle, Washington, is a not-for-profit organization that promotes the ideals of the Basel Convention through a network of global organizations. Its mission is to eliminate the transfer of toxic waste from industrialized countries to developing countries. It has created and promotes what it calls "The e-Stewards Initiative," which is designed to recognize responsible recyclers of e-waste. BAN's e-Steward initiative was inspired by a report authored by BAN, with the Silicon Valley Toxics Coalition in 2002, which found that about 80% of the e-waste collected for recycling in North America does not get recycled in North America, but is instead exported to Asia.

BAN publishes a list of e-Stewards that have signed its "Electronics Recycler's Pledge of True Stewardship" and encourages the use of these organizations for recycling of computers and electronics. Recyclers that sign the pledge agree to:

▲ Ensure that e-waste does not end up in landfills or is not incinerated.

▲ Not export e-waste from developed to developing countries.

▲ Not use prison labor for recycling.

▲ Follow best practices for environmentally friendly recycling.

▲ Meet all applicable environmental and health regulations.

▲ Provide visible tracking of all e-waste throughout the product recycling chain and agree to third-party audits.

Figure 9-7

BAN E-STEWARD LOGO. (© BASEL ACTION NETWORK 2006)

▲ Provide bonds to cover environmental costs if their facility is closed and insurance for accidents.

▲ Support design for environment and toxics use reduction programs and/or legislation for electronic products.

One major weakness in BAN's e-Steward Initiative is that it is an honor-based system, without safeguards to prevent organizations that sign the Initiative from cheating. BAN is currently working on a certification process to help prevent cheating.

IDC G.R.A.D.E. CERTIFICATION

To help corporate customers pick an asset disposal firm that recycles in a responsible manner, in 2008 the market research firm IDC created a certification program called the "Green Recycling and Asset Disposal for the Enterprise," or G.R.A.D.E. The certification process is based on 34 IT asset-disposal related activities to grade OEMs and recyclers on how well they perform the functions of on-site services, logistics, processing, and treatment of waste. To earn this certification, a company must score a minimum of 75% on a multidimensional weighting of these 34 activities.

The certification is designed to measure how well the recycler can guarantee that it recycles end-of-life IT assets in an environmentally responsible manner and can also guarantee that the organization's intellectual, financial, and other assets are protected from loss or misuse. This is becoming more critical as laws and regulations hold the original owner of the asset responsible for environmental damage or customer data loss caused by inappropriate handling and disposal methods by the recycler. Companies can no longer avoid responsibility just because they turn over the IT asset to the recycler.

The first list of companies that were awarded the G.R.A.D.E. certification was released in July 2008. These companies were Dell, Hewlett Packard,

Figure 9-8
IDC G.R.A.D.E. LOGO. (© IDC 2008)

IBM, Intechra, and Redemtech. Details of the methodology used by IDC can be found in the IDC report "2008 Assessment of U.S. IT Asset Disposal Service Providers." IDC has said that it will continue to evaluate recyclers on a regular basis.

CHOOSING A RESPONSIBLE RECYCLER

So with all the problems and potential liability issues involved in disposing of your end-of-life IT assets, how do you choose an ITAD vendor you can trust? While you can never be 100% sure of the performance of any vendor, the following steps should help you find a responsible recycler:

▲ Trust, but verify. This phrase that Ronald Reagan used when dealing with the former Soviet Union applies in spades to e-waste recyclers. No irresponsible recycler is going to publicize the fact that they are irresponsible, so verification is a must. Review and inspect the processes the recycler uses, from properly destroying data to disposal of unusable toxic material. Visit its facilities and those of any subcontractors – third-party contractors are where many of the problems occur. Your vendor should have rigorous auditing and monitoring processes in place to ensure that its partners are meeting the same high standards it follows.

▲ Transparency. An ITAD service provider should be able to provide you with tools (preferably Web based) that allow you to track your items throughout the process. You should know how each piece of equipment was handled, who handled it and when, and what was its final disposition. These same systems can provide you with details on the services your vendor provides, such as the costs involved and any potential areas for revenue back to your organization.

▲ Security. Confidential or private consumer data left on hard drives or other storage devices can be more valuable than the equipment. If the data ends up in the wrong hands, you could find yourself in a competitively weakened position or face fines for exposing private consumer data. Have your vendor demonstrate how data is destroyed and how a chain of custody is tracked. The vendor should be able to provide you with a complete report showing the tracking and disposition of each storage device.

▲ Size matters. Look for a vendor that can provide service in all areas where you have a substantial amount of equipment. Transportation costs can be a big part of a vendor's cost structure. The partner should have collection sites everywhere you do business. Companies such as IBM and HP have operations worldwide; ITAD provider Redemtech has facilities in the United States, Canada, and Western Europe, while competitor Intechra has a large number of locations, but only in the United States. Match the size of your organization to the size of your ITAD provider; larger vendors are better equipped both logistically and financially to handle the needs of larger organizations.

▲ Look for certifications. While certifications for e-waste handling are still in their infancy, organizations that have earned certifications, such as IDC's G.R.A.D.E., have at least made an effort to meet minimum standards. As these certifications mature, sponsoring organizations will most likely become better at ensuring that their standards are being followed through more stringent audits and other controls.

▲ Get your money's worth. Of course, some of your old equipment may have some value; a good ITAD partner will help you figure out what it is worth. Some companies, such as HP, will sort through your old equipment and give you a report showing its value. If your organization refreshes equipment every three years or less, you could see a significant return on your end of life equipment.

The U.S. EPA has produced a checklist for federal agencies to use when evaluating recycling companies for electronic equipment. The checklist includes the following questions:

▲ Can you provide a general description of the business that includes point of contact, number of employees, years in business, ownership history, number of locations, description of services offered, etc.?

▲ Does the electronics recycler accept the products you want recycled?

▲ Does the electronics recycler service your geographic area and type of organization?

▲ Can the electronics recycler clearly describe its fees for various types of equipment?

▲ Can the electronics recycler offer additional services that you may require? Additional services may include on-site collection support, transportation support, product reuse or refurbishment, product tracking, and recycling guarantee or certificate.

▲ Is the electronics recycler equipped to provide needed media sanitization and destruction services for your electronic equipment and components?

▲ Does the electronics recycler audit this portion of their services for quality assurance?

▲ Can the electronics recycler identify its federal, state, and local environmental agency contacts?

▲ Is the electronics recycler geographically located in an area that is regulated by a state and/or local electronics recycling law? If so, can the electronics recycler provide a description of those laws?

▲ Can the electronics recycler provide information on its compliance history? This type of information should include recent criminal (past five years) or civil (past three years) violations, and how they were, or are, being addressed.

▲ If the electronic recycler exports CRT monitors for reuse and/or mixed CRT glass for recycling, are they able to provide documentation that they are in compliance with the export section of the CRT rule (i.e., notification letter to EPA; consent letter for export from EPA)?

▲ Does the electronics recycler have environmental, health, and safety management systems and/or plans in place? Management systems and/or plans may include: Environmental management system (EMS), environmental risk management plan, hazardous materials management plan, and emergency prevention, preparedness, and response plan.

▲ Can the electronics recycler provide a description of its processes? An electronics recycler should be able to provide an overview of its procedures for disassembly, reuse/resale/donation, secure media destruction, disposal and waste handling, product manufacturing, and storage.

▲ Can the electronics recycler provide a description of what it does with the electronic equipment it receives? An electronics recycler can utilize a variety of processing methods, including brokering (matching buyers and sellers), resale of whole units, remanufacturing (refurbishing equipment), disassembling into parts and subassemblies, material recovery (physical separation to capture plastics, metals, glass, etc.), material processing (shredding and grinding) and donation (school systems, not-for-profit organizations, etc.).

▲ Can the electronics recycler provide the names and/or locations of the downstream businesses to which it sends equipment or components?

▲ Does the electronics recycler, or its downstream vendor(s), export equipment outside the United States? If so, can the electronics recycler supply you with information on the legality of such exports?

▲ Does the electronics recycler practice due diligence for its end-markets, through audit, questionnaire, or other measures?

▲ Does the electronics recycler send materials for disposal in land-fills or for incineration?

▲ Can the electronics recycler supply you with documentation or certification of final disposition?

▲ Does the electronics recycler maintain appropriate insurance/assurance? Types of insurance/assurance may include general liability insurance, environmental liability insurance, and financial assurance (e.g., bonding).

▲ Will the electronics recycler allow you to verify this information through an on-site evaluation? It is critical to have the ability to visit on-site with short notice. Can the recycler provide references and contact information for other businesses that have used their services?

The Federal Electronics Challenge (FEC), a program that encourages federal facilities and agencies to manage the use and disposal of electronics responsibly, has an excellent resource on how to perform on-site reviews of electronics recyclers on-line at http://www.federalelectronicschallenge .net/resources/docs/onsite_review.pdf.

IT Asset Lifecycle Management
The most cost effective and environmentally friendly process for IT asset disposal is to manage the entire lifecycle of these devices with the total cost of ownership in mind. This means considering disposal issues along with energy usage, as well as the environmental impact of the manufacturing process. The entire life cycle from acquisition to utilization to asset disposal must be considered to reduce the total cost of ownership of the asset. IDC, in its 2008 whitepaper "Beyond Power: IT's Roadmap to Sustainable

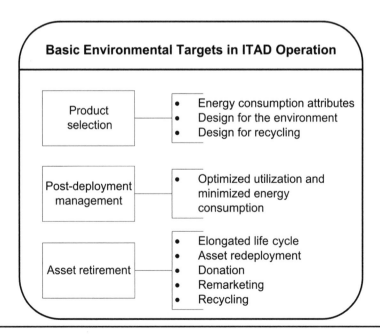

Figure 9-9
IDC BASIC ENVIRONMENTAL TARGETS IN ITAD OPERATION. (© IDC 2008)

Computing," developed a list of environmental considerations for each stage of the IT asset lifecycle. This is shown in Figure 9-9.

The following sections look at things you should be doing to improve the return on your investment in IT assets while doing the right thing for the environment.

ACQUISITION

Companies traditionally make purchasing decisions based on cost and features, with little concern for energy usage or disposal issues. While energy usage has begun to get more notice, the cost of disposal is just beginning to receive the attention it deserves.

The process of acquiring IT assets is typically disconnected from the disposal process, with different parts of the organization responsible for each of these functions. In addition, the deployment of the assets rarely takes into consideration the process of removing the equipment at the end of its useful life. In larger organizations, the facilities management group is responsible for paying the energy bill, so IT and end users have no incentive to reduce power usage. All of this leads to a disconnected process that does not optimize the total cost of owning the IT asset.

Some of the things you should consider at the time of acquisition are:

▲ Energy consumption. Energy usage over the life of the asset is a large percentage of the total cost of owning the asset. Look for equipment that is rated as energy efficient using any of the energy rating standards such as EPEAT or Energy Star.

▲ Design for Recycling (DfR). Look for equipment that is designed to be easily disassembled for reuse or recycling. Equipment designed from the start to be easily taken apart makes it easier to extend the life of the equipment by replacing outdated or nonfunctioning parts. It also reduces the cost of disassembling for recycling.

▲ Standardization. It is more convenient to deal with only one vendor. Therefore, standardizing on a particular vendor for each type of equipment can facilitate turning in old equipment for new with the manufacturer. It also makes it easier for your ITAD vendor to project costs for handling your end-of-life equipment and pass on the savings to you.

▲ Design for the Environment (DfE). Look for equipment that has been designed following best practices in environmentally friendly design. The U.S. EPA leads a number of DfE programs for areas that affect the design of IT equipment. It also maintains a list of

Figure 9-10
U.S. EPA DESIGN FOR THE ENVIRONMENT LOGO

participating companies and allows companies to use the EPA's DfE logo on products that meet its standards.

▲ Consider purchasing used equipment. Buying used equipment avoids the energy and materials consumed in building new equipment. Many business processes do not require the latest and greatest equipment to be productive.

EXTENDING USEFUL LIFE

Keep an IT asset in use as long as possible before disposing of it. This, at least temporarily, keeps it out of the waste stream. It can be as simple as extending the length of time between technology refreshes, or it can consist of a process to refurbish existing equipment on a scheduled basis. Extending the useful life of IT assets provides several financial benefits to the organization. These include:

▲ Improving return on investment (ROI). By spreading out the initial investment over a longer period of time, your ROI should increase. This can be offset somewhat by any costs incurred to refurbish or repair older equipment and any productivity losses that result from poor performance of older equipment.

▲ Reduced total cost of ownership (TCO). Less frequent technology refreshes means reduced costs for support personnel that perform the refresh and less overall user downtime from the disruption caused by replacing equipment.

The organization also benefits for not having to finance the purchase of new equipment, which can be especially important during times of a weak economy. In many situations, the reality is that the while users "want" the latest and greatest equipment, they rarely "need" to have the latest and greatest to effectively do their jobs. Adding memory and upgrading hard disk capacity can go a long way toward keeping equipment good enough to get the job done. Many organizations are also looking at desktop virtualization or the use of thin client technology to lessen the processing power required at the desktop, thus extending the equipment's useful life even further.

REUSE

Another way to keep IT assets out of the waste stream is to find ways to reuse equipment that is no longer needed by the original owner. The first option is to see if the equipment can be redeployed to other areas of the organization. This potentially extends the benefit of the investment made at the time of the original purchase. For redeployment to be most successful, some effort needs to go into making the equipment as "like new" as possible by cleaning up the equipment, reimaging the software, and providing a new keyboard and mouse (and possibly a more energy efficient monitor).

The second option for reuse is to donate end-of-life equipment to schools or charities. While this can be a good option and does seem at first glance a good thing to do, the environmental benefits are lost if the recipient of the donation simply disposes of the equipment. Another challenge with donated equipment is that the license to any software that had been on the machine typically stays with the original organization; the hardware is useless without an operating system and basic productivity software.

To help primary and secondary schools make the best use of donated equipment, Microsoft has created a "Fresh Start for Donated Computers" program to ensure that its donated computers are properly licensed. The Fresh Start program helps K-12 schools eliminate any confusion about whether donated personal computers have a legitimate operating system license. The program provides license documentation and Windows installation CDs at no charge for the Windows 2000 operating system on qualifying donated personal computers. The schools must request the licenses and track the number of systems in use. In addition, note that this program is only available for Pentium II (or equivalent) and older computers.

Another program that allows a new operating system to be installed on donated equipment is the Community Microsoft Authorized Refurbisher (MAR) program. This program is available from (from Microsoft's Web site):

▲ Charities, not-for-profits, and nongovernment organizations (NGOs): These groups must be government certified in their home countries. In the United States, these are 501(c)(3) not-for-profit organizations. In Canada, these can be federal, provincial, or charity-certified not-for-profit companies. Each Community MAR charity recipient must provide a copy of its accreditation document to the refurbisher.

▲ Schools: A Community MAR-eligible school can be any educational institution that is accredited by a regional institutional accrediting agency in its own country.

▲ Public libraries.

▲ Qualifying technology access programs (TAPs): TAPs are eligible recipients only in the United States and Canada. TAPs are recognized mission-oriented programs of a charity, government agency, or school that is providing refurbished PCs to students, families, or individuals for home use for those people who traditionally lack access to technology. Refurbishers can be TAPs themselves.

The Community MAR program (in North America) authorizes eligible refurbishers to install licensed copies of Windows 2000 Professional, Windows XP Professional, and Microsoft Office 2003 Standard on eligible refurbished computers for a cost of $5.00 per license.

RECYCLE

The last option for end-of-life equipment is to transfer the equipment to a recycling firm. The goal is to reuse appropriate parts of the equipment and break down the remaining material into basic raw material that can be used in manufacturing other products. All this must be done while minimizing the damage to the environment and to human health that can be caused by the toxic material that was used to create the equipment or is used to break down certain materials.

The first (and most environmentally friendly) option that a recycler has is to remarket the equipment to organizations that can still make good use of it. While the original purchaser of the equipment could do this itself, most companies are not equipped to handle the refurbishing required and the software licensing issues that must be resolved before the equipment can be resold. A recycler that handles a large volume of equipment has the tools, human resources, and processes necessary to cost effectively recondition older equipment and make it available for sale to new owners.

To remarket used equipment, the recycler must first wipe the hard drive clean and then test and repair any nonfunctioning items. This requires special equipment to perform tests on individual components, processes to inventory functioning parts to reuse in other machines, and procedures to ensure that data is completely erased from hard drives before being sold. And, of course, the hardware is not much use without an operating system. Therefore, Microsoft has developed a program to allow recyclers to legally install Microsoft Windows on used equipment at a lower cost than that for new equipment. High-volume recyclers can take advantage of Microsoft's Authorized Refurbisher (MAR) program, which allows them to inexpensively install a legal copy of Microsoft Windows on a refurbished machine. To participate, the recycler must meet the following requirements:

▲ Have a history of supplying an average of 5,000 refurbished PCs or notebooks per month for the last 12 months.

▲ Have adequate systems for data wiping and Microsoft reporting requirements.

▲ Have technical expertise to preinstall Microsoft Windows operating systems in a large-scale environment.

▲ Have appropriate security measures in place to ensure safe handling and storage of high value assets such as Windows licenses.

▲ Demonstrate conformance with applicable local health, safety, and environmental regulations.

Information about the MAR program and participating recyclers can be found at the MAR Web site at http://oem.microsoft.com/public/seo/mar.htm.

If equipment cannot be reused, it must be broken down into basic raw materials that can be used in the manufacture of other products. With items as complicated as IT equipment, there are multiple steps that must be performed for the equipment to be properly recycled:

1. *Disassembly.* The equipment must be safely dissembled so as not to expose the worker to any hazardous substances; this is especially critical when disassembling CRT monitors. The intact units are broken down to the component level, with any working components that can be resold or used to refurbish another unit separated out. Disassembly is a labor-intensive task. For example to disassembly a CRT monitor, the following steps are required:

a. Manually remove the plastic casing.

b. Depressurize the CRT tube.

c. Remove and separate metals.

d. Separate funnel from panel.

e. Separate leaded panel from nonlead panel.

f. Remove phosphors.

Figure 9-11
DESKTOP COMPUTERS BEING DISASSEMBLED. (IMAGE COURTESY OF REDEMTECH)

Figure 9-11 shows a typical disassembly process.

2. *Sorting.* Next, any parts that cannot be reused are separated into materials of similar types, such as circuit boards, metals, and plastics. Many of these items are shredded into smaller pieces to facilitate the separation of the constituent components and to allow for denser packing of the material for shipment to the foundry for reprocessing.

3. *Reprocessing.* Different refineries are used to process the different materials. Leaded glass from CRT monitors is sent to lead smelters for their silica and lead content. Other metal foundries are used to extract other metals, such as copper, gold, palladium, and silver.

> **STORING USED COMPUTERS**
> Many consumers store used computer equipment rather than throw it away: The U.S. EPA estimated that about 68 million used computers and 42 million monitors were in storage as of 2007. This is the second worst thing you can do with end-of-life equipment (throwing into the trash being the first). Computer technology keeps as well as fresh fruits and vegetables; none get better with age, and they quickly lose any value they originally had.

Other IT Related Disposal Issues

Because of their bulk, computers and printers get most of the attention when recycling issues are addressed, but other items that are a part of the IT food chain can also have a major effect on an organization's environmental impact. Consumables, such as paper and toner cartridges, and portable media, such as CDs and DVDs, while small in size are used in large quantities in most organizations. Other devices, such as flash drives, PDAs, and cell phones, are regularly upgraded to the latest and greatest devices. And probably most important of all is the data that is stored on all of these devices. If the data is not handled correctly at disposal time, the cost to the organization can be significant.

IT CONSUMABLES

Consumable items are used as part of the delivery of information technology services. Much of these consumables support the production of documents used for the creation and dissemination of information. These consumables include paper, toner cartridges, inkjet cartridges, staples, and paper clips The best option is to eliminate the use of paper through electronic document management (see Chapter 7, Reducing Paper Usage), but if that is not possible, at least reduce your environmental impact. Of course, the biggest step for most organizations is to recycle its paper – you are recycling your paper, aren't you? Other steps you can take to reduce the environmental impact of your use of consumables include:

▲ Use remanufactured products whenever possible. Toner cartridges and inkjet cartridges are easily recycled and are usually of the same quality as new ones. New cartridge manufacturers will attempt to convince you that using recycled cartridges may void your warranty, but doing so is illegal. If a poorly remanufactured cartridge causes damage to a printer, the recycling company would be liable for that repair but the warranty would still be intact.

▲ Buy consumables from vendors that will take back depleted consumables for recycling.

▲ Buy brands from manufacturers that design their products to be easily remanufactured or recycled.

CDS AND DVDS

CDs and DVDs are also a major source of waste driven in large part by IT. Since the first compact disk was pressed in 1982, billions of these thin, mostly plastic disks have been manufactured to store audio and video material, as well as data. Originally developed to store audio music, they soon were being used to store data. Their large capacity compared to floppy disks made them perfect for storing large applications and later data. In the 1990s, DVDs became available first to store video movies and, like CDs, later being used to store computer-generated data. With a capacity to store several times more data than CDs, they became the preferred portable medium for data backup and storage.

While CDs and DVDs appear to be simple items, they are actually quite sophisticated products. They are a complicated combination of various metals, including aluminum, gold, nickel, and silver. These metals are then combined with petroleum-based plastics, lacquers, and dyes. These disks are created using several thin layers of different materials mixed together, which make them very difficult to recycle. Most local recycling programs will not accept them, which means you need to make special arrangements to have them recycled. As a result, most CDs and DVDs eventually end up in the regular trash. While one or two here and there does not seem like a big deal, millions of these disks get discarded every year, and most end up in landfills.

The U.S. EPA publishes a list of compact disk recycling resources. At the time of this writing, these include:

▲ The National Recycling Coalition, Inc.
www.nrc-recycle.org/

▲ Plug-in to Recycling Program
www.plugintorecycling.org

▲ Sony's CD Recycling Web page
www.sony.co.jp/en/SonyInfo/Environment/ecoplaza/recycle_c.html

▲ Aural Tech CD Refinishing Specialists
www.nsynch.com/~auraltech/index.htm

▲ GreenDisk Recycled Disks Web page
www.greendisk.com/

The U.S. EPA has also partnered with Best Buy, AT&T Wireless, Dell, Panasonic, Sony, Sharp, Recycle America (part of Waste Management, Inc.), and others to help consumers of electronic products tap into a national network of recycling options.

HOW MANY DISKS ARE IN CIRCULATION?
According to the U.S. EPA, 800,000 disks were sold in the United States in 1983. By 1990, this number had grown to close to 1 billion! The agency also estimates that approximately 50 tons of CDs become obsolete each month.

CELL PHONES

While individual cell phone are much small than a desktop PC or a laptop, their larger numbers and shorter life spans combine to produce a significant amount of waste. Like any other electronic device, cell phones contain beryllium, cadmium, copper, lead, nickel, and zinc, as well as the brominated flame retardant used in the plastic parts. In 2006, more than 1 billion cell phones were shipped worldwide according to IDC's Worldwide Quarterly Mobile Phone Tracker. According to the International Association of Electronics Recyclers, about 130 million cell phone were discarded in 2007; the amount of waste ending up in landfills or incinerated adds up quickly.

While we might refresh our computers every three or four years, cell phones tend to be replaced every year or two, as new models come on the market and everyone has to have the latest features. Their small size also makes it more likely that they will be discarded at end of life rather the reused or recycled. The U.S. EPA has targeted cell phone recycling for special attention because fewer than 20 percent of cell phones are recycled each year.

Figure 9-12 shows the life cycle of a cell phone.

So what are the options for end-of-life cell phones? Like most electronic devices, your options in order of what's best for the environment are:

▲ Reduce. Resist the temptation for the latest and greatest cell phone and extend the life time of your current phone.

▲ Reuse. Pass on the old working cell phone to someone who does not require the latest and greatest.

▲ Recycle. Have the phone recycled by a responsible recycler so that the material can be used to manufacture new electronic items.

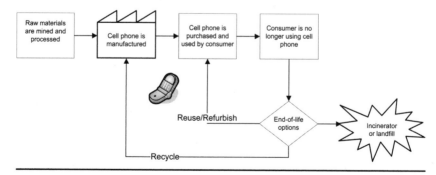

Figure 9-12
CELL PHONE LIFE CYCLE

DATA

Your organization's IT staff spends considerable time and resources protecting your data while your computers are in active service, but is your data protected as carefully once your computers reach their end-of-life and are out of your control? Most companies focus on the dangers posed by hackers and other types of intruders, when in many cases an even bigger threat is the loss of data that remains on hard drives when a computer is taken out of service. It only takes one improperly recycled hard drive for an organization to lose valuable customer information, such as credit card information or sensitive trade secrets. Your organization can be held responsible if private data ends up in the wrong hands. Some of the laws and regulations that apply to this data include:

▲ HIPAA – Regulates the use of personal medical data.

▲ Gramm-Leach-Bliley Act – Governs use of financial information.

▲ Sarbanes-Oxley Act – Requires public companies to establish key internal controls to improve confidentiality of financial data.

▲ The Patriot Act – Access to data by law enforcement.

▲ Identity Theft and Assumption Deterrence Act - Makes the theft of personal information with the intent to commit an unlawful act a federal crime.

So what do you do to prevent data on discarded computers from falling into the wrong hands? One option is to make sure the data is deleted before leaving your control. This can be done several different ways, most of them not very effective. Your options include:

▲ Delete the data.

▲ Overwrite the data.

▲ Degauss the drive.

▲ Shred the drive.

▲ Use secure erase.

The most common method is to use the operating system file delete command. This is what most users do when they want to delete data from their computer. In Microsoft Windows, deleting a file simply moves the file to the Recycle Bin, from which it can easily be retrieved. Deleting the file from the Recycle Bin removes the file from the system file list (in Windows the file allocation table), but does not delete the actual file on the hard drive. Until the data is eventually overwritten by new data, it can still be reconstructed, as in Figure 9-13.

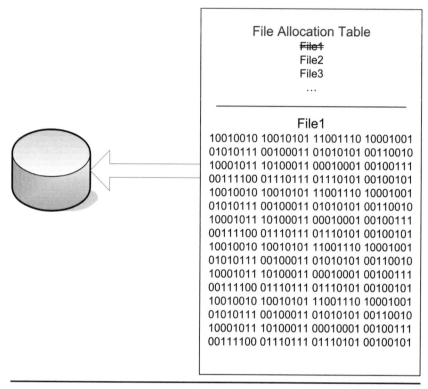

File Allocation Table
~~File1~~
File2
File3
...

File1
10010010 10010101 11001110 10001001
01010111 00100011 01010101 00110010
10001011 10100011 00010001 00100111
00111100 01110111 01110101 00100101
10010010 10010101 11001110 10001001
01010111 00100011 01010101 00110010
10001011 10100011 00010001 00100111
00111100 01110111 01110101 00100101
10010010 10010101 11001110 10001001
01010111 00100011 01010101 00110010
10001011 10100011 00010001 00100111
00111100 01110111 01110101 00100101
10010010 10010101 11001110 10001001
01010111 00100011 01010101 00110010
10001011 10100011 00010001 00100111
00111100 01110111 01110101 00100101

Figure 9-13
DELETED DATA

An option for erasing hard drive data that is considerably more effective is to use a utility to overwrite the data in the file. Data on a hard drive is stored as a series of magnetic imprints that represent ones and zeros. By overwriting the hard drive with junk data, you in theory make the original data disappear. However, because of slight alignment inconsistencies on the read/write heads used to write the data to the disk, the new data may be slightly off on the disk platter from where the old data was written, making it theoretically still possible to read the old data using special equipment. Figure 9-14 illustrates how this might work. To be most effective in overwriting the original data, applications designed to overwrite data will perform the overwrite several times; this makes it less likely the original data can be recovered. See the listing in the useful Web site section at the end of this book for examples of disk cleaning utilities.

The next best option for removing data from hard drives is called degaussing. A hard drive is degaussed by applying a strong electromagnetic field to the drive, which demagnetizes the entire drive. If degaussing is

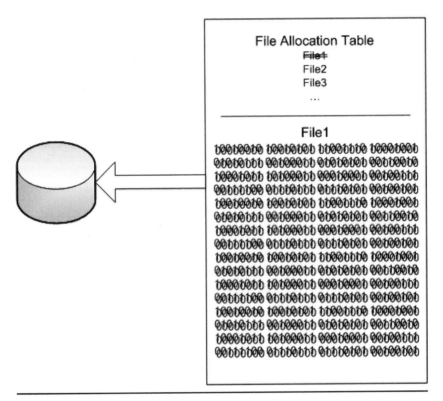

Figure 9-14
OVERWRITTEN DATA

done correctly, it completely erases any existing data. It can also be used to erase data on magnetic tapes. However, degaussing makes the hard drive unusable, as it becomes unrecognizable to the computer. The erasure is so complete that the factory written servo tracks on the disks are erased. As a result, the read/write heads no longer have a point of reference from which to work. The drive cannot be reused and will now have to be recycled. Because degaussing requires special equipment, the work is typically outsourced to a specialized vendor. This can cause chain-of-custody issues if the vendor does not have the proper controls in place to ensure that no hard drives are "lost."

As with paper records, if you want to make it almost impossible for a bad person to reassemble your data, have your hard drives shredded. Many document shredding companies also offer the use of special heavy-duty shredders to rip the hard drive into millions of small pieces. Like degaussing, this work requires special equipment and is typically outsourced to a specialized vendor. And, like degaussing, it can cause chain-of-custody issues if the vendor does not have the proper controls in place to ensure that no hard drives are "lost."

If you want to do the best job possible in erasing old data but still allow the drive to be reused, a set of commands embedded in most ATA hard drives made since 2001 called Secure Erase should do the trick. Secure Erase overwrites every single track on a hard drive, including data that is in bad blocks, directories, and partly written blocks. In short, everywhere that there could be data. The BIOS on most motherboards come with this feature disabled to prevent the average person from accidentally activating Secure Erase, so most people are not aware that it exists.

To use Secure Erase, a freeware Secure Erase utility is available from the University of California at San Diego's Center for Magnetic Recording Research. Running this utility from a DOS boot disk will allow you to activate the Secure Erase commands to erase the disk. Some systems may require changing jumpers on the motherboard; see the readme file that comes with the utility for detailed instructions. The Secure Erase commands are so effective at erasing data that the National Security Agency (NSA) and the National Institute for Standards and Testing (NIST) both highly recommend this method for secure erasing of hard drives.

ERASED DATA?

A 2002 study by two MIT graduate students found more than 5000 credit card numbers, detailed personal and corporate financial records, numerous medical records, and gigabytes of personal e-mail and pornography on 158 used hard drives they bought on eBay.

The Bottom Line

IT asset disposal is becoming a critical component of the management of IT assets. Long gone are the days when you could just fill up a dumpster with your old equipment and have it just go away with the trash. Organizations must now consider the impact they have on the environment as new laws come into effect and important stakeholders begin to demand accountability for the organization's impact on the 90openvironment. Reduce, reuse, and recycle have become the mantra for the day, as organizations reduce their use of energy and raw materials, reuse what they have rather than always buy new, and responsibly recycle what they can no longer use. Managing the entire IT asset life cycle with the environmental impact in mind, from acquisition to installation to decommissioning to disposal, is now required to reduce an organization's IT asset total cost of ownership and increase its return on investment.

VIRTUALIZATION

AS THE NUMBER of applications and systems we use to run our businesses has grown exponentially, it has become increasingly clear that the hardware resources we implement to support these applications are not being used to their fullest potential. As each new application is brought on line, it is typical to dedicate hardware to the care and feeding of the new application. By having each application on its own server, you can prevent a misbehaving application from affecting other applications. By dedicating data storage to an application, you can more easily ensure that the application will have the data storage space it needs. So, as the number of applications grows, so does the amount of hardware in our server rooms and data centers. And all of these new servers and data storage devices require an ever-increasing amount of IT resources, personnel, and energy to keep them running.

Virtualization is the concept of sharing hardware resources among the services and applications that use the resources. At the Gartner Symposium

ITxpo in 2008, this marketing research firm named virtualization the number one of its top 10 strategic technologies for 2009 Virtualization allows you to take a single hardware resource and turn it into multiple resources from the application's point of view. For example, a single physical server can be transformed into multiple "virtual" servers, each with its own CPU, memory, disk drive, and network controller that are not connected to each even though they all run on the same physical server. This allows multiple applications to now run on a single server without the possibility of them interfering with each other. In fact, server virtualization is the most common form of virtualization and is what most people think of when they hear the term "virtualization." Other resources that can be virtualized include disk storage, memory, network resources, and applications. By virtualizing physical resources, you can save energy and money, as well as make it easier to reposition these resources as the needs of the business changes.

Virtualization Basics

To understand where we are today, it is helpful to know a little about how we got here. As a manager you do not need to understand the technical intricacies of virtualization, but it helps to understand the basic concepts as you evaluate options for your organization.

HISTORY

What's old is new again! If you've been around computers as long as the authors have, you'll recall the days of the 1960s and 1970s when to take full advantage of expensive mainframes we partitioned the machine into separate virtual machines. This allowed us to run multiple jobs (applications) at the same time. Because they were so expensive, mainframes were designed from the beginning to use partitioning as a way to fully leverage our investment.

Then, starting in the 1980s, we began to move to inexpensive servers based on the Intel x86 series of processing chips. We also began developing client/server applications to take advantage of the processing power that we now had on the desktop. Windows NT and, later, Linux made it easy and inexpensive to set up a new server for each new application required by the business. Users were happy because they had a dedicated server to ensure on-demand availability for each of their important applications. IT support personnel were happy because it was easy to pinpoint the source of application problems reported by the users.

But now, in the 2000s, we face a new series of challenges. The need for servers has increased even further because of the proliferation of Web-based applications accessed by both internal and external users. Continuing to add more and more servers has created a new set of problems, including:

▲ Poor investment utilization. The market research firm IDC estimates that the typical server spends 85% of the time waiting for a user request and not performing any useful activity. Most applications are only used during business hours, yet servers are left running 24 hours a day. Many servers are lightly used, yet the users require that the application be available when they need it.

▲ Increased energy usage. No matter what is running on a server, energy is required to power the processor, spin the hard drive(s), and keep memory refreshed. As this energy is used and converted to heat, the amount of energy required for cooling the server room or data center goes up.

▲ Facility limitations. Increasing the number of servers may strain the ability of the local power grid to provide enough power to run and cool the facility housing the servers; it also increases the amount of physical space needed.

▲ Increased IT costs. As more servers are added, additional IT personnel are required to manage the servers. The cost of disposing of end-of-life servers can also be a major expense.

▲ Lack of disaster recovery. As the number of servers increases, it becomes more complex and resource intensive to properly protect applications from natural disasters, security threats, and equipment failure. If quick restoration of an application is required, a duplicate set of hardware must be available and ready to go. The expense of doing this makes it more likely that it would not get done properly and restoration objectives will not be met.

To help address these issues, the virtualization of x86 based servers was first made available by VMware in 1999. As of this writing, it is the leader in the virtualization market. Other companies, such as Citrix and Microsoft, have entered the virtualization market with their own products to virtualize all or part of an IT infrastructure.

HOW IT WORKS

Virtualization, as most frequently applied today, essentially uses software to mimic hardware. On a server or a desktop PC, it allows multiple operating systems and multiple applications to run on a single computer. The software that makes this possible is known as a hypervisor. The hypervisor forms a layer between the physical hardware and the virtualized operating system or application. Sometimes, the hypervisor acts as its own operating system and works directly with the hardware; in other cases, it simply sits on top of the operating system installed on the machine. The hypervisor makes the virtual operating system or application think that the underlying hardware belongs only to it and provides an isolated environment so that a problem with one does not affect another running on the same hardware.

Other types of virtualization, such as virtualizing networks, desktops, and storage, all work in a similar fashion. A piece of software, sometimes assisted by specialized hardware, allows you to create a virtual resource from one or more physical resources. You can then manage and allocate this resource to users and applications as needed. Each type of resource that can be virtualized has different reasons for not being fully utilized, but through virtualization we can change that.

WHY IT'S GREEN

Virtualization potentially offers great benefits to an organization without regard to its impact on the environment. However, since this book is about IT's impact on the environment, let's take a look at what virtualization has to offer from a green perspective:

- ▲ Decreased energy use. By increasing the utilization of our computing resources and reducing the number of physical devices, the amount of energy required to operate the devices is decreased. So, too, is the amount of energy required to cool these devices, thereby doubling our reduction of energy usage.

- ▲ Reduction in toxic waste. Most of these electronic devices contain toxic materials such as lead, cadmium, mercury, hexavalent chromium, polybrominated biphenyl (PBB), and polybrominated diphenyl ether (PBDE) flame retardants. These materials can be released into the environment if the devices are not recycled properly.

- ▲ Reduction in facility requirements. If the amount of equipment is reduced, so are space requirements, which means business can increase without having to build ever larger data centers.

So whether you use virtualization to save money or to be green, everyone wins.

Types of Virtualization

Just about anything you can think of in an IT environment can potentially be virtualized. The major categories of virtualization in use today are

(1) server virtualization, which allows multiple servers to run on a single physical server; (2) application virtualization, which allows applications to run independently of the underlying host operating system; (3) network virtualization, which combines resources on a network so they can be managed as a single entity; (4) storage virtualization, which allows multiple storage devices to be combined as one large storage resource; and (5) desktop virtualization, which allows virtual desktops to be centrally managed on a server and run by the end user on a thin client machine.

SERVER VIRTUALIZATION

Server virtualization is the most popular form of virtualization, and it is what most people think of when they hear the term. Server virtualization allows you to run one or more "virtual" servers on a single physical host system. As the power of hardware has increased in accordance with Moore's Law (which states that the number of transistors on a chip doubles every 24 months and, with it, computing power), businesses acquire ever-more powerful servers whether their applications require them or not. If our servers become much more powerful than the applications on them require (which most are) and our servers are not running anywhere near 100% capacity (most are running at 10% to 15%), then it makes sense to run multiple servers on a single machine.

Virtualization can be implemented in two different ways: software-based and hardware-based. Software-based virtualization is commonly implemented using either full virtualization or paravirtualization. In full virtualization, the hypervisor is independent of the operating system and sits between the operating system and the hardware. The hypervisor then acts as the gatekeeper between the multiple operating systems and the hardware to share system resources. In paravirtualization, the operating system is modified to be aware of the fact it is virtualized.

The advantage of using full virtualization is that any operating system can then be virtualized, while the advantage of using paravirtualization is that overall performance is better because the operating systems recognizes and cooperates with the hypervisor.

Hardware-based virtualization adds additional advantages, in that it makes the job of the hypervisor much easier if the hardware is designed with virtualization in mind. This allows for a much simpler, more efficient, and better performing overall virtualized system. Intel began offering its Virtualization Technology (VT) product in 2004, followed by AMD's Virtualization (AMD-V) product in 2006.

Server virtualization provides a host of benefits to both the IT department and to the users that they serve. These benefits include:

▲ Improved investment utilization. Because many virtual servers can run on a single physical machine, you can greatly increase the utilization of your computer hardware investment, as well as reduce the number of physical servers required.

▲ Decreased energy usage. Having fewer servers means less energy is needed to power and cool the servers.

▲ More floor space. Reducing the number of servers can reduce the amount of space needed, or at least allow you to use the space more efficiently.

▲ Decreased IT costs. Less physical equipment means fewer people are needed to keep it running. The cost of disposing of old equipment at end of life is also reduced.

▲ Improved disaster recovery. By using virtual servers, you can create a "hot" standby image of the production machine that is much quicker to get up and running than is trying to restore backup tapes to a physical machine. The virtual standby image can sit idle on a

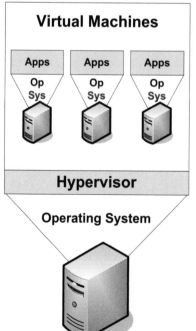

Virtual Machines

Apps

Apps

Apps

Op Sys

Op Sys

Op Sys

Hypervisor

Operating System

Physical Server

Figure 10-1
SERVER VIRTUALIZATION

storage device and be activated when it needs to take over for a production server that is experiencing some sort of problem. You can use replication to keep updated copies of a virtual machine at an off-site disaster recovery site for additional protection.

▲ Safe testing environment. Software testing is simplified by the ease of creating a virtual machine for testing new software. A standard system image can be created that can be quickly set up with the new software installed. As a result, testing can be done without impacting other systems.

While there are a number of good reasons to virtualize your servers, server virtualization is not for everyone. Some issues with virtualization include:

▲ Server sprawl. The biggest issue for most organizations is avoiding "server sprawl," in which the number of virtual servers grows to an unmanageable level.

▲ Licensing issues. You must also plan ahead for potential licensing issues with some operating systems and applications.

▲ Increased complexity. While virtualizing servers can simplify some aspects of your IT operation, it does add a layer of complexity to your environment that will have to be managed.

▲ Hardware compatibility issues. Some specialized programs that work with dedicated hardware, such as point-of-sale (POS) systems, may not work well on virtual machines.

▲ Single point of failure. And last, but not least, having several virtual servers on a single host machine means that if the hardware fails, all servers on that machine will fail. What was before maybe a single department screaming when the machine running its critical application went down, now becomes a chorus of angry users when multiple virtual servers all die at once when the physical server fails. You may need to have a second physical server available in case of hardware failure.

APPLICATION VIRTUALIZATION

In the common client/server model used in most organizations, each desktop PC has to have its own operating system and a number of applications installed. Each application needs its own license and must be updated as required. As more applications are installed or as existing applications or the operating system are patched and updated, problems can begin to occur.

One application may start to misbehave or no longer "play nice" with the other applications. This makes the user unhappy and adds to the workload of the IT support personnel as they try to troubleshoot these problems.

Application virtualization can help you avoid this problem by having each application virtualized onto a central location and served or streamed to the desktop computer when needed. Application virtualization is similar to server virtualization, but instead of having separate isolated copies of operating systems sharing resources, separate isolated copies of an application share resources. Just as in server virtualization, the hardware is hidden from the application, but, in addition, the operating system on the host machine is also hidden.

A virtualized application is not installed on the host machine in the way a traditional application is, but runs as if it were. A virtualized application package is created, which is then copied to the machine on which you want to run the application. Application virtualization also allows the virtualized applications to be moved from one host system to another without disturbing other applications running on the machine. Advantages of virtualized applications include:

▲ Applications can be executed from portable media, such as USB drives on any machine, even if the operating is system different from what the application normally requires (e.g., running a Windows application on a Linux machine).

▲ Because no device drivers are installed or registry entries made, applications can be deployed without having administrative rights.

▲ Because the virtual application exists as a single file, it can be easily removed from a system when no longer needed.

▲ Fewer resources are required than when creating an entire virtual machine.

▲ Applications that are incompatible can be safely run on the same physical machine.

▲ Security is improved because the application is isolated from the underlying operating system.

A few issues should be considered when virtualizing an application. Some older applications, especially those that require special device drivers or that use memory in unsupported ways, may not work in virtual mode. Applications must be packaged using a virtualization tool, such as Microsoft Application Virtualization and VMware ThinApp. Your network must be

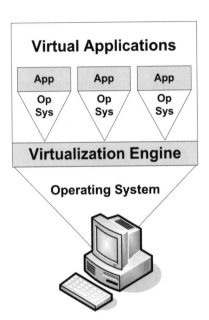

Virtual Applications

| App | App | App |

| Op Sys | Op Sys | Op Sys |

Virtualization Engine

Operating System

Physical Computer

Figure 10-2
APPLICATION VIRTUALIZATION

able to handle the increased traffic generated by streaming virtualized applications to where they are needed. And, although a virtualized application can be streamed to any PC, the receiving PC must still be powerful enough to run the application.

NETWORK VIRTUALIZATION

Network virtualization allows you to combine all of the resources available on a network by splitting up the available bandwidth into independent channels. These channels can then be assigned or reassigned to a particular device or server in real time. Any user or device that has access to the virtual network has access to any other resource on the network.

A virtual network can make the maintenance and administration of the network easier by allowing for centralized access to all the resources in the virtual network. For example, files, folders, storage media, and programs can be centrally managed from a single physical location. Physical devices can be easily added and made available to users of the network. Additional benefits to a virtual network include the following capabilities:

▲ Consolidation of many physical networks into one virtual network.

▲ Partitioning of a single physical network into many virtual networks.

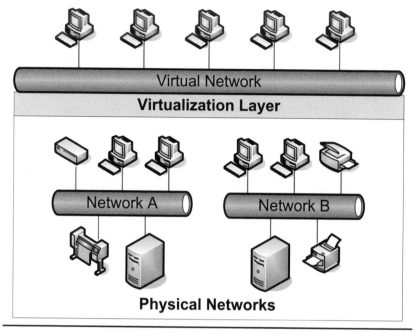

Figure 10-3
NETWORK VIRTUALIZATION

▲ Customizing access for users and groups to the appropriate resources.

▲ Rapid deploy updated services and polices to everyone on the network.

STORAGE VIRTUALIZATION

Just as servers have been underutilized, so have storage devices. Many applications require that some minimum amount of storage be allocated for their use, and then in many cases, only a small fraction is actually used. Storage virtualization allows the physical storage from multiple storage devices to appear to be a single storage device to the operating system or application. The storage can then be allocated as needed for use by users, applications, and servers. Just as with server virtualization, storage virtualization can increase utilization to 75% or better.

There are three basic approaches for virtualizing storage. The most common (called in-fabric) is the use of storage area network (SAN) devices that are connected by a high-speed fibre channel network. Software is then installed on a host server or a storage virtualization device is installed as

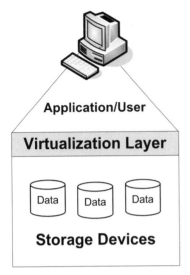

Figure 10-4
STORAGE VIRTUALIZATION

part of the SAN; either provides the layer of abstraction between the hosts performing the I/O and the storage controllers providing the storage capacity. The second method, called host-client, uses software running on file and application servers to detect available storage and to maintain the metadata necessary to manage them. The third method, known as in-array or embedded functionality, uses a special network controller and management software to manage different storage systems as one large resource. All methods provide the advantages of storage virtualization, which include:

▲ Easier administration as virtualized storage can be managed from a single administrative console.

▲ Storage growth can be closely monitored and managed, making upgrade planning easier.

▲ Disaster recovery is improved as storage can be more easily moved around or backed up to other locations.

▲ Data can be migrated to new storage devices without disrupting the application, since the physical storage is not directly tied to the application. This makes it easier to swap out end-of-lease equipment or to refresh old storage with newer devices.

Issues to be aware of when considering storage virtualization include:

▲ If you have heterogeneous storage devices, are they all compatible with the virtualization technology you're considering?

▲ Ensure that the storage metadata is protected and backed up.

▲ Be aware that whichever option you choose, you'll be locked into a particular vendor.

DESKTOP VIRTUALIZATION

Desktop PCs are notoriously difficult to maintain as new software is installed and old applications are removed. It can be difficult to keep track of what versions of what software are installed on any given machine, and conflicts can occur among incompatible versions of different applications. Many organizations use Microsoft Terminal Services or Citrix Presentation Server to provide a managed, stable desktop environment that can be accessed using a standard PC or a less expensive thin client device. Desktop virtualization builds on this by giving the user a virtualized full client environment using a server-based hypervisor. This allows the user to have full administrative control over the desktop environment and applications. Some of the advantages of desktop virtualization include:

▲ Easy to deploy desktops to new users.

▲ Desktop machines can be less expensive PCs or thin client devices.

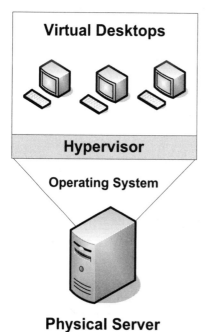

Virtual Desktops

Hypervisor

Operating System

Physical Server

Figure 10-5
DESKTOP VIRTUALIZATION

▲ Ability to use your desktop environment from any PC with network or Internet access.

▲ Access to typical desktop features, such as multiple monitors, USB devices, and so on.

▲ Disaster recovery at the desktop is simplified, as a new device can be quickly installed to use the virtualized image on the server. Backups can be managed at the server level.

Virtualization of the desktop also creates the opportunity to have desktops provided through the Internet, much as many vendors are doing with applications using the "software as a service" (SaaS) model. For desktops, one term being used is "desktop as a service" (DaaS), while others use the term Virtual Desktop Infrastructure as a Service (VDI).

Some issues to be aware of when considering desktop virtualization:

▲ Your "per seat" cost may be initially higher because of the cost of the servers, virtualization software, and Windows licenses.

▲ The OEM version of Windows that comes with most new PCs cannot be used in a virtual environment; new licenses must be purchased.

▲ User resistance to giving up their full client PCs.

Technology Options

As the interest in virtualization increases, so do the technology options available to your IT department. While VMware has dominated the market for virtualization technology since releasing its first product in 1999, other players have recently moved aggressively into the market.

VMWARE ESX

VMware, which started the latest virtualization craze, has jumped out to a commanding lead in the market. VMware's flagship product, ESX, uses the full virtualization approach and installs directly on the server hardware. An advantage of this approach is that almost any operating system or application can run in a virtualized environment without any modification. This approach also allows for more virtual servers to be run on a physical server than other methods. Performance is also better as it does not rely on the underlying operating system. It also supports all Intel and AMD processors, so it will work with older machines. Its VMotion product allows you to migrate virtual machines from one physical server to another while running, which is a huge advantage in high-availability situations. Its management tools are mature and gives it quite the advantage in the market.

The flip side of being first to market is that ESX was not designed with other virtualization systems in mind. As a result, its management and storage tools do not work well with other systems, such as Hyper-V and Xen. Products from VMware are also expensive from an initial licensing perspective and will face increased price pressure from Microsoft and open source alternatives.

MICROSOFT HYPER-V

Just as in the 1990s Microsoft had to play catch-up with the early market leader in the hot new technology (Netscape and the Internet browser), so, too, in the early 2000s did Microsoft have to scramble to avoid being left behind by yet another pioneer in a hot new technology (i.e., VMware and virtualization). Just as the browser was seen as a potential threat to Microsoft's Windows franchise, virtualization technology is potentially disruptive to the "Windows on every desktop" model that has made Microsoft the number one software company in the world. And just like its response to Netscape's browser, Microsoft has used a combination of acquisitions, marketing muscle, and a renewed focus on Windows technology to protect its Windows turf.

Given all that history, what direction do you predict Microsoft will take with virtualization? If you said, "build it into Windows," you get a prize. Microsoft's latest virtualization technology, called Hyper-V, is built into the latest version of Windows Server 2008. Having virtualization built into the operating system cannot help but increase the acceptance and use of the technology. One interesting feature in Microsoft's latest virtualization system is the support in System Center Virtual Machine Manager 2008 for managing VMware virtual machines. While still very new at the time of this writing, the Hyper-V technology appears to be a serious competitor to market leader VMware.

A possible disadvantage of Hyper-V is that it only runs on the newer processors from Intel and AMD that include built-in support for virtualization, and will not work on older servers. Rather than be able to consolidate the servers you have now, you may need to wait until your next technology refresh. And while it may come with Windows, it is still not inexpensive, as users need to buy the Data Center edition of Windows Server 2008 to avoid the additional licensing costs required. These costs apply to any edition of Windows that does not include the right to create an unlimited number of virtual machines in a production environment.

Unlike VMare, Hyper-V also does not support the ability to perform live migrations of virtual machines. At this time, it only officially supports a single flavor of Linux, Suse Linux Enterprise Server 10 from Novell.

XEN

Xen is a free, open source hypervisor for x86-based CPUs. It started as a research project at the University of Cambridge and was first released to the public in 2003. In 2007, Citrix acquired XenSource, the organization that was founded by Xen's creators and had supported its development. While Citrix now leads the development of Xen, as an open source product Citrix has partnered with IBM, HP, Intel, Novell, Red Hat, and Sun in creating the Xen Project Advisory Board to oversee Xen's future development. The Xen Project Advisory Board is also responsible for the Xen trademark and licensing requirements for the hypervisor. It is also responsible for the community Web site at www.xen.org.

The Xen hypervisor makes use of paravirtualization, which means that the guest operating systems are aware that they are in a virtual environment. It supports the most commonly used guest operating systems (i.e., Linux, Windows, Solaris) and some versions of the BSD operating system.

KVM

KVM (Kernel-based Virtual Machine) is another open source hypervisor developed by Qumranet, which was started in 2005. It differs from Xen in that it turns the Linux kernel itself into a hypervisor. This was done by developing KVM as a kernel module, which simplifies the management and improves the performance of the virtualized environments. This also allows higher level software to take advantage of the new hardware virtualization features being built into the latest processors from Intel and AMD. By making use of these new hardware virtualization features, other operating systems, such as Windows, that can run on the processor can be guests running on a Linux-based host using these newer chips.

Management Considerations

Make sure you consider virtualization's impact on your overall organization. It must provide benefits to the entire organization and not be something the IT department does in isolation.

PLANNING FOR VIRTUALIZATION

As with any other IT project, planning is critical. One of the advantages to virtualization from a project management prospective is that you don't have to do everything at once. Take time to think about your objectives and what makes sense to virtualize in your organization. It is important to perform due diligence as you plan for virtualization. Virtualizing a small number of servers and other resources can be a fairly simple task, but the complexity increases exponentially as the number of physical resources to be virtualized grows. Keep the following in mind:

1. *Education is critical.* Learn about the different types of virtualization and how they might apply to your organization. If, like most organizations, you have numerous applications running mostly on their own servers, server virtualization can be great low-hanging fruit.

2. *Focus on the goal.* Remembering to "begin with the end in mind." Map out how the ideal virtual environment would look in your organization.

3. *Test, test, test.* Create a test environment to try things out. The very nature of virtualization makes it perfect for setting up test environments that can be used for testing before going into actual production.

4. *Go slow.* Convert physical resources to your virtual environment as you get comfortable with the technology and gain experience in your test environments.

5. *Process is key.* Because virtual servers and other resources are so easy to create, it can be easy to lose track of which servers exist, who created them, which applications they support, and whether or not they are still needed. Proper policies and procedures must be in place to track and manage the creation of virtual resources.

Keep in mind also that virtualization will not solve all of your problems by itself. A poorly run IT operation will not get better just by implementing virtualization. Virtualization also does not eliminate continued investment in IT – the virtual machines are not free. There are still operating systems licensing costs if using Windows, and you still have to have a physical server somewhere to run your virtual servers. Just like any other piece of software, you'll have cost in the ongoing support and maintenance of the software. Your IT personnel will also require training if you want your investment in virtualization to be managed efficiently.

MANAGEMENT ISSUES

While virtualization solves many technical issues, it only makes sense if it solves business problems. Most virtualization planning tools focus on the technical aspects of workload analysis and configuration issues, but do not address the potential business issues. These issues can include:

▲ Politics. Different departments within the organization may have real or imagined reasons why they will not share hardware resources.

▲ Security. A virtualized server is essentially one large file that any administrator may be able to access. This may cause security issues if the server and the data are on the same virtual machine in that single file.

▲ Compliance. Compliance considerations in some organizations may prevent applications and/or data from being shared by different departments. Putting these servers together on the same physical machine may then violate compliance regulations.

▲ Chargeback process. Charging back departments for use of IT resources becomes much more complicated if these resources are virtualized and shared on an as-needed basis.

▲ Downtime. Applications with overlapping critical uptime requirements might mean that the physical server can never be down for maintenance.

ADMINISTRATION ISSUES

Virtualization dramatically changes how your systems operate and how they are managed. System administrators are used to the one-to-one connection between the software applications they support and the hardware on which they run. Virtualization changes this model, so that the direct connection between operating system and application software and hardware is broken. You can no longer easily point to a particular server and say that "this is application X."

Another issue could be the introduction of performance conflicts when two or more virtual applications sharing the same physical resources all hit their peak usage point at the same time. This can cause overall performance to decrease as the virtual servers contend for the same physical resources. You need to consider how your servers and applications are used when determining which resources to virtualize and combine onto a single physical server.

WHAT SHOULD I LOOK FOR IN A VIRTUALIZATION SOLUTION?

The most important consideration in selecting a virtualization solution is the management tools and resources available to work with in your environment. As the hypervisor technology matures and is no longer significantly different from one vendor to the next, the ability to manage the ever-increasing number of virtual resources will determine the success of virtualization in your organization. VMware is giving away the basic virtualization technology, and Microsoft includes it free or at a very low cost with Windows Server. The marketing is rapidly moving in the direction of vendors differentiating themselves in the tools they provide for monitoring, managing, and making the most efficient use of virtualized resources. These tools should include the ability to manage a mixture of physical and virtual resources to support the ability to migrate physical resources to virtual ones at your own pace. Your focus should be on which vendor provides the best management tools for your business and IT environment.

Virtualization vendors are also moving toward solutions that put all IT resources into a single resource pool. These "enterprise virtualization" solutions combine all the resources that can be virtualized – CPUs, memory, disk storage, networking, and applications – into one large pool of computing resources that can be allocated as needed.

The Bottom Line

Virtualization has the potential to bring dramatic cost savings, as well as to enhance the organization's ability to adapt to business changes. Since the ability of IT to provide the right services at the right time has become increasing important to the competitive ability of an organization, this increased agility can greatly improve an organization's long-term performance. Adding to this is the opportunity for IT managers to spend more time thinking about the strategic use of their computing resources, as they spend less time managing less physical hardware.

11 DATA CENTER

DATA CENTER managers historically have had two main goals when de-signing and operating the data center: availability and security. Users judged the quality of the data center by whether their applications were available when needed and whether the performance level was acceptable. Con-trolling access to important information has also been a high priority. In our interconnected world, the data center manager wages a constant battle to keep the bad guys out while ensuring the availability of information to those who need it.

However, in a world of ever-increasing environmental concerns and with the rising cost of energy, a third priority has emerged—how to control the vast amount of energy required to power today's data centers. Being "green" has become a solution to both the environmental issues caused by data centers and to the rising cost of power. Part of this problem is caused by the fact that in a typical data center, 60% to 70% of the energy used is not for the computers, but to power to the facility and cool the data center. A green data center can also make it easier to upgrade and support increasing computing demands. This chapter explores these issues and looks at some of the solutions available to make your data center "green."

The Problem

The problem itself is simple – an ever-increasing need for energy. As our need for computing power increases for everything from running our businesses to streaming video over the Internet, so has our need for energy to power and cool the servers. Most of this computing power is housed in specialized facilities known as data centers, which centrally manage a large amount of computing power. While there are numerous advantages to concentrating computing power in a single location, it also creates its own set of energy-related problems.

The first problem is having enough power to run the servers and peripheral devices, such as disk storage arrays, networking equipment, and off-line data storage. Web sites are becoming bigger and more sophisticated, thereby requiring bigger servers and more data storage. System manufacturers want to sell you the biggest and most powerful systems they can, so newer servers tend to require as much or more energy as the ones they replace. As a result, the problem grows more serious over time. In some cases, the software used cannot even take advantage of the additional computing power, so this extra power is wasted. Some organizations do not fully allocate the true cost of new applications to the user community, so new applications are created requiring ever more computing resources without thought to their impact on the data center.

The second problem is dealing with the large amount of heat generated by all of these devices in a confined space, as it also takes energy to remove the heat so that the equipment can operate properly. High-density servers are creating hot spots that can be as high as 30 kilowatts per rack for some high-end systems. Older data centers may have been fine when initially built, but are now having to jam more and more equipment into a confined space.

Not only can the power be expensive, but in some areas the local utility company may not be able to provide the power needed. It may simply not be available at any price. Compounding the problem is that data center managers in many organizations do not see the power bill; it is under the budget of the facilities department. If energy usage is not properly allocated to the data center, IT has little incentive to reduce power consumption.

HOW MUCH POWER DO SERVERS USE?
Total power used by servers represented about 0.6% of total U.S. electricity consumption in 2005. When cooling and auxiliary infrastructure are included, that number grows to 1.2%, an amount comparable to that for color televisions. The total power demand in 2005 (including associated infrastructure) is equivalent (in capacity terms) to about five 1000 MW power plants for the United States. and 14 such plants for the world. In 2005, the total electricity bill for operating those servers and associated infrastructure was about $2.7 B and $7.2 B for the United States and other nations, respectively.

Source: Jonathan G. Koomey, Ph.D., Estimating Total Power Consumption by Servers in the U.S. and the World Stanford University, Final Report, February 15, 2007. Contact: http://www.koomey.com

---

DATA CENTER POWER USAGE

A look at the electrical bill for your data center should confirm that computing resources require a tremendous amount of energy. Power is required for servers, UPS units, telecom equipment, HVAC, and lighting. But do you know exactly where all the power is going? If not, an energy audit will give you a better idea of the scope of the problem and help identify areas in

Census Division	Residential		Commercial		Industrial	
	Jul-08	Jul-07	Jul-08	Jul-07	Jul-08	Jul-07
New England	17.74	16.31	16.14	14.87	14.3	12.29
Middle Atlantic	16.5	14.88	16.24	14.45	8.91	8.34
East North Central	10.83	10.05	9.03	9.05	6.78	5.77
West North Central	9.73	9.08	8.04	7.63	6.07	5.74
South Atlantic	11.24	10.44	9.77	8.77	6.94	5.9
East South Central	9.69	8.36	9.26	8	6.47	5.47
West South Central	12.85	11.42	11.09	9.55	9.39	7.16
Mountain	10.56	9.94	8.95	7.94	6.87	6.23
Pacific Contiguous	12.96	12.86	12.62	12.78	8.74	8.2
Pacific Noncontiguous	28.92	21.59	24.52	18.02	25.17	17.17
U.S. Total	12.09	11.06	11.08	10.2	7.75	6.61

Figure 11-1
U.S. ELECTRICAL POWER COSTS PER REGION. (SOURCE: ENERGY INFORMATION ADMINISTRATION, FORM EIA-826, "MONTHLY ELECTRIC SALES AND REVENUE REPORT WITH STATE DISTRIBUTIONS REPORT")

which the biggest impact could be made. An energy audit looks at the complete process of providing computing resources and the power required to do so. It should include the following:

- ▲ An inventory of all devices that use power in the data center and their locations.

- ▲ The amount of power required by each device both at peak usage and when idle.

- ▲ The utilization rate for each device.

- ▲ The organization's plans for growth and the computing resources required.

- ▲ Existing or planned energy regulations that could affect access to and cost of electrical power.

- ▲ Your organization's green goals for reducing the organization's carbon footprint, as well as timelines for meeting these goals.

When looking at power usage the following areas must be considered:

- ▲ Overall energy use.

- ▲ Computing equipment and software used.

- ▲ Heating and cooling system.

- ▲ Airflow management.

- ▲ Lighting.

As you begin your energy reduction initiative, be sure to look at the affect of each change on the entire system. You don't want to optimize one area just to discover that your savings are being spent in another area.

BENCHMARKING

As with any major initiative, management support is critical to getting the time and resources necessary to make something happen. Management may be interested in an energy reduction initiative because of a desire to be more "green." As Kermit the Frog once said, "It's not easy being green," but it has become more popular because of its positive connotations and its real ability to save money.

You can't manage what you don't measure. This old management adage is never truer than when looking to save energy in the data center. Before getting started, you should benchmark the efficiency of the data center against organizations of similar size and operational requirements. This gives you a starting point from which to measure energy efficiency improvements. It can help you identify "low-hanging fruit," where small changes will have the biggest impact. Benchmarking can also be valuable if expansion plans are in your future, because it identifies what you are doing right and wrong today. This can help improve energy efficiency in the future of the additional space. Once you have baseline benchmarks in place, you can use them to show progress in your green efforts. Below are some of the most common data center energy efficiency benchmarks.

POWER USAGE EFFECTIVENESS (PUE)

Power Usage Effectiveness (PUE) is used to measure how efficiently energy is used in the data center. It was created by the Uptime Institute and promoted by the Green Grid. It is a simple calculation done by taking the amount of power that enters the data center and dividing by the amount of power used by the computer equipment in the data center.

$$PUE = \frac{power\ entering\ data\ center}{power\ used\ by\ computer\ equipment}$$

Computer equipment includes anything necessary for the delivery of computing services, such as servers, storage devices, and telecommunications equipment. The power usage of the data center is more efficient as the PUE value comes down to 1.0. To determine PUE for your data center, use the following steps:

1. Measure the power coming into the data center at or near the utility meter. Make sure you only measure what is going to the data center and not any offices or other areas shared with the data center. If the data center is not on a separate meter from the rest of the facility, estimate the amount of power used by these other areas and subtract this from the total power coming in.

2. Measure the power as it arrives at the server racks. This is most effectively done at the output of the power distribution units.

3. Divide the value in item 1 by the value measured in item 2.

According to the Uptime Institute, the typical data center has an average PUE of between 2 and 3. This means that for every 2 or 3 watts that are provided by the utility company, only one watt is actually used by the computer equipment. The Uptime Institute estimates that most facilities could achieve 1.6 PUE using the most efficient equipment and industry best practices.

DATA CENTER INFRASTRUCTURE EFFICIENCY (DCIE)

A metric that is the reciprocal of PUE, called Data Center infrastructure Efficiency (DCiE), is also sometimes used. It is defined as:

$$DCiE = \frac{power\ used\ by\ computer\ equipment}{power\ entering\ data\ center}$$

DCiE is expressed as a percentage, with the target value being 100%. This equation tells you what percentage of the power you are paying for is being used by the equipment providing computer services in the data center. A typical data center has a DCiE of 40%.

COMPUTE POWER EFFICIENCY (CPE)

While PUE and DCiE measure the efficiency of the data center for energy usage, they do not measure how efficiently the power is being used for computing. Another metric, Compute Power Efficiency (CPE), attempts to measure this. It is calculated by dividing the PUE into the utilization percentage of the computing equipment:

$$CPE = \frac{computer\ equipment\ utilization\ rate}{PUE}$$

Or

$$CPE = \frac{computer\ equipment\ utilization\ rate \times power\ used\ by\ computer\ equipment}{power\ entering\ data\ center}$$

Computer equipment utilization rate is usually determined by the average CPU utilization percentage of all the servers in the data center. This metric connects the efficiency of the computer equipment in the data center with the efficiency of the entire data center. In many data centers, CPE is typically 20% or less.

CADE (CORPORATE AVERAGE DATACENTER EFFICIENCY)

Another metric that was recently developed to rate the overall energy efficiency of a data center is CADE (Corporate Average Datacenter Efficiency). It was designed by the Uptime Institute and the management consulting firm McKinsey to compare the energy efficiency of one data center with another. It is calculated using the following formula:

$$CADE = Facility\ Efficiency\ (FE) \times Asset\ Efficiency\ (AE)$$

Facility Efficiency (FE) is determined by taking the amount of power used by computer equipment divided by the power entering the data center (DCiE), multiplied by the amount of power used by computer equipment divided by the maximum amount of power the facility can support to the computer equipment.

$$Facility\ Efficiency\ (FE) = \frac{power\ used\ by\ computer\ equipment}{facility\ power\ capacity\ for\ computer\ equipment}$$

Asset Efficiency (AE) is the utilization percentage of the installed computer equipment, using the average CPU utilization percentage.

McKinsey and the Uptime Institute are promoting CADE as a metric to be used in a similar fashion to the way the automotive industry uses the CAFE (Corporate Average Fuel Economy) for measuring corporate fuel economy. Like DCiE, CADE is expressed as a percentage, with a higher CADE indicating a more energy efficient data center. McKinsey has defined a five-tier rating scale for CADE values:

▲ Level 1 – 0% to 5%.

▲ Level 2 – 5% to 10%.

▲ Level 3 – 10% to 20%.

▲ Level 4 – 20% to 40%.

▲ Level 5 – >40%.

Most organizations today are at Level 2 or below. McKinsey believes that most organizations will get to Level 3 or Level 4 by 2012 as data center efficiency becomes increasingly important. Another important step to take is to change how costs are allocated for power usage in the data center. It is critical that the true cost of the energy used by the data center is captured and charged to the users of that power. You can then modify the internal chargeback systems so that energy usage is included in the costs calculated for new systems and applications. It is important that you charge per kW of power used in data center facilities and not for power based simply on the square footage of the facility.

Powering Your Equipment

The vast array of equipment required to operate today's data centers use a tremendous amount of electrical power. Servers, hard disk storage, memory, and even your network all require ever more expensive energy to operate. Let's take a look at each of these types of equipment and see what energy savings we can find in each.

Servers are the top users of power of all the computer equipment in the data center and, for most data centers, the first and best place to look for energy savings. The annual energy costs for a single server can be estimated based on its rated power and the price of electricity ($0.11 per kWhr commercial average in the United States, see Figure 11-2 for power costs in your area) as shown in the following equation:

$$Annual\ power\ cost = 8760\ \frac{hrs}{yr} \times \frac{\$0.11}{kWhr} \times server\ power\ in\ KW$$

Once you know how much each server costs in ongoing energy costs, you know how much you can save for each server you eliminate or replace with a more energy efficient one. It's quite simple in theory, as you have only two options for reducing the amount of power used by servers:

1. Reduce the number of servers.

2. Make the remaining servers more efficient.

Of course, these goals are easier said than done. You had a very good reason for every server installed in the data center, and you probably focused on meeting the user's needs by ensuring the server had plenty of horsepower to run its applications. But because energy usage was probably not high on the priority list, what you ended up with was too many inefficient servers drawing lots of power and generating lots of heat that has added up to today's huge energy bill.

First, look at how many of the existing servers can be turned off. In most data centers, as many as 10 percent of servers are no longer actively used and can be turned off. Since idle servers still use a significant amount of power just waiting for something to happen, this wastes a huge amount of energy. Implementing a formal decommissioning process to eliminate these unused servers can realize immediate energy savings.

Another way to reduce the number of physical servers is through the use of virtualization. Server virtualization (see Chapter 10) allows you to run multiple "virtual" servers on a single physical server. Since most servers have a utilization rate of 10% to 15%, two or three virtual servers can on average be hosted on a single physical server.

The next consideration is enabling power saving features that are available on newer servers. In many data centers, power management is not a factor because administrators have historically focused on uptime and performance metrics, with little regard to the amount of energy being used. Support for power management in servers is relatively recent and should

US Electricity Costs per kWh in July 2008

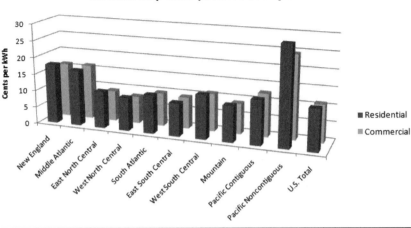

Figure 11-2

U.S. ELECTRICAL POWER COSTS PER REGION. (SOURCE: ENERGY INFORMATION ADMINISTRATION, FORM EIA-826, "MONTHLY ELECTRIC SALES AND REVENUE REPORT WITH STATE DISTRIBUTIONS REPORT")

be done with caution. Some things to consider when evaluating the use of power management are:

▲ Begin with a test environment to see how well power management works for your servers and to look for any problems. You want to have a process that is automated and still reliable.

▲ Check with your hardware provider about support for sleep and hibernate modes for servers. These functions may not work exactly as you are used to them working on desktop machines.

▲ According to Microsoft, sleep and hibernate functions are turned off automatically when using Windows Server 2003 and 2008 on machines with more than 4 GB of memory due to performance issues. Details can be found in the Knowledge Base article available at: support.microsoft.com/kb/888575.

▲ While turning servers off with scripts is easy, turning them back on can be more difficult. Check with your server vendor to see what options are available.

Power supplies are the main source of energy waste in servers. Server manufacturers are in most cases oversizing power supplies and, since power supplies are most efficient at 100% capacity, much energy is wasted. Energy efficient power supplies are 15% to 20% more expensive than the commodity power supplies used in most servers, so servers purchased with low purchase price in mind waste a lot of energy. In low-cost power supplies, efficiency peaks at about 70% to 75% when the server is 100% utilized, but drops into the 65% range at 20% utilization. Since the average server is 10% to 15% utilized, almost half the power used is wasted as heat and never reaches the rest of the server. Just by using smaller power supplies that will run closer to peak power levels where it's more efficient can save a significant amount of energy.

PG&E CORP.

PG&E Corp., the San Francisco-based utility, offers a "virtualization incentive" program that pays $150 to $300 per server removed from service as a result of a server consolidation project. PG&E also offers rebates for data centers that use Sun Microsystems Inc.'s energy-friendly Niagara T1000 and T2000 servers, and for virtualization software used to consolidate servers.

DISK STORAGE

Disk storage is the third largest user of power in most data centers, after cooling and powering servers. Storage in the average data center consumes 20% to 25% of the total power used. As storage needs have skyrocketed, the number of file servers and direct-attached storage devices has also increased dramatically. These devices require an ever-increasing amount of power to operate. Many are poorly utilized either because too much unused space is allocated to specific applications or on-line storage is being allocated to applications that are rarely used. Industry estimates of storage utilization rates range from 25% to 40%. This means that 60% to 75% of the storage capacity that is being powered is not being used. Compounding the problem is the fact that in many cases, storage allocated for a particular use

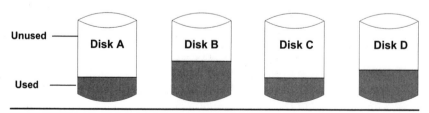

Figure 11-3
TYPICAL FILE SERVER STORAGE UTILIZATION

cannot be easily changed to meet other needs. This also results in over allocation of storage to avoid having to allocated more storage later. All of this only adds to the problem

Steps you can take to reduce your storage power requirements include:

- ▲ Replace existing direct-attached storage with a storage network. Removing file servers reduces the amount of power required for storage, as well as increases flexibility. Instead of adding new servers, new disks can be added to increase storage.

- ▲ Move to higher capacity drives. Higher capacity drives give you more bytes per watt.

- ▲ Use SATA (Serial Advanced Technology Attachment) drives rather than Fibre Channel drives. While Fibre Channel drives have a higher data transfer rate, they use twice the power of a SATA drive per terabyte and many applications do not require the higher transfer rate. SATA drives also have a higher storage density than Fibre Channel drives.

- ▲ Move rarely used data to near-line or off-line storage from on-line storage that is always powered.

- ▲ Eliminate as much redundant data as possible. Use deduplication technology to reduce redundant data.

To measure the efficiency of your storage power system, determine the amount of power used per usable terabyte. This takes into account the utilization rate of your data storage and allows you to directly compare the storage energy efficiency among data centers or a single data center over time. While manufacturers will use watts per terabyte (W/TB) as a measure of power efficiency, it does not take into account how efficiently that storage is used. The formula for calculating this is:

$$watts\ per\ usable\ TB = \frac{\frac{watts\ per\ system}{total\ terabytes}}{utilization}\ rate$$

MEMORY

Another user of power in the data center is memory. The memory used in the vast majority of servers requires power to constantly refresh the contents of the memory, whether or not it is being read or written to. The most common type of memory is known as DRAM, or dynamic random access memory. This memory is configured in dual in-line memory modules (DIMMS) and provides virtually instantaneous access to data. In addition, conventional hard drives are used for data that is not needed immediately, such as lower ranked search information. DRAM offers fast access to data, but consumes tremendous amounts of power.

Another problem with DRAM is the limited amount of this type of memory that can be used in a single server because of energy constraints at the DIMM level and the limited number of DIMM sockets within the server. Increases in the amount of data that needs to be in memory for quick access also requires servers to be added to meet this need, increasing the overall amount of power being used.

Several companies are working to reduce the amount of energy required to power server memory. Spansion, a spinoff of AMD and Fujitsu, produces memory based on flash technology that does not require power to retain its contents. It offers lower energy consumption as well as higher capacity, but is not as fast as traditional DRAM. Other companies, such as Micron Technology, are working on traditional DRAM that requires less voltage to maintain its contents and, therefore, uses less power and generates less heat. These alternative memory solutions use 15% to 75% less energy than traditional DRAM, potentially saving a significant amount of power in the data center.

ECOMMERCE EXPERIMENT

An experiment conducted by content hosting provider Ecommerce demonstrates that you do not always need the biggest and most powerful systems to run your applications. Rick Gideon, Ecommerce's VP of Systems Operations, created a "server" out of laptop components and used it to host some of his customers' Web content. The test server uses a power efficient Intel Centrino chip as opposed to the Xeon chip that is used in his typical production server. Because of limitations inherent in the Apache/Linux environment used, no more than approximately 700 users can be supported on a single server – no matter how powerful the server. While the test server maxed out at about 600 users, it used much less power than the standard server (2/3 to 1 amp at 110 volts vs. 2 1/2 to 3 amps) and was 1/3 the cost to operate considering power and cooling requirements ($3/month vs. $10–$12/month).

NETWORK

The routers and switches that move data around and in and out of the data center also require power to operate. Data bits are represented by different energy levels that represent the 0s and 1s that get moved around in vast quantities. The exact amount of energy consumed depends on the technology used and the amount of data being moved around.

A framework for measuring the energy efficiency of network and telecom devices called the Energy Consumption Rating (ECR) Initiative has been developed by Ixia, a provider of performance test systems for IP-based infrastructure, and Juniper Networks, which provides network infrastructure equipment.

The ECR framework grew out of the development of an earlier efficiency standard called IxGreen, developed by Ixia to measure the amount of power required to run a telecom device at a given performance level. The ECR initiative is open source, designed to be vendor neutral, and able to be applied to any networked hardware setup. The first iteration of the ECR standard itself has been posted on-line at www.ecrinitiative.org. The framework covers routers, WAN, and broadband aggregators, Ethernet switches, security appliances, and application gateways. The goals of the framework are to:

▲ Define a test procedure for measurement and estimate of energy efficiency for network and telecom equipment.

▲ Establish a common energy efficiency metric for the network and telecom industry.

▲ Promote energy awareness and competition among OEM vendors.

When looking to reduce the power consumption of network equipment, consider the following guidelines:

▲ Look for equipment with the best ECR rating.

▲ Consider cooling requirements of the equipment.

▲ Avoid excessive capacity reserves.

▲ Avoid multifunction equipment, as such pieces of equipment are often the least efficient user of power.

▲ Consider local energy costs and trends as your calculate the total cost of ownership.

Cooling Your Equipment

As your need for computing power increases, so does the need to remove the heat being generated. As servers become more powerful and are more densely packed into data centers, the heat being generated increases. Each watt of power used by the server generates one watt of heat, which then requires one watt to cool. Servers require a proper balance of temperature

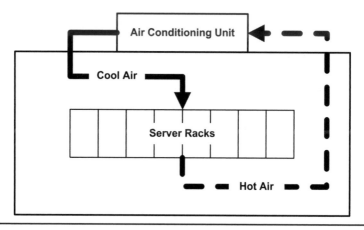

Figure 11-4
TRADITIONAL AIR CONDITIONER COOLING. HOT AIR IN THE FACILITY IS COOLED AND RECIRCULATED

and humidity to perform properly, as an excess of either can cause computational errors or outright failure of certain components. Maintaining the proper environment can dramatically increase overall energy costs if temperature and humidity are not controlled in an efficient manner. Most computing equipment used today is air cooled, so the focus is on bringing cool air to the equipment and removing the hot air heated by the equipment.

CALCULATING COOLING COSTS

Heat generated by equipment is typically measured in one of several ways: BTU per hour, tons per day, or joules per second. Since joules per second is equal to watts, watts is becoming the standard for measuring both power usage and cooling capacities. This makes it easier when looking at both the energy needs of the data center and its accompanying cooling requirements. Because the power used for transmitting data is negligible, all of the power provided by incoming lines is converted into heat. By knowing how many watts the equipment in the data center is using, we know how much cooling capacity we will need if our cooling process is 100% efficient.

To calculate the cooling needs of a data center, several factors must be considered in addition to the needs of the equipment. You must also take into consideration:

▲ The size of the room. The room itself will also require cooling. To determine the cooling requirements of the room, determine the area of the room in meters and multiple by 330 to get the BTU required. Then, divide that number by 3,412 to calculate the kilowatts of energy required.

▲ Any windows in the room. Windows that let in sunlight will increase the energy needed for cooling. Calculate the area of the window in meters, then multiply by 165 for a north facing window and by 870 for a south facing window. This will determine the BTU required. Then, divide the BTU required by 3,412 to calculate the kilowatts of energy needed.

▲ People. People generate about 400 BTU of heat, so you need to determine the average number of people in the room and multiple by 400. You can then divide this number by 3,412 to calculate the kilowatts of energy required.

▲ Lighting. Multiply the total wattage of the lights by 4.25 to calculate the BTU generated, and again divide by 3,412 to calculate the kilowatts of energy required.

Add up all of the calculations made above to see the total wattage required to cool the data center. By multiplying this value by the cost per kilowatt, you can determine the total cost to cool your data center.

HOT/COLD AISLE

The most common method of cooling racks of equipment in the data center is call hot/cold aisle, or hot aisle/cold aisle. Equipment racks for servers and other heat generating devices are arranged in parallel rows sitting on top of a raised floor system, where every aisle between rows of racks has exclusive hot-air outlets or exclusive cool-air intakes. Air is brought into the cool aisles from underneath through perforated tile in the raised floor and exhausted from the hot aisles overhead. This produces a constant flow of cool air through the racks, assuming there is no interruption in the air flow. Figure 11-5 shows how this works.

In a hot/cold aisle configuration, the hot aisles are always at a much higher temperature than the cold aisles. For this to provide the most efficient cooling, internal fans that bring air into or exhaust it out of individual units should be disabled or configured to act with, not against, the overall pattern of air flow in the aisles. It is also critical that as equipment is add or moved, consideration is given to how the air will flow through the equipment. This may require coordination between IT and the facility manager.

For a hot/cold aisle setup to work most efficiently, make sure the racks in the aisles are evenly loaded. As equipment is moved around over time, racks can become inconsistently loaded, with some racks fully loaded while others may be empty. An even distribution of equipment will improve the overall cooling performance.

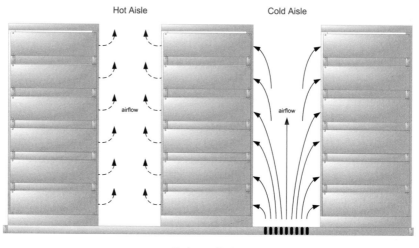

Figure 11-5
HOT/COLD AISLE RACK CONFIGURATION

Other steps you can take to improve cooling efficiency include:

▲ Seal off cable cutouts and holes in the perimeter walls and in the raised floor. You want to ensure that the air is going where it helps the most and is not leaking out somewhere it's not needed.

▲ Make the best use of existing cooling capacity by clearing under-floor blockages and implementing effective cable management.

▲ Ensure that floor openings match the equipment thermal load by adding or removing perforated tiles at the equipment air intakes.

▲ Add ducted air returns to better control air flow.

ECONOMIZERS

In many parts of the world during certain times of the year, the temperature outside of the data center is cooler than the temperature inside. You can take advantage of this temperature difference to let nature help cool the data center through the use of an "economizer" system. An economizer system is any method by which the cooler temperature outside is used to help cool the inside of the data center. In addition to lowering energy usage, an economizer system will reduce the wear and tear on expensive air conditioning equipment.

Two types of economizer systems are in common use: air and fluid-based. Most data centers will use a fluid-based economizer over an air economizer because of concerns over the temperature, air quality, and humidity requirements of the computer equipment. With these environment concerns in mind, most data center managers find fluid-based economizers to be more effective over a wider range of temperature and humidity conditions, especially those using glycol as the heat exchange fluid. But several recent studies have shown that computer equipment is not as sensitive to fluctuations in temperature, humidity, and air quality as commonly thought, so air economizers may be a better choice in some environments.

AIR ECONOMIZERS

An air economizer brings in outside air directly into the data center to provide cooling. It is used mostly when the outside air is cooler than the inside air, essentially it means "opening up the windows" for almost free cooling. According to GreenerComputing.com, the widespread use of air-side economizers has the potential to reduce annual cooling energy consumption costs by more than 60 percent. Figure 11-6 shows how such a system works.

A data center can also benefit from cooler daytime and nighttime temperatures, as a data center requires cooling around the clock. It works by opening an outside air damper and blowing outside air into the data center when the outside air is cool enough to lower the temperature inside. A return air damper closes as the outside air damper opens. A third damper connected to the return duct helps avoid overpressurization of the room. Filters are used on the outside air before entering the space to remove contaminants in the air.

The first thing a data center manager is likely to worry about with an air-side economizer is that contaminants, such as pollution from the outside, will cause problems with delicate electronic circuits. Particulate particles

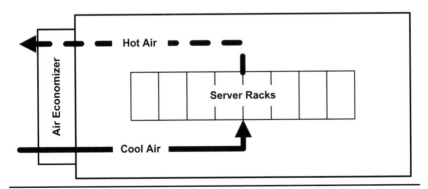

Figure 11-6
AIR ECONOMIZER COOLING. HOT AIR IS FLUSHED OUTSIDE, AND
OUTSIDE AIR IS DRAWN IN

in the air could cause conductor bridging and damage to the circuits. Humidity is also a concern as too much moisture in the air could also play havoc with sensitive equipment. But studies performed by the Lawrence Berkley National Laboratory, Intel, Microsoft, IBM, HP, and others have demonstrated that servers are not nearly as fragile as once thought. Servers running with no humidity control and in temperatures up to 90 °F have functioned fine with little or no increase in failure rates. Savings of 60% to 70% in cooling costs were reported in these studies.

FLUID ECONOMIZER

A fluid economizer also takes advantage of cooler outside temperatures to help cool the data center. It is incorporated into either a chilled water or glycol-based cooling system. It works with a cooling tower or dry cooler to remove heat from the fluid that was captured from the air inside the data center.

Fluid economizers are popular in many data centers because they are not affected by outdoor humidity levels and are also effective over a wide range of temperatures and humidity levels. They also do not require a filtration system as no outside air enters the building. For an overview of a fluid economizer, see Figure 11-7.

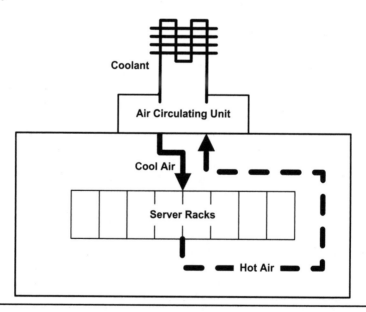

Figure 11-7

FLUID ECONOMIZER COOLING. HOT AIR EXCHANGES HEAT WITH COOLANT THAT HAS BEEN PIPED OUTSIDE TO COOL

SUPPLEMENTAL COOLING

Another option to improve the efficiency of cooling in the data center is the use of supplemental or on-demand cooling. Supplemental cooling brings cooling right to the source of the heat. By reducing the heat output at the source, the amount of power needed to cool the room is greatly reduced. Supplemental cooling also eliminates the need to over chill the data center to remove hot spots, an issue with the raised-floor cooling approach. Another advantage is that the units can be placed when and where they are needed, without making changes to the existing infrastructure.

There are two basic types of on-demand cooling; air-to-air and fluid-based systems. In a smaller air-to-air system, a wheel mounted unit can be moved to exactly where the cooling is needed, limited only by access to a window for removing the heat generated by the system using a flexible hose. Air-to-air units can also be mounted directly above the racks where the cooling is needed to supplement air coming up through the floor. Larger systems are mounted outside and use a flexible hose to take the cooling to where it is needed. The smaller mobile systems offer up to 3.5 kilowatts of cooling power, with the larger outside mounted systems offering up to 17.5 kilowatts of cooling power.

Fluid-based systems use either water or refrigerant running through pipes to bring cooling to where it is needed. Water-based systems offer inside and outside options, with the inside systems using a standard garden hose to bring water to the unit and another to carry the heated water to a drain. These portable units have a capacity of up to 17.5 kilowatts. Outside systems are connected to the building's chilled water system pipes and have a capacity of over 800 kilowatts.

Refrigerant-based systems, such as the Liebert XD from Emerson, use refrigerant-filled pipes that snake around the server racks in a data center. The refrigerant absorbs the heat coming off the computers, turns it into a gas, and then pumps it back to a cooling unit. The cooling unit then turns it back into a liquid to be cycled back again. Emerson claims that this system reduces the power for cooling required by 30% to 50%.

The choice of an on-demand cooling system depends on the amount of cooling needed and the logistical considerations of access to outside air and water. A small air-to-air system is the easiest to set up, requiring only access to the outside or unused space to exhaust the waste heat and a standard 110V electrical outlet. Water-based system will remove a greater volume of heat but expose the data center to the possibility of a water leak. Outside systems require greater technical expertise to install. Refrigerant-based systems are more difficult to move around if your cooling requirements change.

DUCT WORK: AN EFFICIENT OPTION?
Inexpensive duct work to take airflow where you need it can be cheaper that expensive units from vendors. Hosting provider Ecommerce spent one-third of the cost of buying specialized equipment by using cheap duct work to put cooling air where it is most needed.

Green from the Ground Up – Change the Rules

As the cost of energy continues to rise, organizations are becoming very creative in solving the problem of providing power to operate their data centers. New processes and technologies are being tried the world over to reduce the cost of providing computing resources as well as reducing IT's impact on the environment.

COOL IDEAS

Innovative ideas for reducing a data center's carbon footprint run the gamut from incremental improvements of standard processes to radical new ways of doing things. Some of the more interesting ideas include:

- ▲ Augmenting the capacity and efficiency of chilled water systems by using a thermal storage system that stores energy generated at night, when chillers are usually more efficient and power is cheaper. This can be as simple as making ice at night and then using it during the day for cooling when energy costs are higher.

- ▲ Make use of available renewable energy sources, such as hydroelectric, wind, solar or biomass-generated energy to reduce dependency on fossil fuels.

- ▲ Use man-made lakes as cooling ponds to use with heat exchange coils. Similar to using a cooling tower but uses less energy.

- ▲ Turn up the temperature for the general space and make better use of spot cooling to bring cooling only to where it's needed.

- ▲ Build the data center underground to take advantage of the natural coolness of the Earth.

- ▲ Google has filed a patent for creating ocean-going data centers that would use the movement of the waves for power and the ocean for cooling. This also eliminates the cost of real estate and potentially saves on taxes, as it would not physically be in a state or county.

GREEN DATA CENTER RESOURCES

A number of organizations research and promote ideas to "green up" data centers. They are a tremendous source of best practices and leading edge ideas for the efficient use of energy in the data center. Some of the most important of these include:

▲ Association for Computer Operations Management (AFCOM). AFCOM is an association dedicated to providing education and resources for data center managers. Its mission is to enable data center management professionals to share industry best practices by providing a forum for dissemination of critical information; to provide education on key data center management issues; to provide the industry's most comprehensive insight and analysis in key areas affecting all data-intensive organizations; and to be the most comprehensive and effective resource available to the overall data center community. AFCOM can be found on the Internet at www.afcom.com.

▲ The Green Grid. This is a consortium of organizations whose mission is to advance energy efficiency in providing computing resources to business. Its board of directors is comprised of people from AMD, APC, Dell, HP, IBM, Intel, Microsoft, Rackable Systems, Sun Microsystems, and VMware. It works to develop metrics, standards, measurement methods, processes, and new technologies to improve data center performance. It collaborates with end users and government organizations to ensure that all users of data center technology have their needs addressed. The Green Grid can be found on the Internet at www.thegreengrid.org.

▲ Climate Savers Computing. Started by Google and Intel in 2007, the Climate Savers Computing Initiative is a not-for-profit group of ecoconscious consumers, businesses, and conservation organizations. Its focus is on reducing carbon dioxide emissions from the operation of computers by 54 million tons per year. The group promotes the development, deployment, and adoption of smart technologies to improve the efficiency of a computer's power delivery and to reduce the energy consumed when the computer is in an inactive state. Its board of directors consists of people from Dell, Google, HP, Intel, Lenovo, Microsoft, and the World Wildlife Fund. It can be found on the Internet at www.climatesaverscomputing.org.

▲ Department of Energy. The U.S. DOE's Industrial Technologies Program (ITP), through Save Energy Now, works with U.S. computer data centers to reduce their energy consumption. Information about this program can be found on the Internet at www1.eere.energy .gov/industry/saveenergynow/partnering_data_centers.html.

▲ Environmental Protection Agency. The U.S. EPA supports the research and study of data center power usage and technologies to improve the efficiency of data centers. Its ENERGY STAR program identifies and supports manufacturers of energy efficient products used in the data center. The EPA can be found on the Internet at www.epa.gov.

▲ Lawrence Berkeley National Lab. Managed by the University of California, the Lawrence Berkeley National Lab is a member of the national laboratory system supported by the U.S. Department of Energy through its Office of Science. Some of its many areas of interest include the environmentally friendly generation of power and the efficient user of power in data centers. The Lab can be found on the Internet at www.lbl.gov.

▲ American Society of Heating, Refrigeration, and Air-Conditioning Engineers (ASHRAE). Founded in 1894, ASHRAE is an international organization whose mission is the advancement of heating, ventilation, air conditioning, and refrigeration technologies and the promotion of a sustainable world through research, standards writing, publishing, and continuing education. ASHRAE can be found on the Internet at www.ashrae.org.

▲ SearchDataCenter.com. This is an on-line information resource for news, tech tips, and expert advice for IT managers responsible for operating a data center.

LEADERSHIP IN ENERGY AND ENVIRONMENTAL DESIGN (LEED) CERTIFICATION

The LEED green building rating system was developed and is administered by the U.S. Green Building Council (www.usgbc.org), a Washington D.C.-based, not-for-profit coalition of building industry leaders. It promotes design and construction practices that reduce the negative environmental impacts of buildings and improves the health of the people who occupy the buildings. While not specifically targeted toward data centers, many of its ideals can apply to how data centers are designed and constructed.

LEED focuses on how the entire building impacts the environment by focusing on the following six areas; points are earned in each area toward a certification level:

▲ Sustainable site developments   14 possible points

▲ Water efficiency   5 possible points

▲ Energy efficiency   17 possible points

▲ Materials selection   13 possible points

▲ Indoor environmental quality   5 possible points

▲ LEED innovation credits   5 possible points

Points toward LEED certification are earned by meeting criteria in each of these areas. Certifications are ranked using the following scale:

▲ Certified   26–32 points or >37% of max

▲ Silver   33–38 points or >47% of max

▲ Gold   39–51 points or >56% of max

▲ Platinum   52–69 points or >75% of max

The majority of items that count toward LEED certification are related to design and mechanical and electrical support infrastructure, rather than specifically to the computing portion of a data center. But planning for data center needs while pursuing LEED certification is critical for optimizing the data center's overall impact on the environment.

The Bottom Line

Being green at first seems to be just another burden on the life of the data center manager, but in reality the process of becoming green solves a number of other problems along the way. More efficient cooling strategies produce results that go right to the bottom line, as well as contribute to the overall corporate environmental goals. More effective utilization of servers not only means less power being used, but can also simplify the job of the administrators charged with keeping the servers running. And a green project forces the data center manager to think more strategically about where the computing needs of the organization are going, which makes him/her a more valuable member of the executive team. So while Kermit might be right about the difficulty in being green, the benefits more than make up for trouble.

12 VIRTUAL WORKERS

VIRTUALIZING A data center brings significant savings to a company, but it takes time for IT leaders to absorb how to best apply this new approach. Once the principles are clear and the changes are made, the savings are almost immediate. Imagine applying a similar solution to another expensive area of the company—something that would save money and significantly reduce a company's environmental impact at the same time.

When companies think about being Green, they look at their emissions, their waste stream, and their overall "footprint" on the environment. This is natural since this is what gains headlines in the press. However, there is another area where significant environmental gains can be realized and, yes, for cost savings as well as further Green credits. It is called a virtualized work force.

One of the challenges companies face is the growth of their work force. As success creeps in, companies add floor space, parking lots, break areas, and so on. Over time, departments become fragmented across several floors or over different office buildings in an effort to provide adequate space. All of this floor space is expensive. To this, add the cost of cubicles, furnishings, and computing equipment.

In the days when documents physically moved from one person to another, this approach made a great deal of sense. Work teams that exchanged documents or other work products needed to sit close together. They could quickly ask questions about the work and then move on. This minimized the number of messenger runs and piles of papers waiting to shuffle between desks.

Over the years, office workflows have subtly changed. Physical documents have been replaced with electronic ones. Paper memorandums are no longer dropped into a worker's "in-box." Instead, documents are sent to that person's electronic in-box for processing when they are ready. Equipment and data communications prices have fallen. Who needs a time wasting and irritating rush hour commute?

It is time to think about your work force differently. Consider applying the concept of virtual to your staff, as you will reap immediate Green benefits. Virtual workers are employees who are in the office – virtually. They connect to the company's IT systems and complete their work as before, except that they are not physically present. Rather than people coming to the work, the work (electronically) goes to them.

Figure 12-1 illustrates how high-speed communications has enabled people to work productively from home. Originally, one worker completed a portion of a project, and someone else then physically carried the papers to the next station. For example, the first person might write up a purchase order, which the messenger then carried to the Accounting Department. In the new scenario, the same data is transmitted from the originating PC to another desktop PC over the network. Networks are indifferent as to whether you are sitting at the next desk or in the next county. As a result, the first person at home can write up the purchase order, and someone else at home can perform an Accounting check on the balances.

Working virtually is not a new idea. Executives often work from their hotels when traveling. In addition, key team members also sometimes worked from home for a day or two while attending to family matters, such as taking care of a sick child. The difference now is that team members can work primarily at home and only occasionally come into the office.

Working virtually offers many advantages to the company and employees. For one, it allows companies to retain valuable employees with conflicting domestic requirements that require them to remain close to home. Rather than lose this valuable expertise due to poor attendance, these people can be readily available. With a virtual work force, everyone wins.

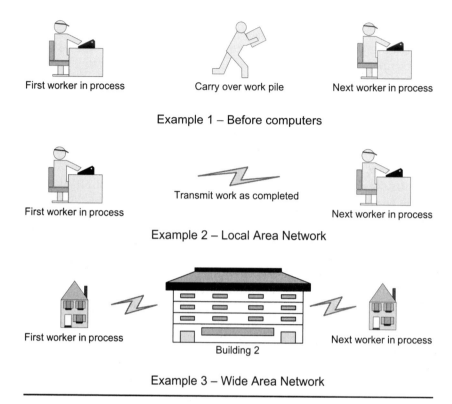

First worker in process — Carry over work pile — Next worker in process

Example 1 – Before computers

First worker in process — Transmit work as completed — Next worker in process

Example 2 – Local Area Network

First worker in process — Building 2 — Next worker in process

Example 3 – Wide Area Network

Figure 12-1
THE CHANGING TECHNICAL LANDSCAPE

Company culture, however, is an essential element of a successful virtual work force. If the company values workers and holds them accountable for completion of work to a commonly accepted level of service, then virtual teams can succeed. If the company views workers as lazy, then distrust will quickly unravel the whole idea.

A virtual work force is scalable to the demand. For example, if the East coast office needs workers and the Midwest virtual team needs work, they can connect to each other and begin working. If more work is available in Dallas, then the virtual workers supporting New York can log into that office and begin working. If the work requirement is temporary, then it is easier to hire temporary virtual workers regardless of where they are located.

Virtual workers are ideal for assignments that have a definable deliverable, such as a code module, a document, or a users' manual. When an assignment is made, a time estimate to completion is also submitted. This approach allows virtual workers to set their own deadlines. It also encourages workers to focus on results and managers to evaluate them on those results (not on whether they are appear to be busy working or not).

Virtual work is also suitable for data entry. This works well with the local work force. A Web-enabled screen with VPN access is provided for all workers. This removes the variability of the equipment that they use at home and minimizes company investment. They can be compensated by the page or the hour.

Virtual workers are more successful if their efforts do not require close coordination with others. Save those jobs for a traditional work environment.

The Green Problem

The problem is people. People who drive to work (often one person to a car) pollute the atmosphere with car exhaust. Then, they sit in their office all day using the company's electricity, heating, air conditioning, floor space, and desktop computers. At the end of their shift, they climb back into their vehicles and add more air pollution by driving back home. The commute to and from work, the walk to and from the parking lot, and the occasional traffic tie up can easily add two hours to every workday.

The challenge is how to reduce this polluting action that is currently required by the company? How can this process be Green'd? The key is to revise the idea that people must be seen to be present and seen to be working before they can be counted as present. Companies looking for a quick way to reduce their CO_2 emissions and to bolster their Green credentials can do so quickly by converting part of their staff to a virtual work force.

VIRTUAL WORK FORCE METRICS

Companies can save money by virtualizing a part of their work force. This reduces office space, furniture, and utility costs. Workers do not need a place to sit – they sit at home. They do not need a work area to shuffle paper, as everything is accomplished electronically. They use the same data center servers and internal network as before. The one difference is the potential need for a higher capacity network connection from the data center to the outside world.

The metrics for a virtual work force savings are:

▲ The company is improving its Green contribution. The company may be able to claim the number of miles each person no longer drives round trip to work daily as a carbon credit, since their action have reduced emissions.

▲ The place of work becomes secondary to work performance. Big offices in areas with high rents can be exchanged for smaller facilities.

Depending on your virtual strategy, a few smaller offices can be maintained in low rent areas for occasional face-to-face meetings.

▲ Less office space is needed. If office work space is in short supply, this is a good thing. If your company owns its building and there are plenty of empty seats, then this is not an advantage. The loaded cost for office space, furniture, and so on may be as high as $75 per square foot. (Remember that utilities run around the clock in all seasons.) Remember that floor space that sits idle is still a cost. It must be released to the landlord or used for another company purpose for true savings to be realized.

▲ A prorated amount of the company's utility bill. For example, if floor space is reduced by 10%, then this effort might claim an amount equal to 10% of the company's utility bills.

▲ Reducing office furnishings may lower your local property tax burden.

▲ A wider labor pool is available. Instead of being restricted to local people, talented people can be hired almost anywhere,– so long as they meet your technical conditions.

▲ A virtual work force enables the gainful employment of homebound people who have much to contribute but find it difficult to commute to a job every day.

▲ A virtual work force may earn a company valuable tax credits by recruiting its workers from economically depressed areas, such as Appalachia. The difference in pay between city workers and those farther out in the sunshine may be significant.

Figure 12 – 2 illustrates how eliminating the need to commute potentially opens employment opportunities to homebound people, no matter where they live.

MATCHING WORK AND WORKERS
Virtual teams open other possibilities for IT departments. Applications development is an area that has long suffered from a shortage of skilled workers and slower schedules for systems development than customers find acceptable.

By creating virtual teams, the company can match the available work with the available labor. If JAVA programmers are needed in Boston and these people prefer to live in Casper, Wyoming, virtual teaming may be the answer. The programmers in Wyoming can submit their work to Boston for review.

For rapid software development, two teams can be used. Applications can be coded by the local team, and the new code can be tested the same day by a virtual team around the globe, even in India. This can significantly shorten the application development cycle.

REASONS WHY COMPANIES AVOID VIRTUAL EMPLOYEES

Think about how companies operate today. Office space is rented and work areas are equipped. People are hired, assigned work, and given specific work hours. As the work progresses, supervisors walk through to ensure goals are accomplished. Since everyone appears to be busy, the big bosses are happy.

However, a virtual office is much different. Depending on the electronic tools used, supervisors can see at what point virtual employees are logged into the computer system, but they may not know if they are working or watching their favorite soap operas. There are ways to measure work, but the idea that someone may be comfortable at home while the office-bound supervisor works away is quite a mental adjustment.

From the company's point of view, virtual workers upset proven business practices. Supervisors see the disadvantages as:

▲ The company cannot tell who is working and who is not. Supervisors are nervous because they are still accountable for their teams' productive output. Lazy employees in the office are obvious. Dis-

A virtual work force helps companies to fulfill
their Corporate Social Responsibility Strategy
by employing homebound workers and
reducing air pollution.

Figure 12-2
MEETING CORPORATE SOCIAL RESPONSIBILITY GOALS

tant workers could be working at a half pace or less and still receive full pay.

▲ Communications with coworkers becomes more difficult since the nonverbal dimension of communications is not present. How people stand, the looks on their faces, and their gestures all help us better understand what they are trying to communicate.

▲ Individuals may short cut purchasing the necessary equipment and services for their home office, which may result in lower productivity because of inadequate tools.

▲ Virtual workers have a difficult time contacting team members in the office. This can bring productivity to a halt. Everyone has worked with someone who never answers the telephone or e-mails. In the office, you can drop by this person's desk to get the answers that you need. This is hard to do if you are in different physical locations.

▲ One of a supervisor's responsibilities is to cultivate company loyalty. This reduces the expense and reduced productivity of training new people. Companies have hard times, just as workers do. Loyalty keeps the teams together until the problem has passed.

IMPROVING EMPLOYEE MORALE

To improve employee morale, some companies allow employees to work from home one day per week. Although this does not save on office expenses, it does reduce absences since team members can schedule their personal appointments for those days, save the expense of commuting to work for 20% of their work week, and reduce carbon pollution by 20%.

The Virtual Department

Permitting employees to occasionally work from home does not require a special support team. These workers use the same tools and processes and report to the same supervisor as during the rest of the week. However, a permanent virtual work force requires an in-house support organization to smooth out routine issues that arise.

Keep in mind that no company can be entirely virtualized. Customers expect a storefront of some kind at which they can meet you and discuss business. (Try to avoid this, and you will be suspected of shady activity.) In addition, some types of company business should never be conducted outside of the office's walls. Every company will have at least a central office staff to interact with customers and support the virtual team. In most cases, the virtual team will make up only a small portion of the company; the remainder will be polluting-commuting office workers.

VIRTUAL TEAM SUPPORT STAFF

Virtual teams need a designated leader to be their advocate to upper management. This person ensures that virtual personnel are properly supported by in-house staff and that their work is done on schedule. Virtual team members are not immune to the company's routine administrative details, such as time sheet reporting, expense submission, absence requests, and materials request forms.

An important trait in the virtual team leader is trust. A lack of trust between the virtual workers and their supervisor will limit candid communications and hinder productivity. Another important trait is patience. Someone may be trying very hard but not achieving the desired result. Patience together with trust will help to identify and overcome obstacles.

One way to build trust is to properly regulate workflow. Virtual workers should be given work that results in a verifiable product (e.g., data records entered, programs written, documentation written.) Evaluation of virtual workers must center on these results. To simplify work tracking, try to break deliverable results into chunks of one week or less. This way, the verifiable results validate the time card submitted.

FACE TO FACE

There is no substitute for face-to-face relationship building. Ideally, this is accomplished before problems arise. Some companies bring their virtual team members into the main office periodically to meet face to face and address common issues. This helps build team cohesion. Later, when conversing on the telephone, you can "imagine" the person to whom you are speaking.

The team's administrative assistant addresses routine issues. For example, the timekeeping system will also have exceptions that must be resolved (such as how to code jury duty). Other areas of assistance include expense reports, purchase orders, and the odd question about company benefits.

The team administrative assistant also maintains contact information for each team member, including telephone numbers (land line and cell), e-mail address, and instant message service ID). Another important piece of information is the worker's established working hours. During this time, workers must be available for contact by team members.

The administrative assistant assists the virtual team by chasing down people who do not return calls. Every company has some key employee who either intentionally or inadvertently never seems to answer his or her telephone or e-mail. This person also rarely returns messages. The only way to communicate is in person. Without someone on-site who can visit these reluctant people, the virtual team will slowly grind to a halt.

When you need technology the most, it gives you the biggest problems. Virtual teams need access to technical support people who know all about their situations. Someone must be available to address workstation, telecommunications, and network issues. This is normally addressed by the company's IT Help Desk, but depending on the uniqueness of the technologies used, it may be a dedicated person.

A virtual team member cannot complete his or her work without prompt communications. If equipment breaks, it must be repaired promptly. The virtual team manager must have an equipment plan. If the company owns the equipment, keep a spare cell phone and a PC loaded with software and ready for immediate shipment. In a crisis, it can be sent by overnight delivery to exchange for a broken unit. Otherwise, the worker sits and waits while time drags on. If virtual team members provide their own equipment, then they should arrange in advance for local hardware repair.

CRITICAL BUSINESS FUNCTIONS

Never assign a critical business function to a virtual worker. Such things as legal compliance, data security, sensitive customers, or unique business processes must be kept on-site and in sight of the company at all times.

VIRTUAL TEAM TOOLS

Virtual teams need a set of tools to facilitate their work. One already mentioned is an up-to-date contact directory for everyone on the team; another is critical company contacts. A third tool is a central repository for all their work products. A product such as Microsoft's SharePoint enables team members to check out documents for update, track who has checked out which document, post announcements, and so on. This reduces time lost shuffling a document between team members through e-mail. Supervisors can see progress on-line by what is complete and what is checked out. Also, if someone leaves the team, his or her documents are already available for the replacement person to work on.

Instant messaging (IM) is a very tool for virtual workers. When someone is stuck on a long conference call, with the mute button engaged, that person can monitor the meeting and still exchange information through IMs. Instant messaging is ideal when a quick answer is all that is needed. An on-line "Break Room" provides a place where team members can gather to swap ideas and discuss work, processes, or anything else on their minds. This is a place where the virtual team can exchange stories, much as they might do in the company lunchroom. The team manager must monitor the content exchanged to ensure that nothing violates company guidelines. This is also a great place to post notices, celebrate company anniversaries, and share other information.

Some companies establish Wikis that can be used by both virtual and on-site office workers. These are places to gather and share ideas about company processes, problems, benefits, and best practices. Team members can jump in and out of these to add information or research issues. Wikis also help to build team cohesion, as individual ideas are discussed, validated, and expanded.

IS A VIRTUAL OFFICE IN YOUR FUTURE?

Long ago, virtual workers were called telecommuters. This was because they used dial-up telephone connections to communicate with the main office. The communications were slow and were designed to be very basic. Complex tasks were held until the workers came into the office and used a directly connected terminal.

This arrangement was a big leap forward for people who traveled constantly to visit customer sites. For example, salespeople could enter orders directly into the order processing computer instead of mailing or calling them in. However, the equipment was bulky and slow. It was not suitable for working from home.

Modern technology has changed this situation. Most people have at least one personal computer at home, and they are experienced at using it. They likely also have a high-speed internet connection. Another enabling technology is a personal cellular phone, along with a dedicated telephone line at home. Taken together, these tools enable people to communicate verbally and electronically at a speed and capacity equal to equipment in the office.

As Figure 12-3 illustrates, people working from home have a higher quality of life. No more stressful commutes through severe weather. They stay snug at home and ready to work.

Virtual workers function about the same way as other office team members. They participate in meetings, interact with customers, create software, solve technical problems, work toward objectives, and deliver their work product to the people responsible for the next step in the process. All of these things can be accomplished without their physical presence.

Working from home

Commute

The office

Figure 12-3
BENEFITS FROM WORKING AT HOME

People prefer to live where they wish. Many competent workers in rural areas would love to work from home. City noise and pollution is not for everyone –and living far away from the big cities can limit job opportunities.

WORKERS LOVE VIRTUAL WORK OPTIONS

1. No commute to work means that the workday is shorter. Time spent driving to and from work now belongs to the employee. Let it snow! No commute means you do not need to drive through it.

2. Employees save on fuel and reduce wear and tear on their vehicles. They find more money in their pockets and vehicles require less frequent visits to the service center.

3. Work is less stressful if you are wearing a bathrobe and bunny slippers instead of being stuffed into a too-snug business suit that used to fit. Some business attire is a daily expense, such as men wearing starched shirts with the business suits or clothes that must be dry cleaned.

4. Think of all of the reasons workers need to leave work early. When working virtually, they do not need to take off to wait for a repairperson. They are already home. The same holds true for staying home if they feel slightly ill or need to be with an ill family member.

VIRTUAL WORKER INFRASTRUCTURE
SAVES THE COMPANY DURING A DISASTER

No one likes to contemplate a disaster befalling his or her company. After all, the company's financial health is tied to an employee's well-being. A disaster that closes the company for any length of time may also threaten employment. This, however, is the exact reason why disaster recovery or a business continuity plan is so important. An established business recovery plan reduces the amount of time that a business is out of business.

DISASTER PLANNING

A disaster plan documents the steps a company will take to recover from a catastrophic event. It focuses on planning how the company's critical processes might be recovered within a period of time determined by the company. This is called the company's Recovery Time Objective. A disaster plan is only invoked when there is significant damage to the organization.

Business Continuity Planning involves planning for quick recovery or avoidance of problems that would reduce the availability of a critical business function. For example, a common business continuity practice is to train a backup technician in critical skills that are the specialty of only one person.

Both disaster and continuity plans include mitigation actions that reduce the likelihood of a problem occurring, minimizes its impact if it does occur, and/or increases the warning time before disaster strikes. For example, a short-term power outage for an office building is mitigated by a power generator that kicks in the instance that electrical power is removed.

Government offices refer to Disaster Recovery and Business Continuity as "Continuity of Operations" (COOP).

Most disaster recovery planning is focused on the recovery of the data center. This collection of computer servers, disk drives, tape drives, and mounds of network equipment is an essential part of any modern business. Its recovery is time consuming and complex. However, it is only half of the story.

Recovering a data center is only useful if there is someone ready to use it. All too often companies focus on the difficult data center recovery issue and neglect that the fact that work areas must also be recovered. A work area must be established for employees with computer equipment, telephones, and network connections. This temporary office needs the space and furnishings of the old office. Just as only critical IT systems are recovered, only the most critical people in the company can be accommodated at an emergency site. As can be imagined, suddenly plucking a hundred or more people into a conference center with new PCs is one thing, but providing adequate Internet connection is something else! This is where the virtual work force comes in.

Data centers are typically recovered at a site distant from the original building. Sometimes, this is hundreds of mile away. Most workers do not care where the data center is located so long as their work station knows where to find it. Virtual workers are already prepared to work from anywhere – and connect to anywhere. Once the data center is back on-line, virtual workers are ready to work.

Therefore, companies with a virtual worker program in place already have emergency workers ready to restart business. If the company routinely permits all workers to work from home at least several days per month, then, in a disaster, a larger portion of the company is ready to log in and return the company to at least a minimum level of service in a shorter period of time.

Finally, there is the threat of a pandemic – a widespread serious disease that disrupts business. Pandemics occur several times each century and typically last for 18 months or more, as people who avoided the illness think it has passed, begin mingling with people again, and become infected. A significant source of the disease spread is contact with other people. Working from home minimizes this contact.

THREE OTHER INNOVATIVE WORKER OPTIONS

Hoteling is office space provided to outbound workers as they need it. Some workers are always on the road, visiting customers, addressing problems, and so on. Why dedicate the floor space, furnishings, network connections, and other resources to a person, or group of people, who is rarely in the office. Think Green! Instead of paying for the utilities and materials for these idle work areas, consolidate the many down to the few.

Outbound workers use hoteling when they have time to stop in the office for meetings and to submit paperwork. Just as a room is reserved for an overnight stay in a hotel, office hoteling requires a reservation. Outbound workers connect to the company servers and reserve office space for as long as they need it. Some companies will route that person's telephone calls to that space during the reservation period. Hoteling provides Green benefits by only providing the office space needed. In large cities, hoteling is provided by third-party companies that rent office space by the hour.

A common variation on Hoteling is Hot Desking. Both techniques provide office space as needed (thereby contributing to a company's Green efforts by reducing idle office space). The primary difference between Hoteling and Hot Desking is that the former is reservation based and the latter is first come first served. This means that Hot Desking can be a bit chaotic if too many people show up at the same time and scramble for a seat. However, it imposes the minimum management requirement on the company sponsoring it.

Distributed work is a third variation on virtual working. It provides small office facilities in low-cost areas close to where the workers live. This addresses the company's concern about worker attendance, provides a co-worker support network, and still reduces pollution through reduced commutes and less congestion. These smaller offices provide the same services as larger offices, such as a receptionist, office supplies, and break areas. This approach is more common in large metropolitan areas when the central city office space (and traffic congestion) is high and the suburban office space closer to the homes of the workers.

THE DARK SIDE OF WORKING VIRTUALLY

The case for working virtually seems very compelling. However, not everyone has the self-discipline to stay focused on work with so many interesting distractions at home. There are some disadvantages to working out of sight.

From the worker's point of view:

▲ Few homes are quiet places. Barking dogs, chiming clocks, loud neighbors, and traffic noise all conspire to distract the virtual worker. When children come home from school, typically before the workday ends, can the work area be effectively isolated?

▲ Family members expect you will run errands for them "since you are home" and not appreciate that your home is in your work area.

▲ Virtual workers feel isolated. People are social creatures. They enjoy interaction with others. Friendships among coworkers are common. Working virtually removes much of this. Telephone conversations are an inadequate substitute for face-to-face discussions. Informal communications (such as encounters between coworkers in the hallway), where most of the company's "inside information" is exchanged, becomes difficult.

▲ Virtual workers lack reassurance from their manager that they are valued workers. Traditional positions usually involve daily contact with supervisors. Verbally and nonverbally, these interactions reassure the individual that all is well. Without this, doubts creep into the supervisor-worker relationship.

▲ The primary reason that virtual workers abandon their home-based job and return to working in an office is a feeling of isolation.

Creating a Home Work Area

IT professionals who are working from home requires a dedicated space similar in size and equipment to an office. Before trying to work from home, ensure that there is an adequate dedicated area for spreading out papers around a computer and printer. Home offices should be as Green as the primary work place. Used toner and inkjet cartridges, used equipment, and used paper should all be properly recycled.

Look around an office and you will see cubicles that are approximately 36 square feet in area (even if it doesn't feel that large). There is a flat surface for a personal computer, keyboard, mouse, and monitor. There is also a telephone; a writing surface; shelves to hold reference materials, and file drawers for storing documents. To work as effectively at home as you do in the office, you will need at a minimum the same arrangement in your house.

The work area must be in a quiet area of the house where everything can be left out all of the time. A spare bedroom is ideal. It provides a door to keep noise out and to keep curious children away from stacks of paper. To the extent possible, ensure that the other sounds common in a home, such as barking dogs and chiming clocks, are not heard during telephone calls.

A shelf of reference materials is important. There isn't anyone over the cubicle wall available for a quick chat. Although team members may be available on-line for quick questions, keeping a set of company policies, work process documentation, and other information on hand will make life easier.

COMMUNICATIONS MADE ALL OF THIS POSSIBLE

In the past, people who worked from home performed only tasks that could be measured by output. It might be to edit the drafts for books, such as the one you are reading, or to audit transportation bills for application of the correct tariff. These assignments required no interaction with other employees. When the task was finished, the result could be sent on to someone else. However, very little office work falls into this category. Most responsibilities require a good deal of interaction, involve completing many different tasks in a day, and vary widely in the amount of necessary team contact.

Virtual workers are enabled by the widespread availability of high-speed internet communications and inexpensive long-distance telephone communications. A second telephone number (line or a cellular) dedicated to the virtual job is essential.

There are three basic ways to equip a virtual work force:

1. Use a virtual session to provide the home worker with a browser window into a virtual desktop in the company's datacenter. This provides the company with maximum control and allows the end user to use a home computer as long as its browser is compatible. This reduces the likelihood that a virtual worker's computer will pass a virus to the company's servers.

2. Some companies find that a virtual work force is easier to support if the company provides the computer equipment with standard company software. Shipping the entire package to the worker's house ensures that technical problems can be resolved by the company's tech support staff. Otherwise, workers will attempt to connect and exchange documents with whatever old equipment and "unusual" software they may have on hand. However, providing equipment creates an asset management issue for recovering equipment when someone leaves the team.

3. Require workers to buy a standard equipment setup from the company. Deduct the price of a new standard computer system from their paychecks over a period of time. This provides a standard setup and relieves the company of responsibility for recovering the equipment. There may be licensing issues for software.

OFFICE SUPPLIES

A company is responsible for providing virtual workers with the same supplies available in the office, such as pads of paper and toner for the printer. Some companies provide a set allowance and turn the worker loose to obtain everything locally. Otherwise, some workers will refuse to accept these expenses, delaying work because of a lack of tools.

Company data is not all top secret. Most is routine information of little value to anyone other than the company. However, the effort required to screen out those elements that must remain confidential (such as customer information, company costs, and future bids) would be tedious and error prone. Instead, a company should provide virtual employees with a Virtual Private Network (VPN) connection. This establishes an encrypted "tunnel" through the Internet ensuring private communications between the virtual worker and the company computer servers.

UNINTERRUPTIBLE POWER SUPPLIES

Working from home requires that virtual workers assume responsibility for some of the background tasks provided for them in the office. An Uninterruptible Power Supply (UPS), either supplied by the company or purchased by the worker is essential to filter electrical power and protect it from data losses and damage during a power outage. The need for data backups is minimized if all company data is maintained on the company servers.

Finally, a high-speed data connection enables the use of a video camera so that team members can see each other during communications. This helps to humanize the conversation and slightly reduce the feeling of isolation.

TELECOMMUNICATIONS REQUIREMENTS

After a PC with a high-speed connection, the telephone is the next most important tool in the home office. While the computer visually connects the virtual team, the telephone audibly connects them.

First, the company needs to publish a telephone number for every virtual worker. This information may long survive after an employee no longer works for a company, so family telephone numbers should not be used. In addition, calls may come in at all hours, so arrange for a second telephone number at home. An alternative is a cellular telephone dedicated to this work. In both cases, an unlimited outbound long distance capability is needed. In the case of the cell phone, there must be unlimited minutes. Many teleconferences run more than an hour. Participate in a few of these each week, and the minutes provided with most cell phones are long gone.

Telephone ear is that numb sensation from holding a telephone instrument to your ear for long periods of time. To avoid this, obtain a headset and or a speaker. In either cases, include a mute button. This also frees your hands to take notes (or to do other work) during an endless phone call.

Every virtual team member should be assigned a teleconference number so that they can arrange meetings as needed. This simplifies arranging meetings and allows members to get together for short chats.

HOME OFFICE SECURITY.

Most office workers are not concerned with security arrangements. That is handled by someone else in the company. However, a home office is responsible for its own security. It is the responsibility of each home worker to safeguard the company data in his or her possession. This includes:

▲ Shredding documents and CDs with company data.

▲ Protecting the computer and equipment from theft. A theft is bad enough, but not being able to work for days until everything is replaced can be even more expensive. In addition, the company must immediately determine the sensitivity of any data lost inside of the machine.

▲ Any data backups maintained on-site must be safeguarded and properly destroyed when no longer needed. Ideally, all data is maintained on the company servers where it is backed up and protected.

DO YOU HAVE IT IN YOU TO WORK VIRTUALLY?

Few people find their work more fascinating than the many distractions that exist around their homes. That is why even people who can afford to work from home often prefer the mental and physical distance of a company office. Working from home requires self-discipline. Some people find the physical movement to an office places them in a "work state of mind" and that sitting at home makes them think of household chores.

Virtual workers must be skilled communicators, both written and spoken. The tone and inflection of their voices when speaking substitutes for body language. They must be skilled at picking up conversational nuances. Virtual workers must also possess an optimistic outlook on life and not see dark purposes from every request they receive from coworkers.

Virtual workers must possess the self-discipline to ensure that family members do not dump their errands on them. Everyone must respect that during the posted hours, virtual workers are dedicated to an employer's business.

The Bottom Line

When companies think about being Green, they focus on machines and materials. They often overlook the possibilities of a Greener work force.

Creating a virtual work force creates new capabilities for a company. Just as virtualizing servers has opened new possibilities for the data center, a virtualized work force can save money for both the employer and the employee. The work force becomes scalable as the work comes to the people instead of the people traveling to the work.

The enablers of Virtual Workers are a high-speed internet connection and inexpensive modern telephone capabilities at home. These tools are used to communicate with customers and coworkers, as well as to exchange work products. High-speed data connections enable workstation performance equal to that achieved in the typical office.

Virtual workers are not an all or nothing situation. Few companies can prosper without a storefront somewhere and a receptionist to greet visitors. Therefore, it would be a truly rare company that can be entirely staffed virtually. Instead, virtualization is applied in those jobs where the type of work can be measured and the temperament of the workers is appropriate. Properly led, a virtual team can be very productive.

Companies benefit from a virtual work force in many ways:

▲ The first is by reducing their operations' impact on the environment. People driving to work create pollution. If they can still work and no longer need to drive to work, then the company can rightfully claim that their efforts have reduced CO_2 emissions.

▲ The second benefit is that it enables homebound and handicapped workers to work in an environment that fits their situations. Single parents can work from home while watching their children. Handicapped individuals who might be challenged driving to and from a job will be empowered to work.

▲ The third cost savings is reduced office expenses. If people work at home, there is less of a need for office floor space and furnishings. Further, a company's Green credentials are burnished by using less power, heat, and cooling technology.

Another advantage of virtual workers is their readiness to assist during a disaster. They are set up to connect to the company's servers through its Internet address as soon as one is provided at the recovery site. This same connection process and VPN services can be used for critical employees to sign in from home until a work area recovery site can be located, furbished, wired, and readied for use.

A disadvantage is that virtual workers feel that they less a part of the company without the regular face to face contact. This translates into less company loyalty and they are more likely to jump to other companies. Another problem is the safeguarding of company data in the worker's homes, just from printing reports on a local printer or downloading data files to work. Managers feel that if they cannot see people work, that they must be lounging in front of the television. From the virtual worker's perspective, the work is harder since connecting with people who refuse to answer the telephone or email requires significant effort just to complete simple tasks.

Finally, an important benefit is the work force that is prepared to log in to a recovery site during a disaster and begin work immediately. The value of this capability cannot be overstated.

GREEN IT DEPARTMENT

IT DEPARTMENTS deal with both processes and projects. A project is a one-time event, such as installing a new inventory management module, refreshing all of the UNIX servers, or implementing an ERP. Processes are actions that are repeated over and over, such as requesting a new user ID, making tape backups, teaching a class the latest version of a spreadsheet program, or repairing a desktop computer. To a degree, even projects have repeated actions that act the same as a process.

As repeatable actions, processes strive to be effective (provide the desired outcome) and efficient (use the minimal amount of resources with no waste). All processes require the inputs of material, time, and labor. The output of a process is the desired result, plus any waste created. The more waste that is eliminated from a process, the greener the process is.

Imagine sitting in traffic for an hour trying to get to work, but something has blocked the road. Your car slowly creeps ahead, then stops, and then creeps again. Valuable time passes, expensive fuel is wasted and, eventually, you move past whatever blocked the road and complete your journey. The same is true for processes. Eliminating the roadblock does not change the desired output; it just makes it cheaper to arrive at the desired destination.

An efficient operation is greener than an inefficient one. The efficient operation uses only as much energy and materials as is needed to do the job. An efficient process leaves little waste, because waste represents lost value to the company. It creates a negative impact on the environment without benefit. An inefficient IT operation is quite common, although all processes are inefficient to some degree.

IT departments regularly address business problems using technology. These solutions include developing a set of processes designed to accomplish a specific task. Logical steps within software have long been an IT department focus. The goal is to use the least amount of processing time that is practical to produce a given amount of work. This same approach needs to be applied to the department's business processes as well.

To Green an IT department, follow the same steps used to establish a Lean quality program. Lean seeks out and eliminates waste from a process. It mobilizes all workers to drive effectiveness and efficiency across all processes. Greening a process does the same thing. It eliminates unnecessary movement of materials and economizes on materials used – just like a Lean process initiative! Every waste that is uncovered represents an unnecessary expenditure of energy or materials.

The Lean quality initiatives described here can be used individually to improve processes. However, the recommended sequence is to begin with 5S to clean out clutter and simplify processes. Second, study the details of the Seven Wastes to identify easy-to-recognize process steps to eliminate. Finally, use Process Mapping to examine processes and to identify non-value added steps. Taken together, these programs will improve process efficiencies and reduce wastes. Resources (time, materials, etc.) that are now available from reduced process steps can be applied to provide new customer services.

5S is the First Step

The first step to Greening an IT department is to clean it up. It is a truly rare IT department that makes full use of its many assets. IT departments are cluttered with parts, partially disassembled equipment, tools, manuals, software, and many other things used to address day-to-day issues. Most of this can be placed in shared storage areas away from IT work spaces with no loss of customer service. A primary obstacle to any program, such as 5S, in an

IT department is the presence of many strong-willed and fragile egos among the technical staff. With patience and firmness, this too can be overcome.

5S was developed to improve the efficiency of Japanese factories. It is based on the idea that a sloppy work space is filled with many types of waste. It organizes work areas to focus on the work at hand, so the employee is not working around clutter. These factory principles are easily translated to an office. The five "Ss" roughly translate to: Sort, Straighten, Shine, Standardize, and Sustain.

An excellent example of eliminating clutter is moving one's home. Packing everything you own into cardboard boxes for the movers is a lot of work. So, as you need to purchase more and more boxes, you become more selective in deciding what to move. Soon, a small mountain of old clothes, dishes, exercise bikes, toys, furniture, personal finance records, and other items accumulates. These items, you realize, can be sold, donated, or trashed. However, if you were not packing things up, you would never have sorted your possessions and the clutter would still be there. A 5S program performs a similar service for work areas. By examining everything that the department has, surplus items are easily identified.

The benefits of 5S include:

▲ Visual work place – know when something is done; see the progress of a process.

▲ Empowered employees taking responsibility for the maintenance of their work areas.

▲ Consolidation of spare equipment, tools, parts, and supplies for shared use. Before purchasing something new, see if it is already in stock.

▲ Increased floor space – this leads to better use of this limited resource.

▲ Streamlined processes with fewer things to walk around, fewer places to check before acting, etc.

▲ Uncovering equipment and supplier problems that were disguised with excess parts inventories. By purchasing more parts and materials than are immediately needed, the IT department can cover for the poor performance of suppliers, such as vendors who take too long to deliver.

▲ Improved employee morale – who wants to work in the middle of a mess every day?

Even if your IT offices seem orderly, they can still be quite cluttered. Look for the many signs of a clutter problem. One is "rush" ordering of parts or supplies because no one knew the inventory was too low or where the shipment received last week is now stored. How many times have you looked and looked for something that you knew was "around here somewhere?"

5S is just one of the Lean process programs for improving your process quality. Three significant signs of quality problems are:

▲ Rework because documents are sent back to the originator for changes before it can be reviewed

▲ Scrap material left over from a process after the required goal has been met

▲ Rejected items returned by the customer as defective, such as software that introduced new bugs when fixing old ones.

THE PROBLEM IS CLUTTER

Some of this clutter is the result of poor leadership by middle management. There are few rewards or accolades for efficient operations, but there are many condemnations for late performance. Therefore, extra materials are stockpiled "just in case." After all, if some are never used and thrown away, those same big wigs will never know! The basic leadership principle is that you get what you reward. In this case, the reward is for effective but inefficient (and not green) processes.

5S is based on the concept that a simplified work area will operate more efficiently, cheaply and safely. From a Green perspective, it will use less energy, maximize existing resources, and generate less waste. Clutter is a significant waste of everyone's time, as employees shuffle things here and there out of the way. Money is lost with overnight shipment of parts because no one knew where the local cache for that component was hidden. Clutter hides things of value amid the nonessential material that never goes away.

Types of IT clutter include:

▲ Spare parts in various places. Unless they are in an unopened manufacturer's container, no one knows if spare parts are good or not. Individuals establish personal caches of spare parts for "their" equipment.

▲ File cabinets full of documents that have little current relevancy. Some people fill out their day filing every document that crosses their desks so that they appear valuable to the company.

▲ Tools are scattered about on desks, cabinets, and work areas, but no one can find an important tool when it is needed.

▲ Technical documentation and software "inherited" from the last person to who used a desk, but with no idea of what it related to or goes with.

VISUAL WORK SPACE

The first question of a manager walking into a work area is, "how is work progressing". Are the technicians stuck waiting for something or are they making progress toward their assignments? Is everything working fine or are they crucial support issues to be addressed?

The purpose of a visual work area is to provide quick information to anyone who wants it – without their having to ask anyone else. The concept is easy to understand, and many of the tools are already in use in many places. You just never thought of the process this way. Visual indicators are another way to enfranchise the wider IT team by helping to avoid confusion and enhance team communications.

A primary objective of a visual work space is process status. If the CIO walked into the room today, what sort of status information is available to all. For example, a popular approach is to hang a large screen monitor on the wall and display reports of any significant outages, volume of calls into the Help Desk, if the network capacity on any segment has exceeded a certain threshold, and other information. Such a screen helps members of the IT team feel they are part of the larger group and can see how their efforts impact overall operations. To build this screen, access to real time data is essential. (In days gone by, some of this same data was on a marker board in the corner, but it was often out of date.)

A visual work place also requires marking everything in the office. Every cubicle and office has the occupant's name on it. Every shelf, closet, and closed cabinet is marked with its purpose. Signs are also posted showing the floor plan so anyone entering the area can see which office belongs to the person for whom they are looking.

Every location on storage shelves is marked to show what properly belongs there (such as a specific tool or material). If that item is missing, then it must be time to order more. There is no need to check additional storage areas or ask other people if it might be in another place. If it is not in its assigned location, it is not there.

Visual controls include color coded labels, signs, and even flashing lights. When improving your areas, think bright and bold when an urgent communication is required. For example, you might use flashing lights to tell everyone that a server is down.

ROLLOUT YOUR 5S PROGRAM

The easiest way to roll out a 5S program is to hire a consultant to lead the effort. This reduces fumbles during start up. Bringing in an outsider reduces some of the internal politics and accusations of favoritism. The 5S consultant teaches the program principles to the 5S teams and provides follow-up mentoring. These classes include:

▲ Explaining the program details to each team member.

▲ Providing examples of what has worked elsewhere.

▲ Explaining the many tools available.

▲ Facilitating communications between team members and their executive sponsor.

An executive champion is an essential team member who is responsible for breaking down internal barriers. For the IT 5S program, this might be the CIO or someone even higher in the organization. Every program has at least one prized employee who insists on exemption from any company activity that does not interest them – whether it is mandatory or not. Compliance with the 5S program must be mandatory, so do not waste time arguing.

A 5S roll out is a team effort. Each department's workers must design their own work areas. This reduces the chance of 5S seriously damaging productivity. If the workers design the solution, they will take ownership of it and keep it going with minimal supervision. Ensure that all workers are involved to the extent possible.

COMMUNICATIONS FOCUSES THE TEAM

A valuable communication tool is the 5S information board (refer to Figure 13-1). Each team customizes this board to some extent, but typically it includes:

▲ Pictures of what the work areas looked like before and after the 5S effort.

▲ Floor plans showing the original work layout point and the ideal configuration.

▲ A list of current issues hindering the program, along with the names of the persons responsible for addressing each one.

▲ Copies of all maintenance requests, such as painting, replacing stained ceiling tiles, wet vacuuming of carpets, moving electrical or network connections, etc.

▲ A picture of the 5S team, and a team roster of their names.

▲ Team assignments to complete and/or maintain the 5S actions.

▲ Inspection checklist used by team members, in turn, to ensure that the improvements made are still in effect.

Because work areas reflect the preferences of the people employed there, they may not be optimized for clear work flow. Create a simple sketch of the work area floor plan as it exists today for each IT function. Indicate work benches, tool and materials storage, manuals library, and the software storage point. In an IT office, separate work spaces might include: Help Desk Area, Desktop computer repair, data center, server support team, network team, office spaces, and storage spaces (to include closets).

A 5S roll out can be disruptive to a department's productivity. During the Sort and Segregate steps, most work stops for several days. Plan it for the company's slow season.

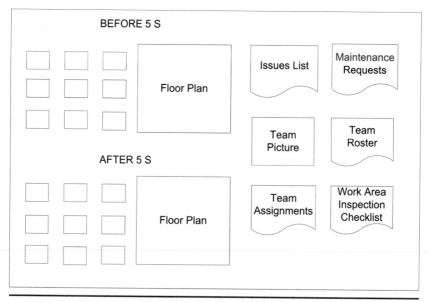

Figure 13-1
5S COMMUNICATIONS BOARD

SORT

To remove the clutter, we need to identify it. Begin by sifting through everything to see what to keep and what to move on. Anything not needed to meet current customer requirements must be moved on. Much of the clutter is "just-in-case" material. If it is needed to support your company, then mark and store it. Otherwise, send the excess "stuff" for disposal.

Sketch out the existing floor plan and add it to the communications board. Note the location of all work benches, desks, equipment, and shelves. Make a note of where the electrical and network outlets are located. 5S teams are empowered to move equipment, shelves, and desks. Just about anything is fair game, except walls and doors. If additional

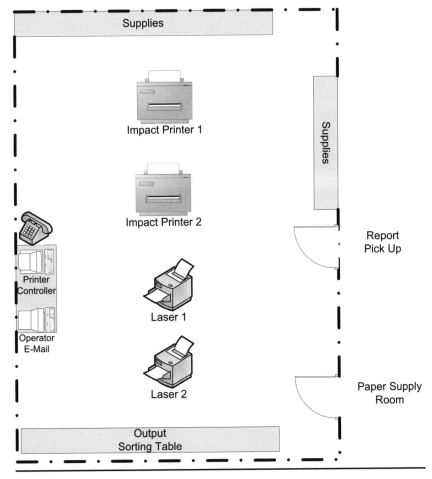

Figure 13-2
"BEFORE" 5S FLOOR PLAN

wiring is needed to support the new locations, then the executive sponsor arranges for prompt skilled trades support. Refer to Figure 13-2 for an example of a "before" floor plan for a printer room.

The steps in sorting are:

1. Make a sketch of the current floor plan that identifies all work areas, storage areas, etc.

2. Select collection points for material that is used occasionally and should be kept nearby and for material that needs to go to disposal. Some sites also select an intermediate disposal area. Things are placed here for six months or a year; at the end of that time, anything not used becomes trash.

3. Purchase piles of red, yellow, and green tags at the local office supply store. Green is for things that stay, yellow for nearby storage, and red for donate, sell, or trash.

4. Decide how to address disposal items. A paper recycling hopper is recommended, along with collection points for batteries and small electronic parts. Surplus equipment must be properly removed from the company's asset books before disposal. Excess devices may be recycled through the company's equipment disposal program.

5. Open all cabinets, boxes, drawers, closets, and wiring cabinets. Tag everything to stay or go. Be thorough – look everywhere. If something does not have a tag, it must have been overlooked. Sometimes the most value things that are found are the ones that were best hidden.

6. Make a list of "found" material and what was done with it. Assign a value to found material that will be kept for local use, including the value of donated goods and the weight of trash sent for proper disposal.

> **REWARD THE EFFORT!**
> Every time an area is cleaned up, someone in another department tries to shove overflow junk into it. Be sure that the 5S IT champion enforces the policy, so that areas cleaned out stay that way. Reward departments based on how much space is freed.

Many work spaces consist of a series of piles. Even the systems documentation in desk drawers is more likely to be stuffed in one place rather than organized for easy reference. In the midst of this cleanout, keep sight of the people side. Some people are emotionally attached to their "stuff" and become very hostile or emotionally upset at its examination or departure. Be sensitive, but firm. Watch for people who shuffle junk to another department for safekeeping until 5S blows over. People attracted to IT jobs are sometimes very possessive of their work spaces, and perceived status.

Set aside storage space for IT materials that are only used once per year. Income tax W-2 forms are often printed on an impact printer. This is because the software is rarely used and the company may not want to spend much money reformatting the individual form to a laser printer. The same is true for documentation and process instructions that may only be used during fiscal year closing time.

STRAIGHTEN

Think about the problems you may have experienced trying to find things when the key support person is not available. Sick days, vacations, training, and many other circumstances pull people out of their work areas – often at the least convenient time. In this situation, the people on-site must do the best they can with what they can find to work with. This is very frustrating when the regular support person keeps information or parts in a "private" location.

Straighten is the step in which everything is placed in a dedicated space, where it is easy to find. Only an item assigned to that space can be put in that location. All spaces are marked—a shelf, a container, a spot on the floor – everything.

A very powerful result of the Straighten phase is the concept of the visual work place. If everything has a place, and only one place, it is quickly obvious if it is missing or in the wrong place. This has many applications:

▲ Warranty parts for pick up or return to the manufacturer.

▲ Out of stock parts are immediately obvious since the place where they sit is now empty.

▲ Shared tools – a shadow board indicates where each tool goes and if it is missing – the shadow shape also indicates what is missing.

▲ Color-coded labels on shelves indicate which team owns a manual or component.

IT departments use shared work areas. Sometimes it makes more sense to keep materials in a specific work area rather than in one central location. In these situations, make a sign at the central site that indicates where to find materials in these satellite locations.

IT shared spaces:

▲ Files – only current files should be maintained in the IT department. Obsolete documents should be moved to paper recycling. Historical records should be moved to off-site storage (often the same place that archive data tapes are sent). Once the cost for off-site storage is known, many of these documents in file drawers head for disposal.

▲ Manuals library – a central place for all manuals, with some signed out to people who are their primary users.

▲ Spare parts – in marked containers on marked shelves. Materials not in a manufacturer's box are tagged as good, with the most recent test date.

▲ Tools –inexpensive hand tools do not need to be tracked. Expensive shared tools and meters should be on shelves with a label underneath. If something is missing, it is obvious at a glance.

▲ Incoming material drop zone – all deliveries go here. This provides a visual signal that something has come in so people can check to see if it belongs to their project.

▲ Outgoing material drop zone – everyone can see if their shipment has left yet. This is important for the return of warranty parts as at some point, that part is billed.

▲ Surplus electronics drop zone – this is for equipment no one wants; it should be examined for disposal

▲ Battery recycling collection box – does not need to be big but must have a sign above it explaining its purpose – or it will be used as a trash can.

An important part of straightening is to label the proper location for things. In many 5S exercises, the doors on cabinets are removed so everyone can easily see what is stored inside. The goal is to quickly find what is needed in a crisis, with a minimum of searching. If pilferage is an issue, use wire mesh doors and padlocks. At a minimum, the shelf labels should indicate what goes into that location and if it has a part number, IT departments should use color coded labels to indicate which IT team is the primary user or custodian of that item, such as blue for applications development, white for management, red for networking, and so on. This will also reduce duplicate storage locations.

HELP DESK AREA

In the Help Desk area, consider labeling the software documentation binders as to the proper book case and shelf. Store the most commonly used items at eye level and the lesser used items at the bottom or top.

IT Teams will want their unique parts located close to their work areas. For example, the Network team will want their components in a separate cabinet or storage area from the desktop computer repair team. Reduce the time spent traveling to pick up something by always storing materials (tools, parts, manuals, etc.) close to their point of application.

Set aside an area for coats, lunch containers, and so on. In wet or snowy weather, items strewn about the work area create obstacles, such as umbrellas that are left open to dry or bulky coats hanging from cubicle walls. By providing an area for these items, accidents are avoided and the amount of mud tracked into the office is reduced.

Now is the time to analyze the workspace to see how it might be changed for more efficient operations. One tool for doing this is the Spaghetti diagram. It tracks the flow of people and work through a work area. Refer to Figure 13-2 for an example floor plan for a printer room. In this example, there are two large laser printers (with voracious appetites for paper) and two impact printers for big jobs that are not used as often. On the left wall is a set of network attached PCs: one to manage the printers and the other for the operators' convenience. There are shelves for supplies along the north and east walls. Of the two doors, one provides access to paper supplies; the other leads to a pick-up point to which reports should be delivered.

The question is, how can this work area be improved? Use the sketch and follow the workers around for a couple of hours. First, measure the number of steps between each major item in the drawing, such as from Laser Printer 1 to the supplies shelf, or the report distribution door to the operator's PC.

As the operators work, draw a line to represent where they walked to do something (to get more paper, to check the printer status, deliver reports, etc.). Refer to Figure 13-3. You can quickly see how these lines make the chart look like a lot of spaghetti. As you draw the lines, keep a list of how many times the workers move from each point to another. After the study is concluded, tally up the number of steps required for each trip between two points.

Based on the 5S team's review, it was decided to move some things closer to the doors, as shown in Figure 13-4. Traditionally, things like the PCs were located next to the wall for esthetics, but for efficiency, they should be closer to the machines. The shelf at the top of the drawing has been removed; its rarely used contents have been moved to the shelf on the right. This frees a significant portion of the room. (Even if there is not an immediate need for this free space, it becomes an asset for future IT service expansion.)

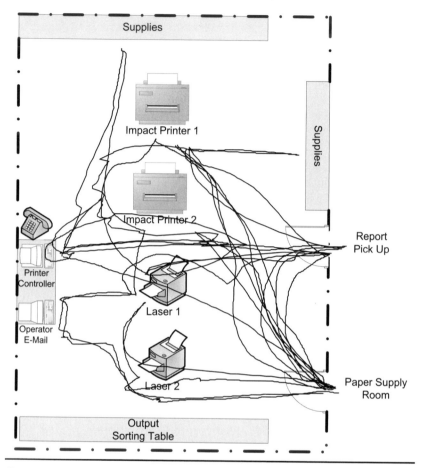

Figure 13-3

SPAGHETTI LINES SHOWING OPERATOR MOVEMENTS

To make the work status visible, a big screen monitor is posted on the wall so everyone in the print room can quickly see the print jobs, both pending and completed. A duplicate of this monitor is mounted outside of the door where customers pick up their reports.

The final step in this phase is to present the team's findings to the executive sponsor for approval and action. Moving this equipment around will require some work by company electricians. The large displays that provide a more visual work status for all are also an expense. This is where selling the proposed changes to your executive 5S sponsor comes in.

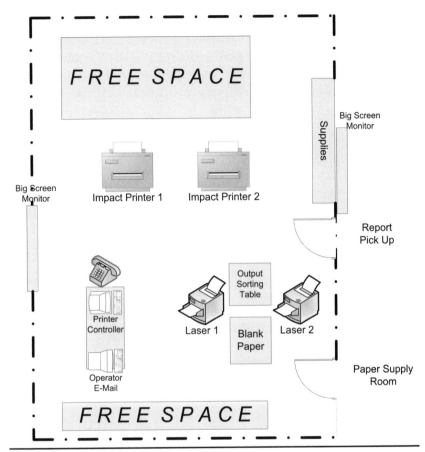

Figure 13-4
REORGANIZED ROOM FOR BETTER EFFICIENCY

IMPROVING THE NEW FLOOR PLAN
After the new floor plan is in place, rerun the spaghetti chart study. Estimate the number of steps now required, and calculate how much time will be saved on a typical shift. A few steps saved here and there can add up over time, especially if some of those involve toting heavy boxes of paper to the printers. Put that value on your 5S communications board. Then go back and see if the new floor plan can be made even better!

SHINE
Everyone wants to work in a clean work space. Sometimes companies use a minimal cleaning staff to save money. Most IT work areas are fairly clean,

as dirt damages electronics. However, if your area is in bad shape, then this step empowers you to fix that. For example, request that dust be removed from all work areas, including storage closets. Wet-vacuuming of carpets will remove much of the office dirt. In some cases, painting may be necessary. Leave no place in the work spaces untouched.

Cleaning becomes a daily process. The facilities cleaning staff will still do their job, but work areas must be tidied after use. The basic rule is to clean as you go and do not leave it for later. For example, promptly dispose of packing material from incoming parcels.

The Shine step also includes maintenance issues. Leaky windows or pipes, wet spots on ceiling tiles, and broken furniture are all reported and logged. If action is not forthcoming, the issues are escalated to higher management. After all, if an adjacent work area is dirty, then its dust will blow into where you work. That situation must also be addressed.

Another maintenance issue is the amount of adequate lighting and electrical outlets in the work area. If possible, use natural light as it requires less energy (Greener!). If adequate electrical outlets are not available, then extension cords tend to be strewn about. This is a tripping and electrical safety hazard. If more electrical circuits are needed, then begin planning for them now.

The Shine step emphasizes finding the root cause of problems and resolving them. Perhaps the office is dirty because filters on the air handling system have not been regularly changed. It might also be wise to place a sound muffling enclosure over a very loud printer or to replace loud cooling fans on some computers.

STANDARDIZE

Using the same practices over as wide an area as practical makes it easier to reassign workers to address the most urgent problems. In this step, all of the best practices developed by the 5S teams are collected and provided to everyone else. (This assumes the IT department is large or that 5S is a companywide initiative.) An easy example of standardization is to develop one label format for all shelves, drawers, and files. Keep standardized processes simple and easy to understand.

In a large IT department, rolling out 5S to one team at a time will use the previous team's standards to ensure consistency. 5S team meetings are an excellent way to pass on information about standards, as are visual aids posted on the team's 5S communications board.

Everything cannot be held to a single standard. There will always be some measure of individualization. The goal is to minimize how often this occurs. Whenever an exception is made to a published standard, the exception becomes a part of that standard.

> ## VISUAL WORK PLACE
> A valuable concept to try in your IT environment is the Visual Work place. A work place is "visual" when someone can walk into the room and know what is going on and how work is progressing.
>
> Besides the large screen monitor, another way to make the work place more visual is through signage. Many cubicles use name plates so that people are easier to find. If a particular person is not in his or her office, a visitor would understand that the employee might not be present that day. Similarly, if visitors need to refill office supplies, a sign tells them the proper location of each item. If a shelf location is empty, there is no need to look anywhere else. The item is out of stock!

SUSTAIN

The whole point of the 5S program is to create a permanent change in work processes. The Sustain step is how the company holds on to its gains. This can be tough. Often, company executives lose interest in completed programs, and people tend to drift back into old habits.

Ways to Sustain 5S Gains include:

▲ Update the 5S communications board to reflect the "after" picture (the results you wish to hold on to) and any pending changes.

▲ Include responsibilities for 5S practices in individual job position accountabilities,

▲ Periodically audit IT areas and include the results in the manager's work evaluation.

▲ Include a discussion on 5S impact for all new projects.

▲ Keep adding to the issues list and request executive assistance for issues that linger too long without resolution.

▲ Schedule a brief weekly team meeting to discuss current 5S issues.

▲ Create an inspection check sheet. Rotate responsibility among the team for a daily 5S review of the workplace.

The 5S program will only survive if the team members believe in it. They must see how the Issues sheet has raised executive awareness of their problems and improved their work spaces. They must see how their ideas are valued by the team and by management. After living in a 5S environment for a while, few workers ever want to return to the old ways.

A successful 5S program is a giant step toward a green IT department. It reduces waste that results from hidden and duplicate materials order. It identifies and properly disposes of unneeded material that may have been casually thrown away in the normal trash bin. It improves the efficient use of labor by redesigning work areas.

The Seven Wastes

The Seven Kinds of Waste grew out of the Toyota Production System. Although Toyota is a manufacturing company, these principles can be profitably applied to all IT processes regardless of whether they result in the creation of a tangible product. IT departments supply a range of services to their customers. These services can be accomplished inefficiently (wasting materials and time) or efficiently. Waste is still waste whether in the IT department or in a supply chain. Waste is never Green.

Much of the waste in processes comes from individuals optimizing a process to make their own job easier or, based on their needs, to make a process run more efficiently. In both cases, they rarely tell their supervisors what they are doing or why. Each type of waste describes a non-value added action in a process. Energy and material used to perform non-value added actions can be eliminated to make a process Greener. The Seven Wastes are illustrated in Figure 13–5.

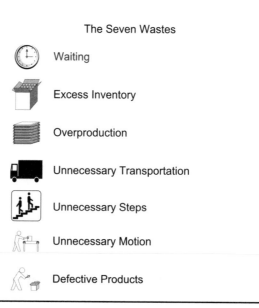

The Seven Wastes

Waiting

Excess Inventory

Overproduction

Unnecessary Transportation

Unnecessary Steps

Unnecessary Motion

Defective Products

Figure 13-5
THE SEVEN WASTES

OVERPRODUCTION

The most common type of waste is overproduction. It occurs when more of something is created than is needed by the customer or by the next step in the process. People naturally think that more is better. For example, if a customer occasionally asks for a fourth copy of a report, the print room operators may decide to always print four copies of the report. This means that one extra copy is printed every time. Although this saves the operators from the occasional interruption to print an additional copy, most of the time the fourth report is simply thrown away as excess.

IT examples of overproduction might include printing detailed reports when only the summary pages are needed, printing too many copies of a form, such as user ID requests, or installing a PC for every seat in a new training room when the old one never taught half that many students at one time. Each of these is an example of a "push" delivery of things we think the customer wants. A Greener approach is a "pull" system, in which something is created only after the customer signals it is needed. The user ID form, for example, should be printed on request rather than preprinted, with many copies stored around the facility for someone to pick up.

Overproduction often disguises other problems in a process. For example, the print room should not have to print 5,000 inventory labels to get 2,000 that are usable because the bar code does not always print properly. The source of the problem needs to be isolated. It may be that the department receiving the labels is careless with them and allows them to be damaged. It could also be that the regular print operator, who is very good at aligning the labels in the printer, is leaving for a week's vacation. Because the customer fears the substitute is poorly trained, extra labels are unnecessarily ordered.

EXCESS INVENTORY

A common IT practice is to make fewer and larger purchases, as purchasing is considered something of an administrative nuisance. For example, paper for the computer room may be ordered by the truck load and taken out of storage as needed. Another example is stockpiling laser printer cartridges. This makes the material conveniently available when needed, but leads to goods that are damaged by moisture, mishandling, and the question of what to do with residual materials when a device is no longer in service.

The most expensive and wasteful excess inventory is the stockpiling of excess electronic parts. Sometimes, individual IT Technicians purchase repair parts to keep on hand "just in case." The same holds for equipment (such as extra network hub cards) that is kept on hand for quick repairs when no down time is acceptable. After some time, these unused devices are declared obsolete and added to the waste stream. What a tragedy – never used, and now in the toxic waste stream.

Some spare parts are essential to keep on hand as the time delay to order and receive replacements is longer than the company can tolerate. In most cases, you can minimize these quantities. To find these idle parts, search everywhere in the IT work space and in some of the customer closets as well. Personal caches can be found in closets, filing cabinets, desks, boxes, and warehouse corners. Look high and low, especially the top shelves of warehouses. Consolidating all of this material in a single central issue point will reduce the number of items needed to be kept on hand. Over the short term, the company saves money by drawing from this stockpile before ordering more components.

IT inventory becomes more wasteful the larger it is and the longer it is held. However, efficiency does not mean that someone will run out of something necessary to complete a job. Electronic parts do not improve with age. Instead, they corrode, are damaged through handling, and slowly deteriorate. Determine the number of parts that are needed on hand by counting your historical usage based on help desk tickets. The team can identify parts that must be kept on hand as too difficult to obtain on short notice.

Excess inventory can also be documents, forms, and other items that accumulate in an IT department. Too many copies of manuals are a waste. Further, manuals should be ordered on a CD. Obsolete documents with no legal requirement for retention should be moved out to disposal. They all consume floor space which in turn is heated, cooled, and maintained. In short, less "stuff" means that more people and work spaces that will fit into existing offices or that the overall IT office space can be reduced.

> **MAKING ROOM FOR PEOPLE**
> Removing the clutter from office space is a good way to fit more people into the same space. Sometimes departments keep hiring people, and you wonder where to put them all. Before requesting more space, be sure what you have is used efficiently.

Suppliers who do not deliver materials on time or deliver materials that are of poor quality are sometimes protected by excess inventories. Instead of ordering extra material in case of a problem, the IT department should identify and correct the problem, remove the waste, and Green the process by eliminating the use of more energy and material than is needed to complete the task.

WAITING

The three drivers for customer satisfaction are price, quality, and delivery. An item at the right price that takes too long to deliver will not be appreciated. IT must strike a balance between price (usually measured in tools and labor) and delivery. Speed is essential to customer satisfaction.

When someone is waiting for something to happen before they can proceed with their work, they are wasting time. Examples are waiting in line, wandering around looking for something not in its proper place, or waiting for a message. This type of waste is common in IT administration, where people need to fill out forms to get something done. An example is the time people spend waiting for an IT technician to repair a dead computer. Another is time lost by IT customers waiting for a server to reboot in the middle of the day. Finally, who has not waited and waited for their boss to finally make a simple decision about their project!

Waiting waste is created by a number of factors. One is saving up user ID request forms until you "have enough" to process them or to only work on them on Tuesday mornings. In either case, the focus is on the convenience of the operator rather than on the amount of time the customer is kept waiting for needed material.

A variation on waiting waste comes from employees who have not been assigned a full day's work (or are avoiding an unpleasant task). They will putter around working on low value tasks just so they "look like they are busy" when the boss is around. This not only decreases worker moral, but diminishes their opinion of the manager's leadership. There are times when waiting is unavoidable. In those cases, the IT Manager should look for ways to detect situations as far in advance as possible to minimize the waste of waiting.

Look for ways to detect delays built into a process and then figure out how to eliminate them. Process maps are excellent tools for identifying waiting waste. Few waits are justified as business needs. Often waiting waste is the result of processing work in large batches according to personal preference. Waiting waste is also a sign of a processing bottleneck.

IT workers must be sensitive to the fact that their actions create waste in the processes of other departments. Although the application programming backlog is not technically a cause of waiting waste, it is a place where others must wait for the result before they can benefit from the software process improvement.

UNNECESSARY TRANSPORTATION

Anytime material takes a circuitous route rather than moving directly from the receiving dock to the end user, there is unnecessary transportation.

Think about buying a truck load of copier paper to feed the voracious appetite of the computer room's large laser printers. Purchasing by the truck load spreads the cost of delivery over a larger number of items (paper boxes) and lowers the unit cost. Purchasing agents are rewarded for reducing the unit cost of the things they purchase. That savings, however, shifts the cost from the delivery truck to local storage space and labor for material shuffling.

First, labor is needed to move the paper from the delivery vehicle to the storage area. Every time more paper is needed, someone must fetch it from the storage zone causing another unnecessary move. Often, the material in storage is subject to wide temperature differentiation which, together with moisture, may lead to corrosion or material decay (in the case of paper).

A variation on transportation waste is the distance to move material from the point where it enters the facility to the place where it will be used. Consider the distance that a completed form travels from the desk of the person requesting a new computer to the IT manager to the purchasing agent. Each hand off is a potential waste of transportation. Therefore, the goal is to minimize the distance something must travel, and the number of times it must be transported. (Often, at each destination, it enters another in-box where it waits for someone to notice it.) Sometimes, it seems like paper documents move a longer distance in a day than most chair-bound workers.

In the case of the paper, ideally it should be delivered to a loading dock within a few steps of the print room, so it can be moved directly from the delivery truck to the print room for use the same day. This is not as far-fetched as it sounds.

TRANSPORTATION WASTE
Chapter 14, "Green Supply Chain," shows how transportation waste can be minimized by using nearby suppliers and reducing the number of times something is reshipped. Waste is minimized by shipping directly from the manufacturer to the customer and avoiding the intermediate shuffling in warehouses along the way.

UNNEEDED PROCESSING STEPS

Always ask, "What if we never did that step in this process again?" Some people will think you "just don't understand" or that you are trivializing their work. However if you ask this question often enough, you will be pleasantly surprised how often people will realize that you have a valid point, and the entire process can be discarded.

Processes grow over time as a result of many factors from an executive's demands to the preferences of the workers. Sometime, these processes originally addressed a transient requirement that no longer exists, but the steps have become cemented in the process. Therefore, in evaluating the efficiency of a process, always ask "why." Over and over again, keep asking. If no one has a satisfactory answer, then stop performing those steps for a few days and see if anyone complains.

For example, many IT departments place large trash containers outside of their data center print rooms to collect all of the unnecessary copies of reports that were printed. Perhaps the person receiving the report is new to the process and is afraid to change the number of copies printed. Other people may not know how to request a reduction in the number of reports, especially if the number of copies printed is embedded in the software and is out of the computer operator's control. In either case, waste is the result.

A good rule is to always ask if your customer would pay you to print that extra report or to perform that extra step in the task. If not, then maybe the step should be reconsidered or the process redesigned. After all, if we are not doing this task for the customer's benefit, then why are we doing it at all?

UNNECESSARY STEPS

An indicator of an unnecessary step is when someone says, "Because we have always done it that way." Process steps came from somewhere. Try to figure out who may have requested a process change, and why. This will reduce the chance that the processing step is necessary, but that workers do not understand how their efforts fit into the final product.

UNNECESSARY MOTION

This waste focuses on unnecessary movements by an operator. In an IT department, this usually occurs when people must step around or over things because they block the aisle. It can also be the result of a poorly designed work area. Perhaps operators waste time sorting through unlabeled or poorly organized files to locate a specific record.

Unnecessary Motion waste is endemic in an IT department. Imagine the various servers that must be logged into to perform some tasks. Some of them time out and need to be logged into several times per day. Others want you to enter a number up here and then press a button down there. The mouse pointer flies around the screen, and windows are changed. Have you ever asked if all of this is really necessary? How many IT staff members still use multiple computers at their work areas?

Clutter causes a lot of unnecessary motion. Imagine trying to locate a tool in a crowded cabinet. To find what you need, many small boxes must be moved around. The same may be true of rooting through a bookcase full of unmarked binders to find the one with the desired manual.

The solution is to rearrange desktops and data entry screens to keep things in logical work groups adjacent to one another. Minimize the amount of motion required between process steps. Relocate every tool, work input (such as documents), and work output locations so all are within reach of the person who needs them.

DEFECTIVE PRODUCTS

Easily, this is the one thing that people think about most when examining waste. How many calls per day do IT departments receive about something they did or did not do or that failed to fulfill the customer's expectations? Who has patched a bug in a program only for the customer to call back complaining about a new one that has just appeared? Consider a programmer who prints a source code listing, makes a change, runs a small test, and then prints another listing. A Greener approach is to only print those few pages that have changed or, better yet, to keep the entire listing on-line.

This type of waste is about finding and fixing defects in a product. Because defective products exist, we introduce quality checks. These actions verify that data is plausible, that printed documents are complete before delivered, and that programs appear to be free of defects. However, if the IT processes delivered results with fewer defects, time now spent on inspection could be applied to providing more customer services.

A common tool for eliminating this type of waste is mistake proofing. An old IT technique to achieve this is data input validation. Think about entering your address into a data entry screen. Odds are, when you get to the field for entering "state," you choose from a dropdown box rather than complete a data entry field. This approach mistake proof, as it prevents the user from entering an invalid value. Only a value from the list will be accepted.

EXAMPLES OF IT DEPARTMENT WASTE

▲ Repairing equipment by swapping multiple components "because it is faster" instead of skillfully verifying that the existing pieces are properly seated and connected.

▲ Stockpiling old equipment, software, and manuals – just in case they are ever needed again.

▲ Making small purchases that require multiple signatures. Instead, use a company credit card and reconcile once per month.

▲ Making people wait for answers (treat their time as more valuable than your own).

Examples of Green

▲ Maximizing existing resources before buying new material.

▲ Reducing wasted motion, movement of material, decaying material (such as electronic components damaged by corrosion).

▲ Ensuring proper recycling is done as a project instead of on a here-and–there basis.

▲ Making space for recycling collection points (batteries, printer pieces, small electronic parts, and devices) and educating everyone on their proper use.

Draw a Process Map

Processes are the actions performed to complete a repetitive task. They consist of a series of actions in which workers combine time, materials, and labor to create a final product or provide a service. Processes are found everywhere, including IT departments. Because people often perform these processes automatically, without thinking about them, the outcome can be a final product that is created using wasteful methods. Sometimes this waste is from taking too long to complete the task. Efficient processes generate very little waste. Focus every material and all labor toward value for the customer.

Asking people to identify the waste and delays in their processes can be difficult. They just cannot "see" the process from end to end. Often, they focus on the portion that causes them the most trouble rather than on the areas that need the most improvement. Then again, there is always the possibility that your question will be taken personally. A visual tool for improving processes is a Process Map. Whether fancy or simple, such maps use graphics rather than text to help people understand the steps in a process. Using basic flowchart symbols, which are easy to draw. Showing encourages workers to review and think about all the process steps in minute detail.

Process maps can reveal many problems and wastes embedded into a process. Many of these are variations on the seven wastes. For example, look for things that delay forward motion of materials, such as bottlenecks.

Bottlenecks are points in a process through which all work must pass. Often, these are approvals. The problem arises when the person approving an action is busy with other assignments and pending requests pile up. In many cases, these approvals are provided automatically, so they really should only be provided as notifications. Instead of everyone signing off on an action, identify one approver and send everyone else a copy. Now everyone has a set time period in which to stop the action. If they fail to act, their opportunity to voice an opinion is lost.

When examining a process map, one of the goals is to improve cycle time – the amount of time required for something to pass completely through the process. Think how frustrated you have been when something you know takes less than an hour to resolve is taking weeks Keep this feeling in mind when examining a process, and work to reduce every process' cycle time. A good place to start is any place where waiting waste is present.

Analyzing a process map is a four-step process. First, draw out the major steps in the process. If several people are involved, then draw one box for each person. For each process step, list the activities required, such as make a file copy, sign the document, or update a database. Next, determine how much time that step requires, including the amount of time lost between steps. Finally, for each activity in a step, label it as:

▲ Value Added (VA) – an improvement to the final product that the customer is willing to pay for.

▲ Non-Value Added (NVA) – an action (usually one of the Seven Wastes) that is performed but that adds no value to the final product. This is something the customer is not willing to pay for.

▲ Required (R) – an activity that must be done, such as to fulfill a legal mandate.

Figure 13-6 is an example of a process map that details a series of steps required to repair a PC. Each step is broken down by the tasks involved and then labels as Value Added, etc. When drafting a process map, it is difficult to include every small step that might sometimes be needed After drawing a few examples, however, you will find the level of detail that you are most comfortable with. Also, remember that not all non-value added steps can ever be eliminated, but keep trying!

Evaluating a process map should be a team effort. However, the person who executes the process every day often finds it difficult to be objective and interprets comments as personal criticisms rather than an objective evaluation of the process. The goal is to eliminate those actions that add no value (from the customer's perspective). This, in turn, speeds the result to the customer.

A process map begins and ends with an event (see Figure 13-7). This illustrates the process for a programmer to submit a changed program for

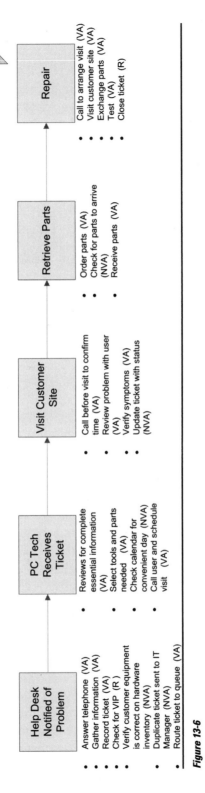

FLOW OF WORK

Help Desk Notified of Problem

- Answer telephone (VA)
- Gather information (VA)
- Record ticket (VA)
- Check for VIP (R)
- Verify customer equipment is correct on hardware inventory (NVA)
- Duplicate ticket sent to IT Manager (NVA)
- Route ticket to queue (VA)

PC Tech Receives Ticket

- Reviews for complete essential information (VA)
- Select tools and parts needed (VA)
- Check calendar for convenient day (NVA)
- Call user and schedule visit (VA)

Visit Customer Site

- Call before visit to confirm time (VA)
- Review problem with user (VA)
- Verify symptoms (VA)
- Update ticket with status (NVA)

Retrieve Parts

- Order parts (VA)
- Check for parts to arrive (NVA)
- Receive parts (VA)

Repair

- Call to arrange visit (VA)
- Visit customer site (VA)
- Exchange parts (VA)
- Test (VA)
- Close ticket (R)

Figure 13-6

TECHNOLOGY PROCESS MAP

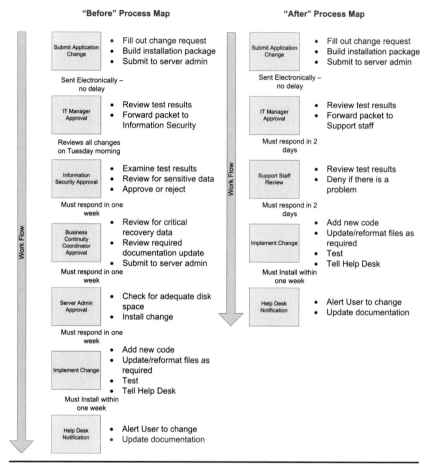

Figure 13-7
BEFORE AND AFTER PROCESS MAPS

installation. Under each step is a comment about the amount of time required before the next step begins. The left side of the figure is the before; the right side is the after.

In the original process, everyone needed time to evaluate the requested change just to be sure that it did not adversely impact their area. In the "After Process Map," all members of the support staff receive the application change request. They only need to reply if they wish to stop it. In this way, the cycle time for installing a change is reduced from more than four weeks to about two weeks. Definitely a Greener and leaner process, and just by cutting out some of the waiting waste.

MAPPING PROCESSES

Many IT processes can be identified and mapped. Some are short, and some are long. IT processes are easily identified as a series of actions that provide value to the customer. Examples are:

▲ Applications software change request.

▲ New equipment request.

▲ User ID or access level request.

▲ Equipment repair request.

▲ Network outage report and resolution.

▲ Stolen equipment report.

▲ Team member vacation request.

▲ Equipment move request.

The Bottom Line

Applying Lean Quality principles to an IT department's normal operations will improve its efficiency and reduce its cost. It also makes activities Green by reducing duplicate material purchases, reducing floor space, and lowering the amount of energy required to complete a task. Companies will find many Green savings hidden within an IT department.

The 5S program cleans up the work area by eliminating clutter, standardizing where and how to find things, and eliminating unnecessary steps in processes. It empowers the individual team members to clean up their areas and request maintenance support. When redesigning areas, include visual indicators to reduce confusion and make information readily available to the entire team. Remember the S5 program must be controlled and executed by the people who work in those areas.

The Seven Wastes list raises everyone's awareness of the many inefficiencies in a process and in daily routines. Wasteful practices are like the excess weight above your belt. Both are fat and endanger health. Waste in a company represents excess that can disappear with no discernable customer impact, just as the waste above your waist provides no benefit to your health.

Process Mapping is so easy to do and requires little start up. However, many people may feel more like a victim of their own processes than a valuable part of them. With patient coaching, these workers can begin to question why things are done they way they are, and why so many simple things take so long to complete.

In all process improvements, keep in mind the people element. They may gripe about how painful a process is, but they are familiar with the pain and prefer to live with the problems than face the unknowns that come with process changes. These people will be inclined to keep the status quo. A second issue is that people become frightened by these changes, as they worry that by removing steps from the process, their jobs may be in jeopardy. Instead, they should be assigned other customer service tasks. If this is viewed as a way to cut staff, no one will ever speak up.

Finally, waste is never Green. Find the waste, and send it on to its proper disposal!

14 GREEN SUPPLY CHAIN

ORGANIZATIONS STRIVING to reduce the environmental impact of their operations sooner or later turn their attention to their supply chain. IT managers will be dragged out of their data centers and into participating in this effort, so an understanding of how a supply chain works will be useful. Supply chain is something that most IT Executives do not spend time worrying about. That responsibility is left to the Purchasing (or Supply Management) team. After all, once the IT manager submits a purchase order, he or she only wants to see the material showing up at the receiving dock. Everything else is not their concern. At least, that is the traditional view. Life has changed.

A company Greens its internal processes because it recognizes its own business actions are having a negative impact on the environment in the following ways:

- ▲ Consuming unnecessary energy that encourages the electrical utility to burn more fuel.

- ▲ Hiring employees whose vehicles burn fuel on the commute to work.

- ▲ Heating work areas.

- ▲ Accepting delivery of materials brought in delivery vehicles that further add to greenhouse gases.

- ▲ Discarding materials into the community waste streams.

All of these activities add to a company's environmental footprint. While Greening the rest of its operations, it is also important for a company to Green its supply chain as well.

A Green supply chain requires working with suppliers and customers to reduce or eliminate the negative environmental impact of creating and using your products. This starts with using environmentally friendly (nontoxic) materials, transforming them into your product using efficient processes that minimize energy requirements, and ensuring that all waste byproducts can be recycled with a minimum of residual material sent to a landfill.

Addressing a company's supply chain is one part of a holistic view of its environmental impact. Creating a Green supply chain means examining a company's materials from sources to the point of final disposal, including how they are packaged for shipment and how they are transported. A properly managed Green supply chain ensures the minimal use of toxic materials, as controlled by the European Union's Restriction of Hazardous Substances Directives (RoHS).

This challenge is worth pursuing - up to a point. IT departments use materials from a wide range of suppliers, from new servers to cables to printer toner to software CDs. Each of these has a unique supply chain, even if purchased from the same company. To ensure the greatest benefit with the least effort, the IT department's Green supply chain efforts should focus on significant materials. Materials such as electronic equipment, cables, software, and consumables are good starting points. The rest is left to the Purchasing Department.

Supply chain optimization is not new. Its origins are found in companies seeking to ensure the predictable delivery (on time, on cost, right quality) of key materials. The justification was reduced costs. Today, that cost emphasis has expanded to include environmental costs to the company and their impact on the community. A well-managed Green supply chain uncovers and monitors hidden costs (such as packing material disposal) and works to minimize their impact.

SUPPLY CHAIN WASTE

How much waste is in the supply chain? As a simple example, take a trip to the grocery store. If you shake a box of cereal, the box seems to be almost 20% empty. A bag of chips appears large and inflated; see-through bags show a great deal of wasted space. Both products are labeled as sold by weight, and not by volume. So why are the containers oversized? For marketing! They are intended to fool the consumer into believing they are purchasing more than is packaged.

The environmental impact of bloated packaging materials is that more delivery trucks are needed to deliver a given amount of material than is actually necessary—and this wastes fuel. Sometimes, this is also true for IT materials. Compare the package size of a stick of RAM purchased from a parts supplier and one that is delivered in a "retail box." In addition, the extra packaging material will require disposal. Guess who pays for this? Was that expense considered when comparing the price of competing products?

The major obstacle in the path of Greening a supply chain is the lack of a clear mission tied to business benefit. Executives view Greening it as a positive activity, but one that can wait in times of tight budgets. They are unsure what metrics accurately measure the degree of "greenness" and are convinced that it will become a never-ending program. To obtain approval, focus on the many positives of a Green Supply chain.

THE SUPPLY CHAIN PROBLEM

A supply chain includes everything that it takes to create a product or service. It stretches from the point where the original material was created (mined, grown on sheep, trees were cut down, etc.), to the point of its final disposal. It includes all changes made to the material, how materials were combined to create a more complex item, and the transportation to move the material from one step to the next. The sequence of events from beginning to end is considered that product's life cycle.

Each step along the journey from raw material to finished goods uses energy, consumes materials, and creates waste. Pollution and production byproducts represent inefficient or ineffective processes; they mean that more material and energy was used than was necessary. All of this waste adds cost to the product, which is then passed on to the customer. Companies optimizing their supply chains examine this sequence of events and identify the ones that create the most waste while providing the least value. Then, these processes are redesigned to minimize or eliminate waste. This saves everyone money.

> **LEAN QUALITY SYSTEMS**
> The elimination of waste is the goal of a Lean Quality System. It examines processes to reveal the seven wastes (overproduction, excess inventory, waiting, unnecessary transportation, unneeded processing steps, unnecessary motion, and defective products). Each waste adds unnecessary cost without improving the product's quality or adding to the customer's satisfaction.

Consider the steps for creating an inkjet cartridge. It is purchased from a retailer, who purchased it from a wholesaler, who may have purchased it from a larger scale wholesaler, who may have purchased it from the manufacturer that either created the components or purchased them from another facility. Looking back on this supply chain, it is clear that unless your company has gigantic purchasing power, your ability to influence these companies may be limited to the manufacturer.

Greening a supply chain need not be a solo affair. It requires not only cross-functional support within the company, but also with suppliers. A consider amount of time must be spent assisting in the design of products with minimal environmental impact and maximum energy-efficient delivery.

SUPPLY CHAIN MANAGEMENT IS IMPORTANT

A reliable source of supply allows companies to minimize the amount of materials they keep on hand to guard against shortages. This stockpile is known as a "safety stock." If companies felt that paper for their high-speed laser printers was in short supply, they might purchase and store extra paper. If they perceive significant supply chain uncertainty (such as a potential labor strike), they might purchase enough paper to meet their requirements for several months.

In this example, the stored paper ties up money that is then not available for purchasing equipment, investing, or other purposes. In some jurisdictions, a property tax may be assessed. This stockpile, which only exists as a safety stock in the event that a supplier has a problem, is subject to "shrinkage" (pilferage, moisture, rodents chewing on it, and chemical change from excess heat or cold) and storage effects that can jam printers or result in discoloration. When more paper is needed, someone must drive equipment to the storage site, extract the paper, and then transport it back to the point where it will be used.

A second reason to manage the complete supply chain involves the quality of goods. If the company is operating with a low safety stock, a shipment or two of inferior quality materials can halt your operations or require an expensive scramble for substitute materials from a different supplier on short notice. By monitoring the entire supply chain, these sorts of problems (which may have arisen earlier in the chain but were passed on anyway) can be detected and addressed.

Take laser printer paper again as an example. You might monitor the overall business health of the paper factory but still be unaware that a small amount of a special chemical required to manufacture the paper type you use and the factory (farther up the supply chain) that makes that material was just lost to a fire. Therefore, paper shipments will be delayed or of a different quality. The earlier you learn of an adverse situation, the more time you will have to mitigate its effects.

The third reason companies monitor supply chains is to contain costs. By working with the supplier and that company's suppliers, different processes and materials can be investigated to reduce everyone's costs and improve the performance of your own product in the bargain. In this way, a more inexpensive product tuned to your requirements might be obtained.

Why should suppliers allow you inside of their operations? Because it builds a closer bond with customers and facilitates the exchange of information from customer to supplier of fluctuations in demand and potential new business. This valuable information enables the supplier to better tune its own material orders so that it is not caught with large inventories at the start of a business downturn.

In return, the customer receives a smoother flow of information from the supplier. If the flow of material is in question, the supplier understands your material requirements and can recommend different and potentially cost saving substitutes. This regular exchange also changes the adversarial relationship between supplier and customer to one of partnership. After all, you need each other! This is illustrated in Figure 14-1.

EXAMINING YOUR IT SUPPLY CHAIN

Your company uses a wide range of processes to accomplish its goals, some of which are not critical to the company's financial health. Focus your IT supply analysis on those few critical processes, and leave the rest for some other time. Typically, only 20 to 25 percent of all processes are critical.

Next, list the materials necessary to support each of these critical processes. There may be times during your business year when a process needs more of this or that. Combine these lists to create a master list of unique items that should be monitored. For example, several different critical processes may require toner for the company's high-speed laser printer or archive tapes of a specific type.

For each of these critical materials, decide if they are common and easy to obtain from multiple sources or are specific to only a few sources. The former can be managed by monitoring industry publications, since it is

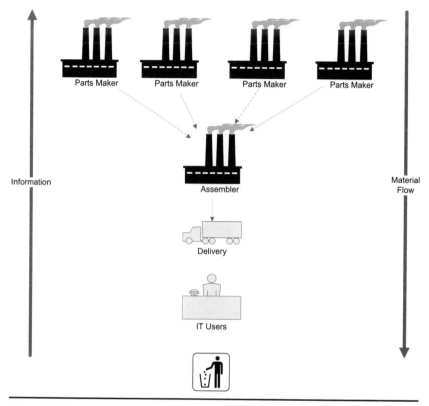

Figure 14-1

SUPPLY CHAIN SHOWING BOTH MATERIAL AND INFORMATION FLOWS

unlikely your purchases will hold sway over many manufacturers. In the case of few sources, the supply chain needs scrutiny.

WHICH PROCESSES ARE CRITICAL?

If your company has completed a Business Impact Analysis, you will know how long the company can tolerate the absence of a process before serious financial damage occurs. This view of the business is created by its business managers, who begin by examining each business process in their department (every department is queried). Next, the loss per hour in idle production is added to lost revenue to obtain a cost per hour for an inoperable process. Then, all of the processes of the company are compared to identify which ones hurt the most financially if idle.

After much discussion, business executives decide which processes are most critical. Each critical (or vital) business function consumes materials, and a lack of these materials, at some point, will cause operations to cease. Once these processes are selected, the IT systems that support them are identified. This is what determines the restoration priorities of the data center in your IT disaster recovery plan. Critical business processes are also known as Vital Business Functions of VBFs.

One example of a critical business function is printing customer invoices, which may require preprinted forms. If this paper is late by one day, then payments will just take longer, but if paper is not available for a week, then the company's cash flow may be seriously hindered.

Another example that hits closer to home is the company payroll. If the supplier that provides blank checks for the organization has problems printing them, then how many days before the work force is serious impacted? If the payroll is late, would the community become nervous that the company may secretly be short of cash? Would the labor union walk out in protest?

Green Supply Chain

Greening the supply chain begins with basic supply chain analysis and then adds in the environmental costs and impact of decisions. In the early days of environmental compliance, the emphasis was on ensuring that suppliers cleaned up their messes. Now, the emphasis is on preventing the mess from occurring. Companies seek to Green their chain to reduce their own costs. To be Green, a supplier's processes must be efficient, as well as environmentally sound. After all, if environmentally friendly operations are good for you, then they must be good for your suppliers as well.

Improving the Green performance of your supply chain may sound like a good idea, but it must be firmly grounded in business logic. You must understand why this is important to your company. Is it being done to improve your public image by encouraging other to be Greener? Is it done to mitigate the risk that an important supplier may be closed for environmental violations? It is being attempted to position a product in the market place as "Greener" than a competitor's offering? Is this necessary to reduce the amount of toxic material found in the supplier's products?

Traditionally, everyone thought of being green as ensuring that every step in the supply chain was environmentally compliant with local laws. The benefit, however, is improved health of the workers (and community) and minimization of the risk of legal sanctions. However, compliance means fulfilling only the minimal requirements of the government. It overlooks the hidden costs and potential process improvements offered by doing more than the least amount. Eventually, some jurisdiction tightens requirements. Then, there is a scramble to catch up. Instead of scrambling, well-managed companies stay ahead of the lawyers by making their processes as green as possible.

Greening a supply chain encourages suppliers to adopt green practices and environmental management systems, as well as to pay attention to the material content and environmental practices of their own suppliers. Companies begin with a sharp eye toward becoming Greener while reducing their cost. All of this must be accomplished without any reduction in customer service. As with most Green efforts, a great deal of the problem is caused by process inefficiencies.

CERTIFICATES OF COMPLIANCE

The fastest way to Green suppliers is to skip the time required to examine their processes and instead require that they provide an independently verified certificate of compliance to ISO standard 14001 (the international standard for environmental management systems). The International Organization for Standards (ISO) publishes standards that detail the best practices for specific areas of business. Companies are rating according to how closely their practices conform to this "ideal." ISO 14001 compliance can be self-declared or certified by a third-party agency. The ISO 14001 standard is flexible enough to apply to all types of business.

ISO 14001 is just one among many of the environmental standards in the ISO 14000 series. They include greenhouse gases, environmental labeling, and how to rate a company's environmental performance. ISO standards are available from www.ISO.org

Greening a supply chain takes time and resources. IT executives must identify how this effort aligns with their corporate environmental goals. As with any process improvement, begin by establishing metrics for the areas to be improved. A baseline measurement must be completed before changing anything, so everyone knows how things were when the effort began. The baseline identifies "how much" of each category (air, water, energy) the company consumes and, in some cases, how much is obviously wasted. A goal is set for reduction and measurements are made along the way to demonstrate progress. Once the goal is reached, monthly maintenance measurements will show if the gains have been maintained

Metrics must be selected carefully, as everyone will work toward what is being measured. If the wrong things are measured or the right things are measured in the wrong way, then those are the results you will get.

Progress to a goal is measured by metrics collected on supplier performance. Some companies include environmental improvement targets on their department balanced scorecards to encourage improvement. This sort of executive emphasis helps to break down internal barriers. Based on your own company's environmental challenges, identify key actions, such as the elimination of a specific material.

Some of the things to measure include:

▲ The amount of toxic materials (by material type) in your product.

▲ The amount of toxic wastes (by material type) created as byproducts.

▲ The carbon footprint for a process, as well as for the overall supply chain.

▲ The number of regulatory violations.

▲ The amount of one-time use packaging materials required.

Greening Your IT Chain

With a goal firmly in mind and a team in place, it is time to begin. Review the various types of materials consumed by the IT department. Of course, the primary material used is energy. Reduction of energy usage is addressed elsewhere in this book. IT materials fall into two broad categories: equipment (anything with a useful life longer than a few months) and consumables. In addition to these groups, a common issue is excess packing and transportation.

IT had several primary supply chains, each with its unique challenges:

▲ Equipment.

▲ Repair parts and cables.

▲ Printer supplies (toner, inkjet cartridges, fusers).

▲ Paper (various types of blank paper and preprinted forms).

▲ Miscellaneous IT supplies, such as tapes.

▲ Telephone instruments (land line and cellular).

▲ Network equipment.

▲ Software.

IT EQUIPMENT

The IT equipment supply chain often begins on the far side of the globe, where circuit cards of all types are created. Along with the integrated circuits mounted to them, they are then packaged and sent to a computer as-sembler. When components leave one company, they are packaged for ship-ment to the next. When they arrive at the next factory (sometimes after a period of storage), they are unpacked, combined with other products, and then packaged again for shipment to the next level of processing. This packaging is used to protect the product in transit and storage and is then discarded as waste.

Unfortunately, even a major corporate headquarters office in Ohio will have little influence on a circuit card assembler in China. However, a ma-jor manufacturer such as Hewlett-Packard, Dell, or IBM can look up their supply chains and influence behavior. This is one way that many IT shops rely on their supplier's Green Supply Chain programs to complement their own.

Make IT purchases greener by selecting equipment that meets pub-lished international standards, such as ENERGY STAR and RoHS. Figure 14-2 shows the environmental compliance labeling for a portable telephone handset. It signifies:

1. *RBRC* – Rechargeable Battery Recycling Corporation – which estab-lishes drop-off points at major retail chains across the country where rechargeable batteries can be brought for proper recycling and disposal.

2. *ENERGY STAR* – a self-declaration of ENERGY STAR compliance.

3. Restriction of the use of certain Hazardous Substances (RoHS) com-pliance label indicating that these substances are at or below the RoHS limitations.

IT supply chains include the recycling of excess materials. Some com-panies, like Hewlett-Packard, include a "Take Back" program with pur-chases. Once a computer or other HP manufactured device reaches the end of its useful life, it can be shipped to the manufacturer for disposal.

However, this equipment does not automatically hit the rubbish heap. Components are removed for recycling. These recyclable materials are ex-tracted from the old equipment, are purified, and then reinserted into the supply chain along with new material. Although not all materials can be economically reused in this way, the ones that can be should be. (The clas-sic examples of recycled materials are aluminum cans and glass bottles that have long been collected and reused.)

Figure 14-3 illustrates how the recycle and reuse process works. Waste is minimized in the creation of the product, which is then transported to the assembly site. The goal is to minimize the transportation distance. Af-ter assembly, the material is sent to the purchaser using the minimal one-use packing and returnable containers where possible. Next, the equip-

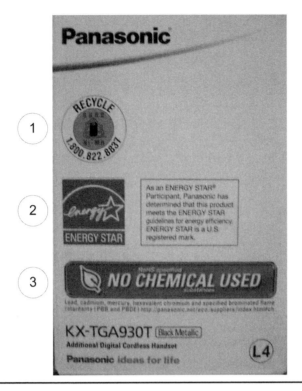

Figure 14-2
ENVIRONMENTAL COMPLIANCE LABEL FOR A PORTABLE HANDSET

ment functions for its full life and is not discarded as "out of fashion." The surplus equipment is sent to a recycling company that separates component materials and sends the results to be recycled or for final disposal. In this way, the Green Supply Chain becomes more of a Green recycling loop.

From time to time, electronic equipment ceases to work. If the device is under warranty, then the manufacturer can send a replacement part. In some cases, the broken part must be returned to the manufacturer as proof of the defect or for recycling. If the component is inexpensive or has little reuse value, the repairperson is told to dispose of it. This is called a "field destroy" replacement. These parts must be included in the regular waste stream to the electronics recycling company.

LOOK FOR THE HIDDEN COST

IT equipment is expensive to purchase and repair. It is also sensitive to rough handling during shipment. This leads suppliers to use lots of packing materials. As a result, the customer ends up with a small mountain of packing material for disposal. (Large facilities, such as factories, may have a

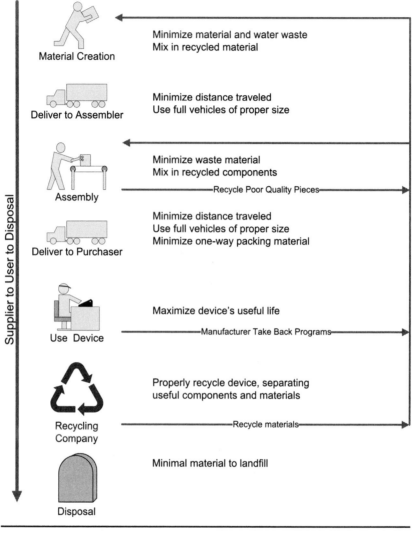

Figure 14-3
RECYCLE/REUSE PROCESS THROUGH THE SUPPLY CHAIN

program in place to recycle the cardboard portion of this heap.) The cost for this disposal is pushed over to the Facilities department, so it is invisible to the IT Executive and, consequently, not included in purchase price considerations.

When purchasing bulky items in quantity, it may be possible to negotiate with the supplier to minimize the amount of packing material. (This is most practical for a direct delivery that does not pass through an intermediate warehouse.) Although the cost of disposing of packing material can be included in the purchase conditions, it still results in excess material heading to a landfill.

Packaging is designed differently to deliver the same product to different markets. Microprocessors sold to a PC assembler are in a tray. This makes it easy to pick them out one at a time, but still at a high speed. The same processors, sold in a single quantity, would be in a "retail box" with internal packing to keep the chip immobile, a CD for configuring the new computer, a manual, and likely some advertisements. Two different uses and a significant difference in the amount of packaging material bound for disposal.

There is a good reason for IT executives to shy away from this issue. Packaging's purpose is to protect the materials sold to you while they are in transit. If you specify the packing method and materials, you assume the risk for any damage to the goods while they are in transit. However, returnable containers can be specified, and they are built stronger to enable them to survive many uses.

EXCESS PACKAGING MATERIALS

The author once received a shipment of several hundred new DEC terminals that were promptly installed. Each of the separately boxed terminals came with a manual and cables, neither of which we needed. So, we boxed the excess materials for delivery to the DEC salesman during his next visit. He had no idea what to do with this material and likely threw it away after leaving our door. We were just trying not to be wasteful, but he was confronted with how to return something to a supply chain that was not geared to receive anything like this back. Most likely, in his mind, it would cost his company more to reinject this material into the packing process than would be recovered in company value.

CONSUMABLES

IT departments consume materials to support their customers. These are generally printing products, with some money spent on CDs and tape cartridges. Paper tends to come in clean and leave for the landfill or paper recycler. (In both cases, it is recommended to shred all documents before they depart since employees are not good at separating confidential from nonconfidential documents.)

Many consumables have a resale value. Printers are a good example. When selecting a vendor, investigate if the company takes back empty toner materials, inkjet cartridges, and printer ribbons. Batteries are another type of material where a return to a vendor or responsible recycler is important. They may also provide some cash back.

CONSUMABLES

The IT industry is constantly improving with the introduction of new products, faster equipment, and updated software capabilities. The same holds true for consumables used in printers. Equipment take-back programs have been in place for some time. Laser printer cartridges purchased from a manufacturer have long included a return shipment label to send the empty back to for proper reuse or disposal.

Disadvantages of Greening an IT Supply Chain

While greening an IT supply chain has many benefits, many challenges must be overcome, including:

▲ Asking an IT Manager to Green a supply chain is like asking the supply chain manager to rebuild his or her own mainframe databases. The training and expertise is not there and the time to acquire it does not balance the lost time and money.

▲ Worrying about how Green a device may be distracts attention from buying the most effective and efficient device for the job. For example, how much of a performance penalty is acceptable to purchase a Green device over one that is not?

▲ Company purchasing policies may not allow deviation from purchasing the lowest cost item. They may also discourage working with suppliers, as "collusion" before a sale.

▲ This Green issue adds yet more complexity into the purchase equation. As purchasing departments strive to accomplish more with fewer people, who has the time to check out suppliers' environmental compliance claims and then the sources of their primary materials?

▲ Returnable containers must be collected, stored, and sometimes inspected. Difficult-to-remove labels must be scraped off. Then, a truck has to be paid to return this material for reuse, possibly to a location thousands of miles away. Returnable containers only work if there is a steady flow of material from the supplier to the purchaser and if the empty containers can be loaded onto the empty truck heading back to the supplier.

The Bottom Line

Greening a supply chain emphasizes identifying and eliminating waste and toxic materials in the processes. Companies will find it difficult to enforce "green" on the entire supply chain from the point that ore is extracted from the ground to the point where the residual material is buried in the landfill. However, many things can be done to reduce the environmental impact of a company's supply chain which is undertaken for their benefit.

Greening a Supply Chain is similar to implementing Lean Quality processes on it. Lean seeks to drive waste out of processes. Driving out waste eliminates unnecessary costs while maintaining the same or offering a higher level of customer service. Green seeks to minimize energy and material usage while changing the composition of goods so they are easy to disassemble and recycle.

Include your Green requirements as optional factors in Requests for Proposals and purchase orders. This might include requesting copies of suppliers' third party ISO 14001 certification. This saves time and leaves the compliance evaluation to the experts.

Consider these actions for Greening your own offices and those along your supply chain:

▲ When ordering new desktop computers, request devices without power cords. Often when replacing old equipment, it is easier to leave the existing cord in place. If you receive new cords, they will just add to the waste stream.

▲ When replacing toner or inkjet cartridges, put the old unit into the new cartridge's box and either send it back to the factory or send it by interoffice mail to a central IT collection point.

▲ When distributing updated paper manuals (including end-user documentation within the company), ask people to place the old documents in the paper recycling containers.

▲ Establish a central collection point for small electronic devices, such as cell phones, cables, telephone instruments, broken keyboards, and broken mice. When the container is full, send it to your equipment recycler.

▲ Ask companies that provide regular shipments (such as of paper) to use reusable shipping skids or at least to take back the ones they provide.

▲ Implement the electronic passing of orders, receipts, and invoices to reduce the flow of paper.

▲ Minimize waste in your processes so you request less. For example, some computer operators will throw away the first few sheets of paper in a ream because, in times past, glue that seeped on to the paper from the seam jammed the printer. This should no long be the case.

▲ Encourage the use of recycled paper for IT printers where the quality and price make sense. The greater the market for recycled paper, the more waste companies can recycle rather than discard.

Energy Usage Resources

ENERGY STAR www.energystar.gov	Encourages the use of power efficient devices.
80 Plus www.80plus.org	Electric utility-funded incentive program for encouraging the use of energy-efficient power supplies in desktop computers and servers.
ACPI Component Architecture (ACPICA) Project www.acpica.org	Defines and implements a group of software components to create an implementation of the ACPI specification.
The Green Grid www.thegreengrid.org	A global consortium dedicated to advancing energy efficiency in data centers and business computing ecosystems.
Climate Savers Computing Initiative www.climatesaverscomputing.org	Promotes the development, deployment and adoption of smart technologies to improve the efficiency of a computer's power delivery and reduce the energy consumed when the computer is in an inactive state.

Less Watts www.lesswatts.org	Energy savings for Linux-based computers. Sponsored by Intel.
US EPA www.epa.gov	Supports the research and study of data center power usage and technologies to improve the efficiency of data centers.
US Department of Energy Industrial Technologies Program (ITP) www1.eere.energy.gov/industry/saveenergynow/partnering_data_centers.html.	Works with U.S. computer data centers to reduce their energy consumption.
Get IT Green Ohio www.getitgreenohio.org	A consortium of industry partners dedicated to promoting best practices, solutions and advocating for policies to maximize energy efficiency in Ohio's technology-enabled industries.

Reduction of Toxic Waste

Basel Action Network www.ban.org	International organization focused on the issue of hazardous and toxic waste disposal.
Electronic Product Environmental Assessment Tool (EPAT) www.epeat.net	Environmental impact rating system for computers and other electronic devices.
Federal Electronics Challenge (FEC) www.federalelectronicschallenge.net	A partnership program that encourages federal facilities and agencies to purchase greener electronic products, reduce impacts of electronic products during use, and manage obsolete electronics in an environmentally safe way.

Green Electronics Council www.greenelectronicscouncil.org	Inspire and support the effective design, manufacture, use and recovery of electronic products.
Silicon Valley Toxics Coalition www.etoxics.org	Supports research, advocacy and grassroots organizing to promote human health and environmental justice in response to the rapid growth of the high-tech industry.
Zero Waste Alliance www.zerowaste.org	A non-profit partnership of universities, government, business and other organizations working to develop, promote and apply Zero Waste strategies.

Environmental Regulations

US EPA www.epa.gov	Regulates the transportation and disposal of toxic waste.
Waste Electrical and Electronic Equipment (WEEE) ec.europa.eu/environment/waste/weee/index_en.htm	Directives 2002/95/EC on the restriction of the use of certain hazardous substances in electrical and electronic equipment and 2002/96/EC on waste electrical and electronic equipment.
Restriction of the use of certain Hazardous Substances (RoHS) www.rohs.eu	European Union restrictions on the use of hazardous substances in manufactured items.
Resource Conservation and Recovery Act (RCRA) www.epa.gov/osw/inforesources/online/index.htm	On-line database to locate documents, including publications and other outreach materials, that cover a wide range of RCRA issues and topics.

Recycling Resources

Consumer Electronics Association www.mygreenelectronics.org	Find recyclers by ZIP Code.
Telecommunications Industry Association www.eiae.org	Map to find recyclers by state and recycling events.
Earth911 earth911.com/electronics	Find recycling site for all kinds of materials.
Redemtech www.redemtech.com	International IT asset disposal company; early proponent of responsible recycling.
Intechra www.intechra.com	Largest electronics lifecycle management company in the U.S.

Hard Disk Cleaning Utilities

Commercial Windows Disk Cleaning Software	
DiskDeleter Pro	www.bluestsoft.com
Norton Utilities and System Works	www.symantec.com
Paragon Disk Wiper	www.disk-wiper.net
Tracks Eraser Pro	www.acesoft.net
Webroot Window Washer	www.webroot.com
Wipedrive	www.whitecanyon.com

Freeware Windows Disk Cleaning Software	
Active@ Kill Disk: Hard Drive Eraser	www.shareware.com
BCWipe	www.shareware.com
Disk Cleaner	www.shareware.com
Eraser	www.shareware.com
Sure Delete	www.shareware.com

Macintosh Disk Cleaning Software	
Norton Utilities	www.symantec.com
iClean	www.aladdin.com
Wipedrive	www.whitecanyon.com

Other Useful Web sites

SearchDataCenter.com www.searchdatacenter.com	An on-line information resource for the news, tech tips and expert advice for IT managers responsible for operating a data center.
American Society of Heating, Refrigeration, and Air-Conditioning Engineers (ASHRAE) www.ashrae.org	An international organization whose mission in the advancement of heating, ventilation, air conditioning and refrigeration technologies and to promote a sustainable world through research, standards writing, publishing and continuing education.
Lawrence Berkeley National Lab www.lbl.gov	A US research lab whose work includes the environmental friendly generation of power and the efficient user of power in data centers.
Association for Computer Operations Management (AFCOM) www.afcom.com	Provides education and resources for data center managers.

5S   A term for the five actions commonly referred to as "Japanese House-keeping." The 5S process is used to remove clutter, introduce the "visual work place," and standardize organizational practices across the company. The 5Ss, roughly translated from Japanese are Sort, Straighten, Shine, Standardize, and Sustain.

7 Wastes   A collection of the various types of waste commonly found in processes. All waste is labor, materials, and time spent for no useful purpose. Therefore, no waste is Green. To Green your process, all waste must be removed. The 7 wastes are Waiting, Excess Inventory, Overproduction, Excess Motion, Unnecessary Transportation, Unnecessary Steps, and Defective Products.

80PLUS   A program that encourages manufacturers to create power supplies that are at least 80% efficient at various loads. The program also encourages consumers to seek out and purchase these products. 80PLUS is a requirement for an ENERGY STAR certification.

Advanced Configuration and Power Interface (ACPI)   A software-based control of an electronic device's power level. The operating system provides an ACPI program that gathers configuration information from all hardware and software components as they start. It uses this information to inform all active components before it reduces power to the unit.

ACPI Machine Language (AML)   A pseudocode language used by the operating system's ACPI interpreter to control ACPI compliant components. These controls, along with a description of a component's power modes, are provided by the device at boot time.

ACPI4Linux   A project to bring the benefits of the ACPI standard to Linux users. This includes kernel modifications and software tools.

Advanced Power Management (APM)   APM is a BIOS-based power management system that preceded ACPI. It was developed to enable notebook PCs to manage their power usage when the unit was idle for a set period of time. It lacks ACPI's robust capabilities for tracking everything that was running at one time and gained a reputation for crashing programs when it could not detect the computer was still in use. APM is still in use by some LINUX systems.

ACPI Source Language (ASL)   A human readable programming language used to create AML controls. ASL is used by device manufacturers and BIOS chip developers as the source code for controls. This code is then compiled into AML.

Air Economizer   A device that brings outside air directly into the data center to provide cooling.

Air Handling Unit (AHU)   A device used to condition and circulate air as part of a heating, ventilating, and air-conditioning (HVAC) system.

ATX power supply   A standard-sized power supply used by manufacturers so that everyone has a chance to compete for providing power supplies.

Basel Action Network (BAN)   An organization focused on the effects of toxic trade (toxic wastes, products, and technologies) worldwide.

Basel Convention on the Control of Transboundary Movements of Hazardous Wastes and Their Disposal   A convention adopted in Basel, Switzerland, on 22 March 1989 to control the movement of toxic materials around the world.

Basic Input Output System (BIOS) chip   Firmware code that executes when a personal computer is first turned on to load the operating system and to provide other runtime services.

Comprehensive Environmental Response Compensation and Liability Act (CERCLA)   Better known as the Superfund law, it mandates that a business or organization that generates hazardous waste is liable for the proper disposal of the waste.

Compute Power Efficiency (CPE)   A metric used to measure how efficiently power is being used for computing in a data center. It is calculated by multiplying the utilization percentage of the computing equipment by the power used by the equipment and dividing this number by the total power used by the data center.

Computer Room Air Conditioning (CRAC) unit   A device that monitors and maintains the temperature, air distribution, and humidity in a computer room or data center.

Computer Room Air Handler (CRAH) unit   A device that monitors and maintains the temperature, air distribution, and humidity in a computer room or data center. This is similar to a CRAC unit but cools the air (re-move heat) by drawing warm air from the computer room through chilled water coils.

Corporate Social Responsibility   A company policy or strategy that de-scribes how the organization will be a positive force in the community. In terms of Green Computing, it addresses a statement that the com-pany will minimize its environmental impact in terms of energy use and waste disposal.

CRT Monitor   A computer device that uses a Cathode Ray Tube (CRT) to display images. CRT monitors contain a considerable amount of toxic material and require proper disposal.

Data Center Infrastructure Efficiency (DCIE)   A metric used to determine the energy efficiency of a data center. It is calculated by dividing the power used by the IT equipment in the data center by the total power used by the data center. It is expressed as a percentage, with 100% being the optimal value.

Desktop PC   A fixed computer that is too bulky to conveniently carry around. It uses a separate monitor, keyboard, and mouse and is the most common computing device.

Design for Recycling (DfR)   Applies to products that have been designed to be easily disassembled and broken down for recycling.

Design for the Environment (DfE)   A U.S. EPA-sponsored program that works in partnership with a broad range of stakeholders to reduce risk to people and the environment by preventing pollution through more environmentally friendly design of products. It includes such items as lead-free solder, cables, and circuit boards.

Discrete System Descriptor Table (DSDT)   Holds the electronic de-vice's power management information, as all software and electronic devices report their ACPI controls upon system start-up or when they are activated.

Dual In-line Memory Modules (DIMMS)   The most common configura-tion of memory used in servers.

Dynamic Random-Access Memory (DRAM)   The most common form of computer memory. DRAM can hold data for only a short time. It must be refreshed periodically to maintain the contents of the memory. As a result, it continuously draws power.

EcoDesign Requirements for Energy Using Products (EuP)   An EU di-rective that sets EcoDesign requirements for any group of products that require energy.

Eco-Management and Audit Scheme (EMAS)   An EU regulation estab-lishing the Eco-Management and Audit Scheme (EMAS) as a voluntary tool for industrial organizations to document their environmental performance.

Electronic Product Environmental Assessment Tool (EPEAT) A tool for gauging the environmental impact of purchasing a product. EPEAT was created by the Zero Waste Alliance through funding provided by the U.S. EPA. It is currently administered by the Green Electronics Council.

EPEAT-Standards Development Roadmap (EPEAT-SDR) This program, under development by the Zero Waste Alliance (sponsored by the U.S. EPA), expands the scope of EPEAT to the wide range of electronic equipment. The road map recommends modifying IEEE 1620 to a range of standards, each with its own focus.

Energy Consumption Rating (ECR) Initiative A framework for measuring the energy efficiency of network and telecom devices.

ENERGY STAR A joint program by the U.S. Department of Energy and the U.S. EPA to improve the energy efficiency of products. ENERGY STAR has programs for consumer goods, buildings, and a wide range of other energy-consuming products.

EOL (End Of Life) Equipment that is at the end of its useful life from the original purchaser's point of view.

Executive Order 13423 (Strengthening Federal Environmental, Energy, and Transportation Management) A 2007 Presidential Order that requires all U, S. federal agencies to use EPEAT when purchasing computer systems. However, it also permits the purchase of non-EPEAT rated items under certain circumstances.

External power adapters A power supply unit external to a device that converts 120 volt line electricity to the lower power levels required by the device. Examples are charging units for cell phones and the "brick" power cord used by notebook PCs.

Federal Electronics Challenge (FEC) A partnership program that encourages federal facilities and agencies to purchase greener electronic products, reduce the impact of electronic products during use, and manage obsolete electronics in an environmentally safe way.

Fluid economizer A device that uses a fluid to exchange heat for outside air to help in cooling.

GPU A Graphics Processing Unit. Essentially, a special purpose central processing unit that is optimized to speed complex graphical images to the screen. It is usually on its own circuit card.

Green A general term relating to the environmental impact of creating, using, or disposing of something. Examples are desktop computers, servers, notebook PCs, and a car used for a worker's commute.

Green Grid   An electronic industry consortium focused on data center energy efficiency.

Greenmark   Taiwan's program that is similar to EPEAT. Unlike EPEAT, Greenmark performs on-site inspections to validate a company's compliance

Gramm-Leach-Bliley Act   Makes financial institutions responsible for the security of their customers' information.

Hard off   Power management mode in which the device has been physically disconnected from its power source.

Hibernation Mode   Power management mode in which the data and operating system context are saved to a special hibernation file on the hard disk and power is stopped for most components. Restarting from hibernation mode takes longer than from sleep mode, as the hardware must be reenergized before the operating system and application context are reloaded from the disk.

Health Insurance Portability and Accountability Act (HIPAA) –   A U.S. federal regulation that requires healthcare providers to protect confidential medical information about patients.

Hot aisle/cold aisle   A method of cooling used in a data center where equipment racks for servers and other heat generating devices are arranged in parallel rows sitting on top of a raised floor system. Each aisle between rows of racks has exclusively hot-air outlets or exclusively cool-air intakes to create a cool airflow through the racks.

Hot desk   A system designed to provide a reduced level of office space for a work force that is primarily outbound. Hot desking means that when a mobile worker is in the office, he or she uses any empty desk from a pool of desks set aside for this purpose. This is an inexpensive alternative to hoteling but with a much lower level of service.

Hoteling   A system that provides a reduced level office space for a work force that is primarily outbound. Hoteling provides temporary office space that is reserved in advance. Often, the reserved space is customized so that an employee's telephone calls are routed to that phone, their files are rolled into that area, and there is a receptionist who can provide administrative assistance.

Hypervisor   In virtualization, a layer between the physical hardware and the virtualized operating system or application.

IEEE (Institute of Electrical and Electronics Engineers, Inc.)   Standard 1680 The international "Standard for Environmental Assessment of Personal Computer Products." It supplies environmental guidelines for purchasing decisions involving desktop and laptop computers and monitors based on materials selection, environmentally sensitive materials, design for end of life, end-of-life management, energy conservation, product longevity and life-cycle extension, packaging, and corporate performance.

ISO (International Organization of Standards)   An international standards organization that collects the best industrial and business practices from around the world and formalizes them into published standards.

ISO Standard 14001   The international standard for environmental management systems. It describes the best international practices for specific areas of business. Companies are rating according to how closely their practices conform to this "ideal." ISO 14001compliance can be self-declared or certified by a third- party agency.

ITAD (IT asset disposal)   The process of disposing of IT assets at the end of their useful life.

LCD monitor   A computer device that uses a Liquid Crystal Display (LCD) to show images. LCD monitors contain a considerable amount of toxic material and require proper disposal.

Leadership in Energy and Environmental Design (LEED) certification   A green building rating system developed to promote design and construction practices that reduce the negative environmental impacts of buildings.

Lean   A term for efficient and optimized work processes. Lean processes minimize waste of all types, which makes them Green. (Of course, this assumes the Lean processes also utilize environmentally friendly materials.)

Metadata   Data about data; describes the context, content, and structure of information and its management.

Metrics   Measurements that objectively describe something. Examples are the amount of energy used by a device over the course of a week, "before" and "after" power management, the pounds of electronic devices discarded in a year, the length of time that equipment is used before replacement, etc.

Network controlled power management   Uses the network to control the power management of many dispersed electronic devices. The network controlled power management software may be configured to set different hibernation delay times for different days of the week or for special occasions.

Non-value added   A term used in Process Mapping that identifies an activity as something that a worker does that the customer would not pay for. The goal is to eliminate non-value added activities, but sometimes that is not practical.

Paravirtualization   A form of virtualization in which the operating system is modified to be aware of the fact it is being virtualized.

Power distribution unit (PDU)   A device that distributes electrical power.

Power management   Software settings in equipment, either customer selected or burned into a BIOS, that automatically moves the device to a low power state after it has been idle for a set period of time.

Power usage effectiveness (PUE)   A metric used to determine the energy efficiency of a data center. It is calculated by dividing the amount of power entering the data center by the amount of power used to run the computer infrastructure in the data center. PUE was developed by the Green Grid.

Process mapping   A way to identify the various activities that make up a process and to categorize them as value added, non-value added, or required. Process mapping is used to identify the waste in a process.

Rechargeable Battery Recycling Corporation (RBRC)   Establishes drop-off points at major retail chains across the country where rechargeable batteries can be brought for proper recycling and disposal

Resource Conservation and Recovery Act (RCRA)   A U.S. law that bans the open dumping of solid and hazardous wastes.

Restriction on Hazardous Substances (RoHS)   An EU directive that bans the sale in the EU of new electrical and electronic equipment containing more than specified levels of six hazardous materials: lead, cadmium, mercury, hexavalent chromium, polybrominated biphenyl (PBB). and polybrominated diphenyl ether (PBDE) flame retardants.

Safety stock   The amount of material that is kept on hand to keep operations working in case the normal resupply of material is late or is of poor quality.

Sarbanes-Oxley Act (Sarbox or SOX)   Requires organizations to make secure all financial information and systems, as well as the IT infrastructure on which these systems operate.

Silicon Valley Toxics Coalition (SVTC)   An organization founded in 1982 in response to groundwater contamination that was discovered throughout Silicon Valley near high-tech manufacturing facilities.

Sleep (or standby) mode   The system state (operating system, applications, data) are kept in RAM supported by a few watts of electricity. Full service can be quickly restarted. However, if total power is lost, so is everything stored in RAM; it would be similar to pulling the plug on a running computer.

Spaghetti chart   A tool for identifying the wastes of unnecessary motion and unnecessary transportation by sketching the work area's floor plan, measuring the distance between various points, and diagramming worker movements for about two hours to determine the number of steps required to complete specific tasks. Based on this data, the work area can be rearranged, after which the test should be conducted again to document improvement.

Storage area networks (SANs)   A network of storage disks. In large enterprises, a SAN connects multiple servers to a centralized pool of disk storage.

Supply chain   Everything that it takes to create something. It stretches from the point where the original material was created (mined, grown, cut down, etc.) to the point of its final disposal. It includes all changes made to the material and how it was combined to create a more complex item. The supply chain includes the transportation to move the material between each step. The sequence of events from beginning to end can be considered as that product's life cycle.

Switched power supply   A type of power supply found in most computers that uses a switched regulator to convert alternating current to the desired voltage levels of direct current.

Tagged Image File Format (TIFF, TIF)   An image file format that does not lose quality when it is saved and compressed.

Telecommuter   A term previously used to describe someone who worked from home by using a telephone to connect to the office computers. The term most commonly used for this type of employment arrangement is now "virtual worker."

Thermal design power (TDP)   A measure of the maximum amount of heat generated by a processor that the computer's cooling system must dissipate under normal operating conditions.

Value added   A term used in Process Mapping that identifies an activity as something that a worker does that the customer is willing to pay for.

Virtual server   A file in a server that thinks it is actually a physical server. Within this executing file is a subset of the operating system. As the application within the virtual server executes, it passes service requests to the virtual machine and then to the physical server. Isolating the applications from the physical server's operating system makes the virtualized servers highly portable.

Virtual worker   An employee who works from home. This person is virtually in the office, but not physically there. Virtual workers are enabled by the ready availability of high-speed Internet service and multiple telephone connections (a combination of land lines and cellular telephones).

Virtualization   The concept of sharing hardware resources among the services and applications that use the resources.

Voice Over IP (VOIP)   The technology for sending telephone conversations through the Internet instead of through traditional telephone equipment.

Wake On LAN The power management capability that enables PCs to idle at a very low power setting over night. When a software patch is sent to that unit, a "wake event" is transmitted to it, and the unit energizes. When the patch is completed, the unit will return to its low power state. This enables software patching at night when no one is around and removes a key objection to power management.

Waste Electrical and Electronic Equipment (WEEE) An EU directive that makes producers of electrical and electronic equipment responsible for what happens to the equipment they make once the equipment reaches its end of life.

INDEX

Larry Webber has more than 30 years of experience in the information services field. He began his career in the U.S. Marine Corps as a digital network repairman and then moved to a position as a COBOL programmer supporting the Marine's Logistics traffic management systems.

After his release from active service, he worked in Kansas City as a COBOL programmer, systems analyst, and IT manager at Waddell & Reed, Temperature Industries, United Telecommunications, and the law offices of Shook, Hardy & Bacon.

For the next 12 years, Mr. Webber held various systems engineering and data processing management positions with International Truck and Bus in Springfield, Ohio, where, among other achievements, he authored an extensive Disaster Recovery plan for the 2-million-square-foot manufacturing facility. He is currently a Disaster Recovery program manager and Six Sigma Black Belt consultant for Computer Science Corporation in Dayton, Ohio.

Mr. Webber has an Associate in Science degree from Darton College in Albany, Georgia, in Data Processing; a Bachelor of Science degree in Business Administration and an MBA both from Rockhurst College in Kansas City, Missouri; and an Associate in Science degree in Industrial Engineering from Sinclair Community College in Dayton, Ohio. He also completed a Master of Project Management degree from West Carolina University.

Mr. Webber is retired from the U.S. Army Reserve as a First Sergeant in the Infantry. He is a certified Project Management Professional by the Project Management Institute, Certified in Production and Inventory Management by APICS, and is a Microsoft Certified Professional. Mr. Webber is an adjunct faculty member at DeVry University Keller Graduate School of Management, and has published several articles on disaster recovery topics.

Mr. Webber can be reached by e-mail at *ljwljw88@hotmail.com,* on his blog at businesstechbooks.wordpress.com, or on Twitter @LarryWebber.

Michael Wallace has more than 25 years of experience in the information systems field. He began his career as a mainframe operator for Super Food Services and then moved to a programming position at Reynolds & Reynolds developing financial applications for automotive dealers.

He became a consultant after graduating magna cum laude from Wright State University (Dayton, Ohio) with a Bachelor of Science degree in Management Science. For eight years he was president of Q Consulting, a custom application development firm. Mr. Wallace has been an application developer, a business analyst, and a technical and business consultant assisting companies in using information technology to solve business problems.

Mr. Wallace has served on the board of directors of various information technology user organizations and is active in the local technical community. He is currently President of the Columbus Chapter of the International Association of Microsoft Certified Partners (IAMCP), is a Competent Toastmaster and Competent Leader with Toastmasters International, and graduated from the Executive MBA program at the Fisher College of Business at The Ohio State University.

After working as a practice manager and director for the last few years, Mr. Wallace is now Vice President of Consulting Services at Result Data, which provides clients with guidance on IT strategy, application development, business intelligence, disaster recovery planning, and policies and procedures. He has also taught in the graduate programs at The Ohio State University and DeVry University Keller Graduate School of Management and has published several articles and books on business and technology topics.

Mr. Wallace can be reached by e-mail at *michaelw@columbus.rr.com,* on his blog at businesstechbooks.wordpress.com, or on Twitter @MichaelWallace.

Your comments and suggestions for improving this book are welcome.